DREAM THEATER
AWAKE

EDITED BY: JOHN PETRUCCI
TRANSCRIBED BY: DALE TURNER, JESSIE GRESS
DREAM THEATER MANAGEMENT: JIM PITULSKI AND ROB SHORE FOR ROUNDTABLE ENTERTAINMENT
PRODUCTION COORDINATOR: AARON STANG
TECHNICAL EDITOR: COLGAN BRYAN
ART DIRECTION: LARRY FREEMANTLE & DONALD MAY
ART CONCEPT: DREAM THEATER AND DON MURO
PHOTOGRAPHY: DENNIS KEELEY

© 1995 WARNER BROS. PUBLICATIONS INC.
ALL RIGHTS RESERVED

ANY DUPLICATION, ADAPTATION OR ARRANGEMENT OF THE COMPOSITIONS
CONTAINED IN THIS COLLECTION REQUIRES THE WRITTEN CONSENT OF THE PUBLISHER.
NO PART OF THIS BOOK MAY BE PHOTOCOPIED OR REPRODUCED IN ANY WAY WITHOUT PERMISSION.
UNAUTHORIZED USES ARE AN INFRINGEMENT OF U.S. COPYRIGHT ACT AND ARE PUNISHABLE BY LAW.

ISBN: 0-89724-608-X

CONTENTS

6:00 · 4

CAUGHT IN A WEB · 22

EROTOMANIA · 49

INNOCENCE FADED · 36

LIE · 103

LIFTING SHADOWS OFF A DREAM · 117

THE MIRROR · 91

SCARRED · 126

THE SILENT MAN · 82

SPACE-DYE VEST · 149

VOICES · 61

6:00

By JAMES LABRIE, KEVIN MOORE,
JOHN MYUNG, JOHN PETRUCCI and MICHAEL PORTNOY

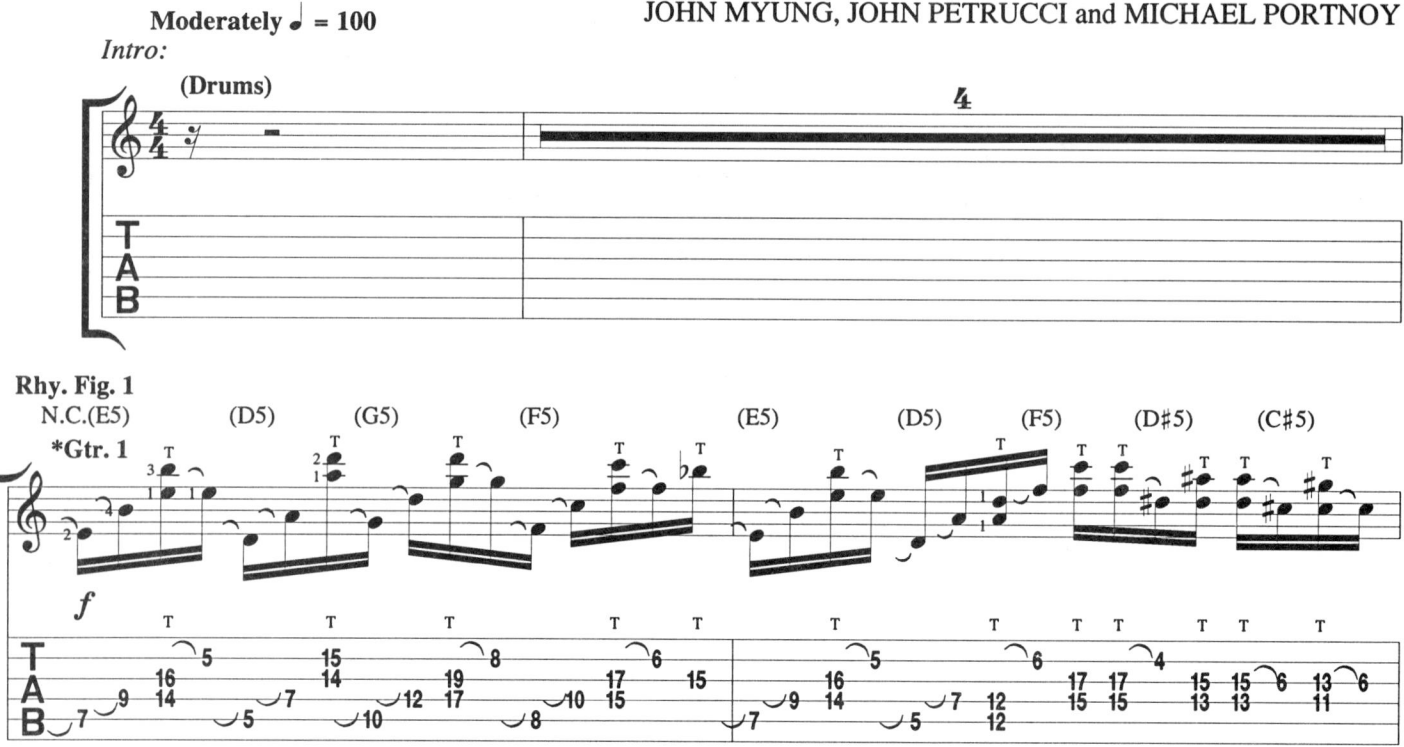

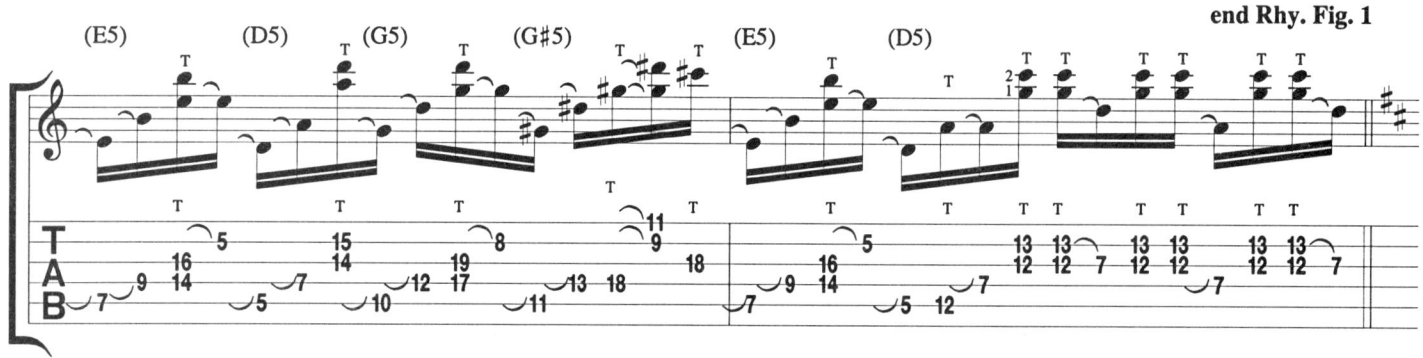

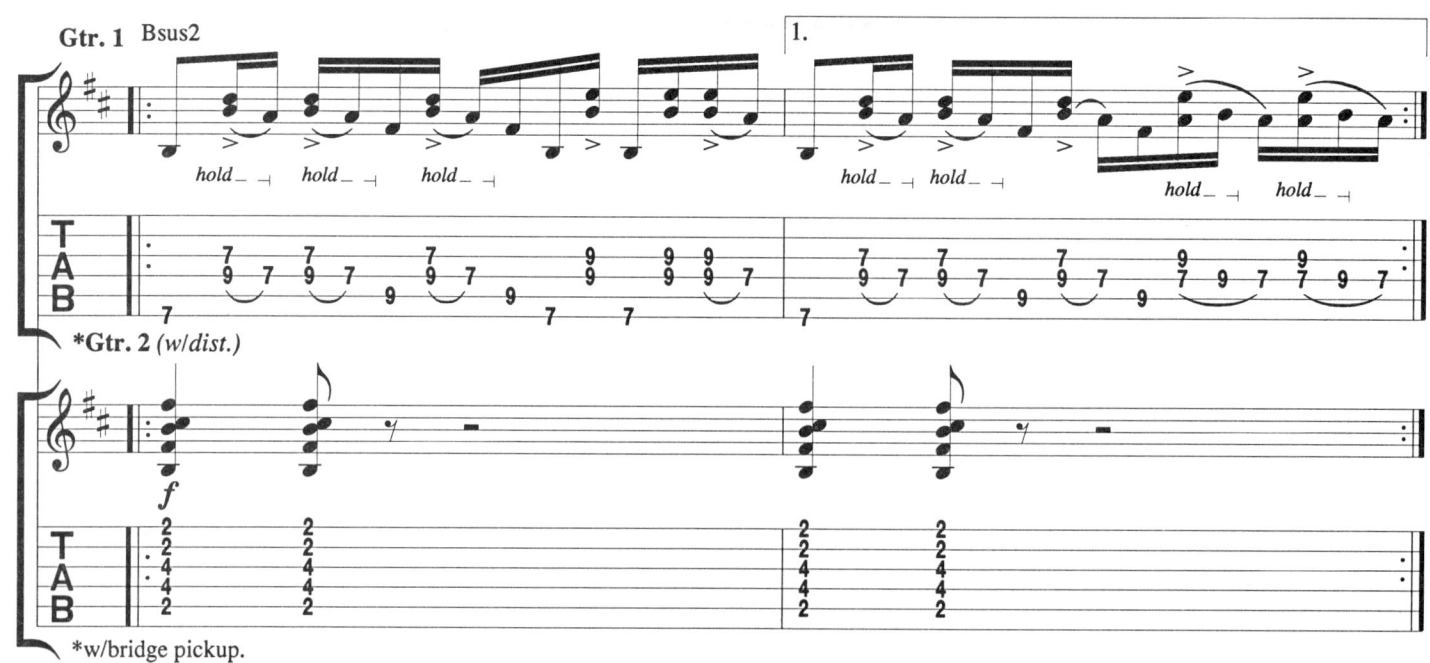

© 1994 OCTA MUSIC, INC. (ASCAP), YTSE JAMS, INC. (ASCAP)
All rights on behalf of OCTA MUSIC, INC. & YTSE JAMS, INC. administered by WB MUSIC CORP. (ASCAP)
All rights reserved

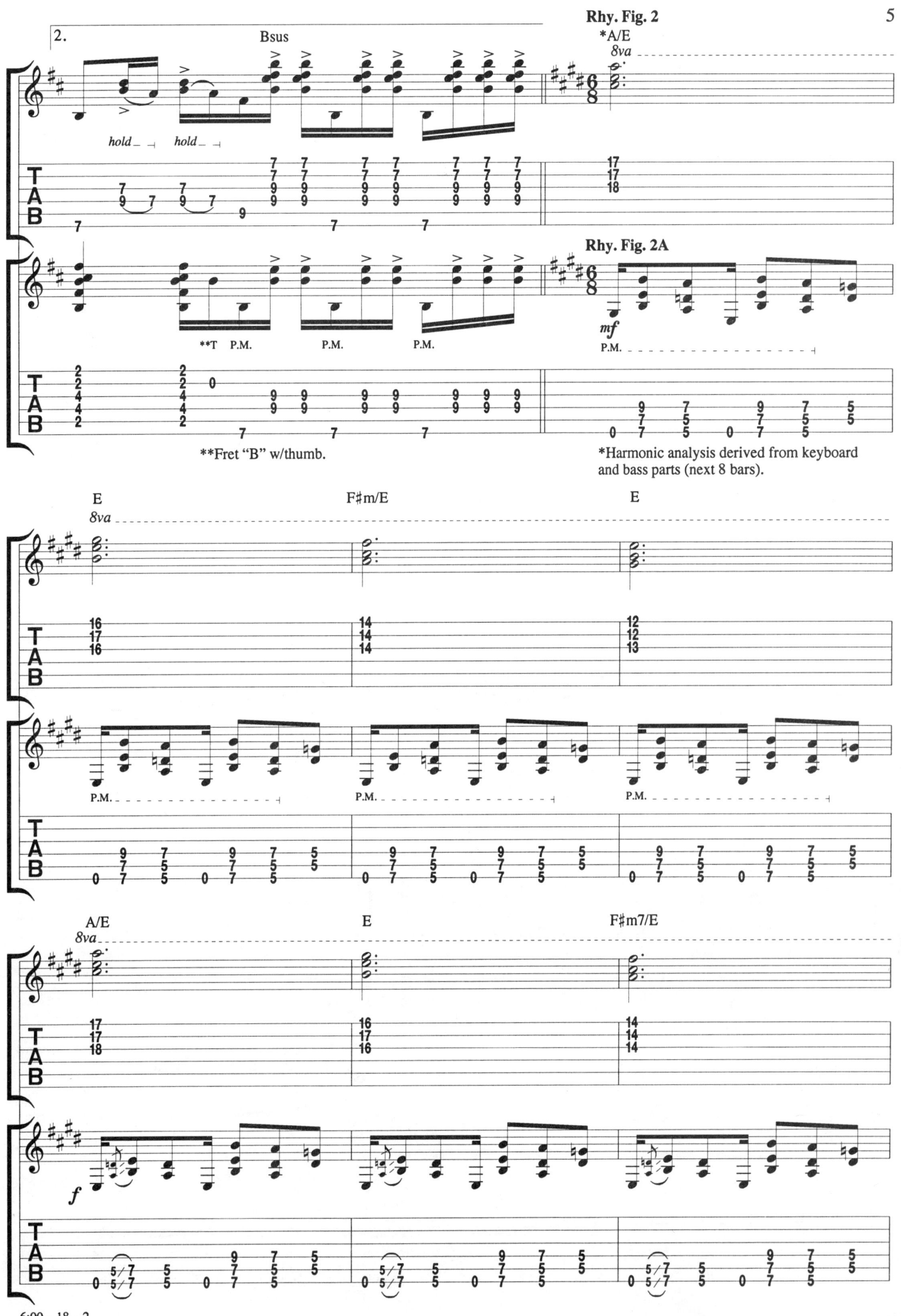

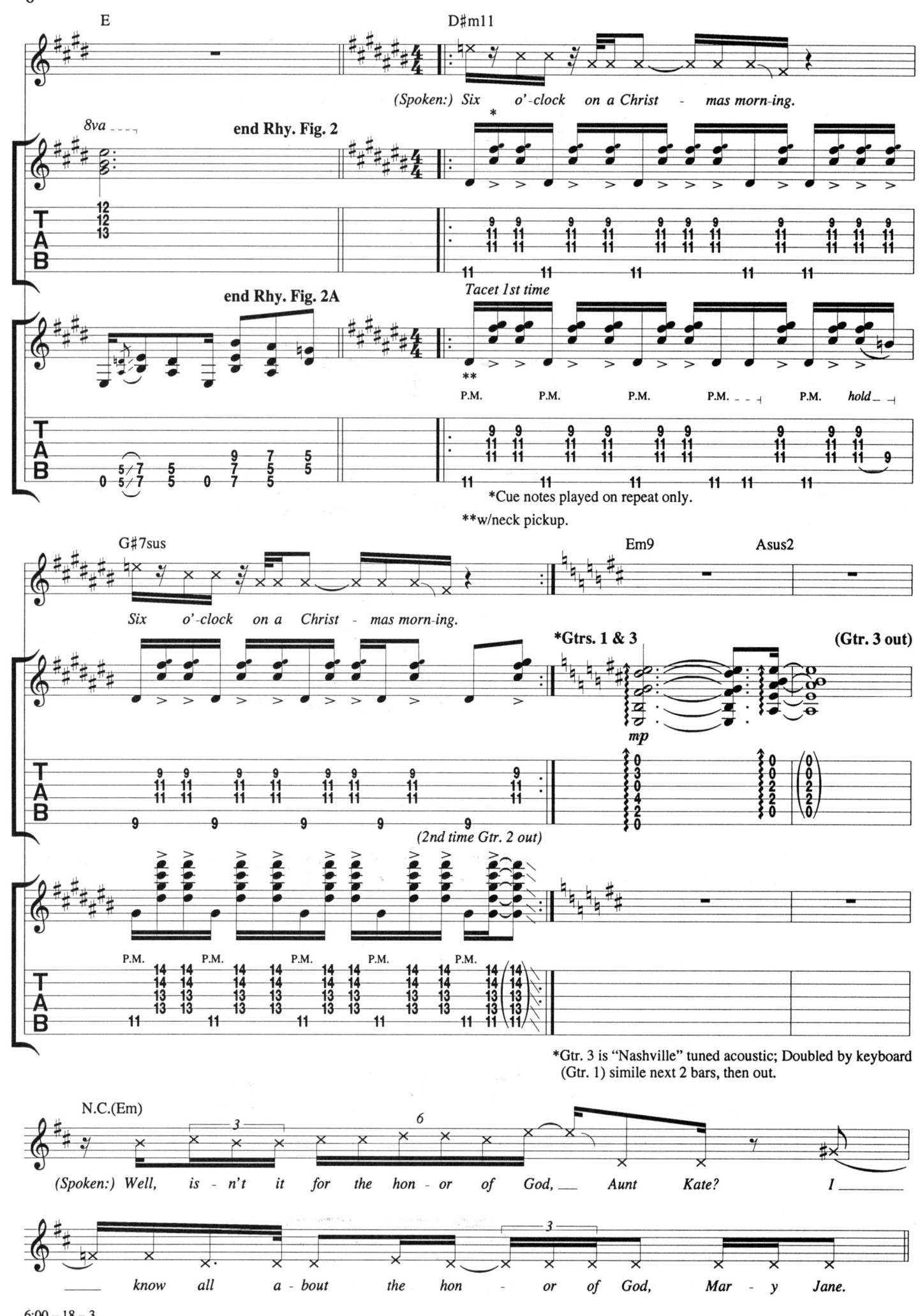

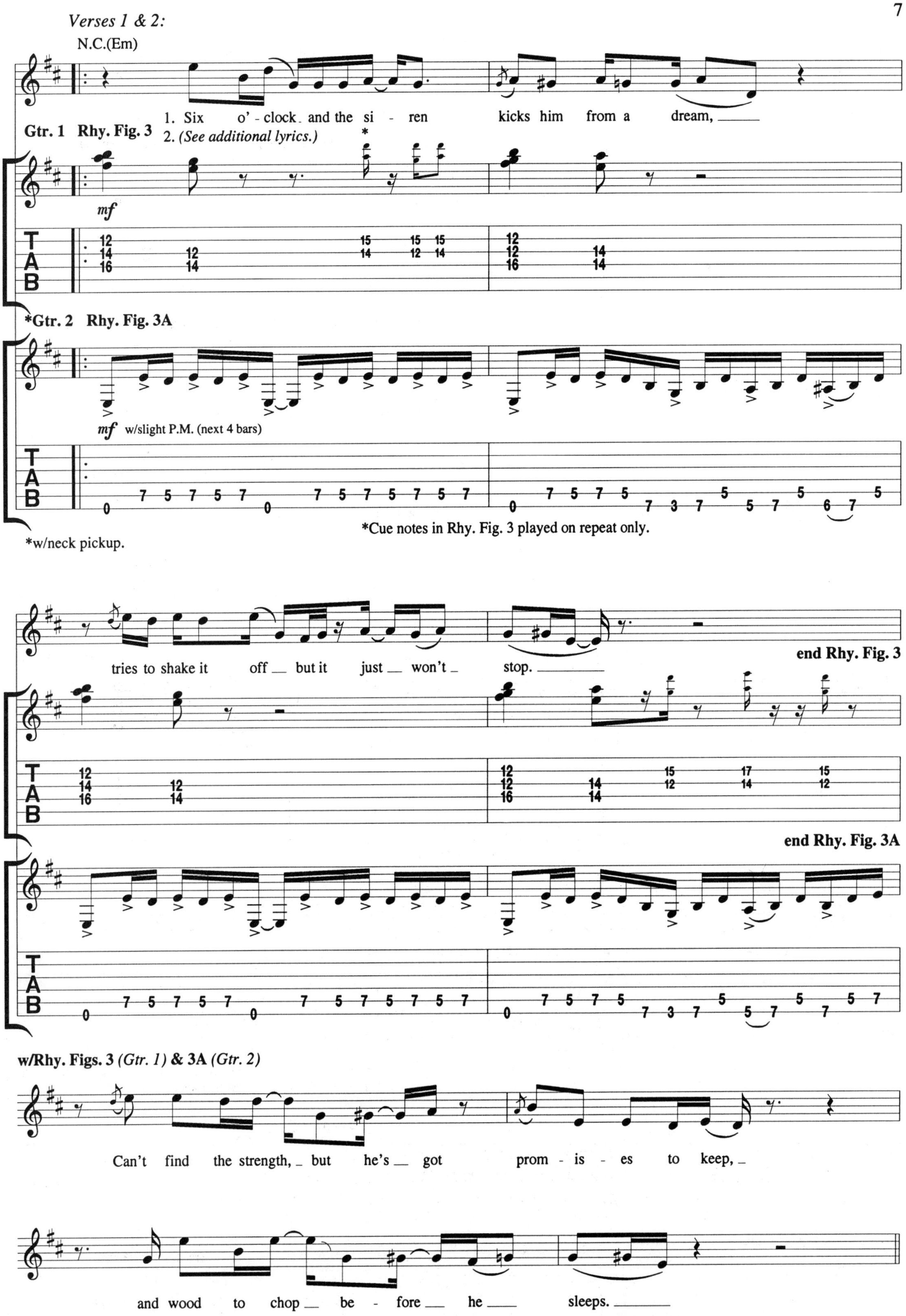
Verses 1 & 2:
N.C.(Em)
1. Six o'-clock and the si - ren kicks him from a dream,
2. (See additional lyrics.)
Gtr. 1 Rhy. Fig. 3
mf
*Gtr. 2 Rhy. Fig. 3A
mf w/slight P.M. (next 4 bars)
*w/neck pickup.
*Cue notes in Rhy. Fig. 3 played on repeat only.
tries to shake it off but it just won't stop.
end Rhy. Fig. 3
end Rhy. Fig. 3A
w/Rhy. Figs. 3 (Gtr. 1) & 3A (Gtr. 2)
Can't find the strength, but he's got prom - is - es to keep,
and wood to chop be - fore he sleeps.

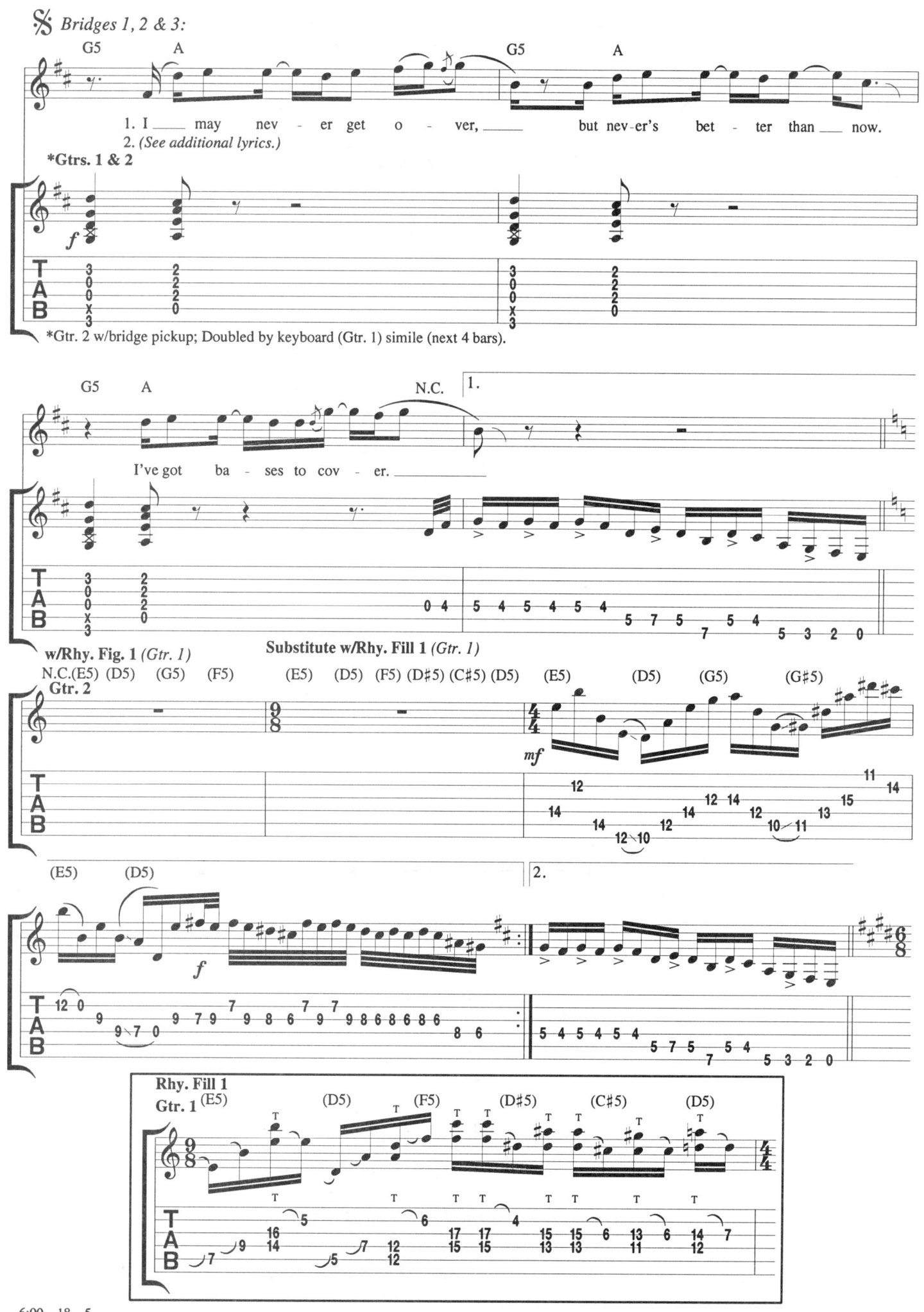

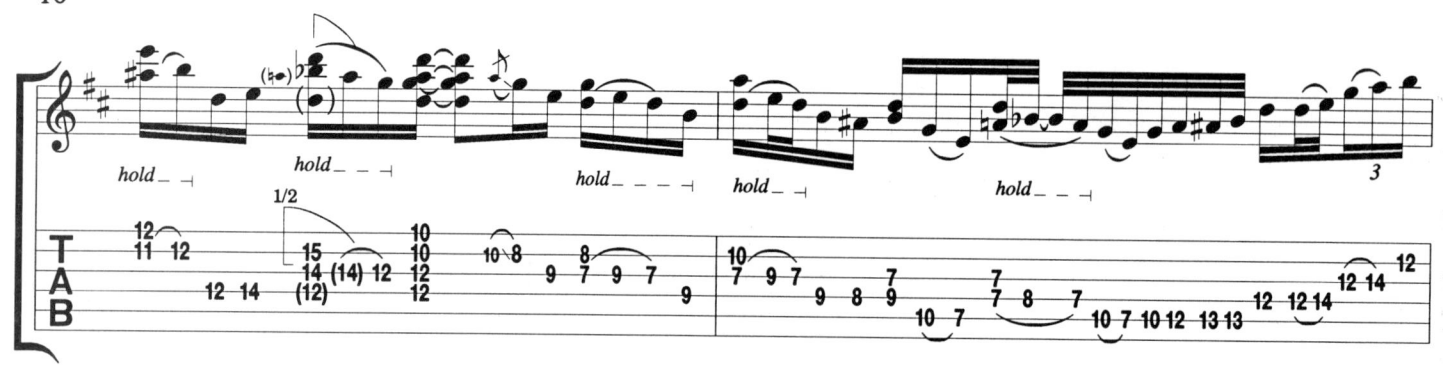

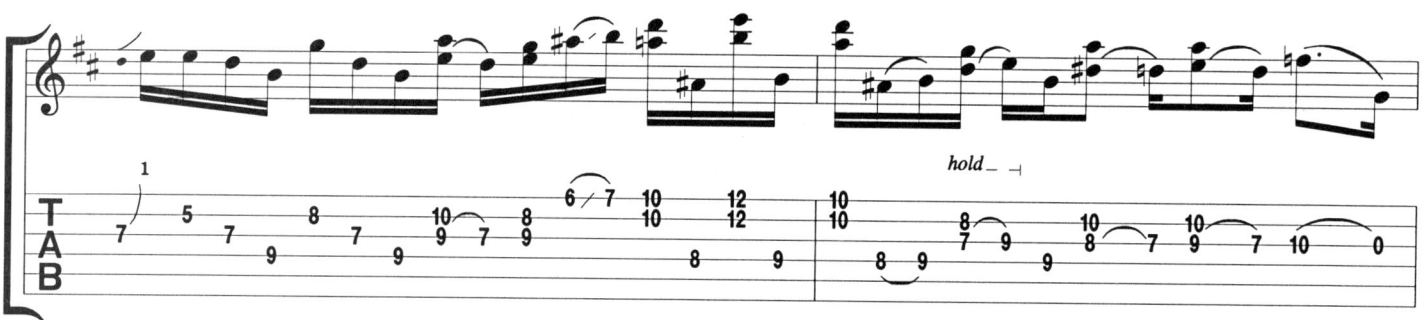

Double-time Feel

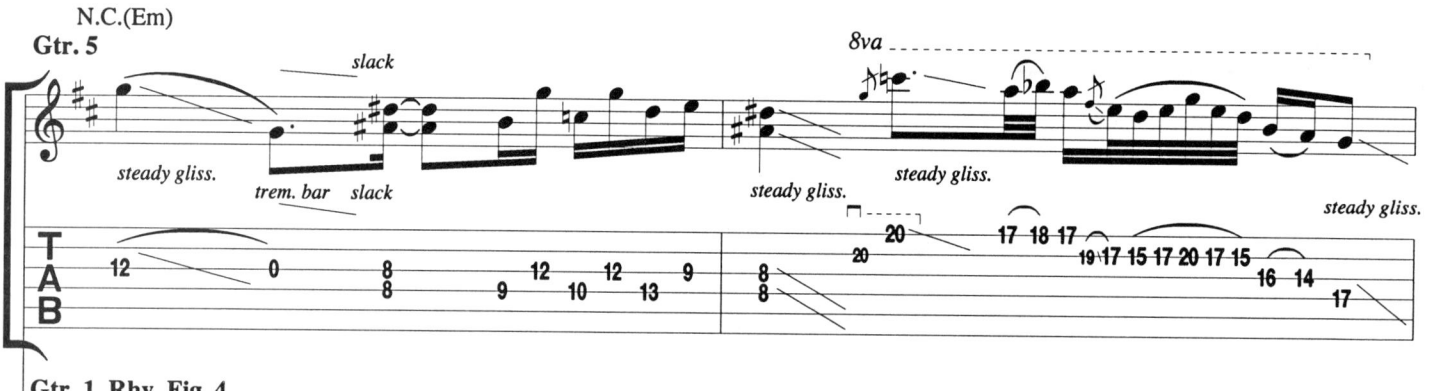

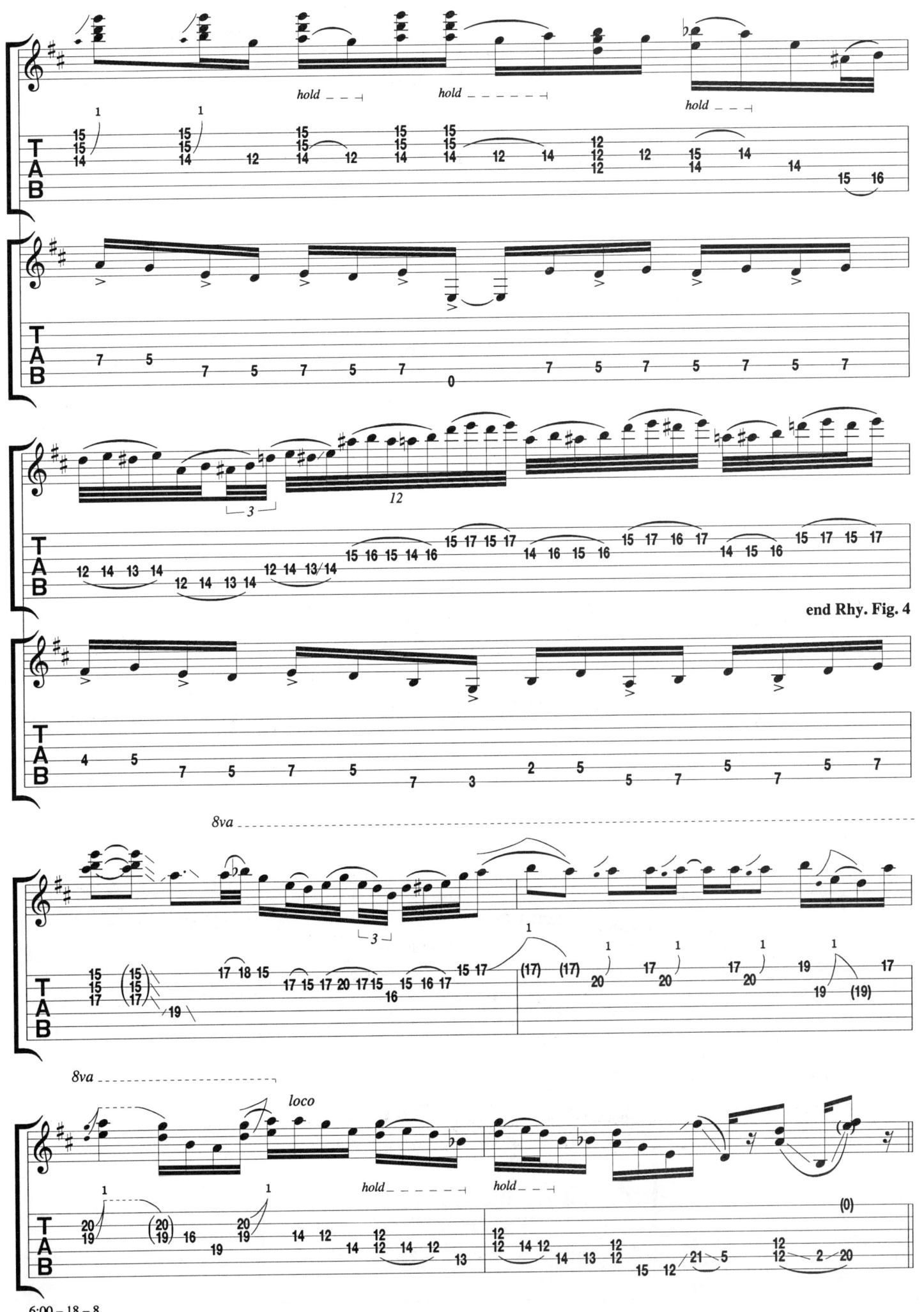

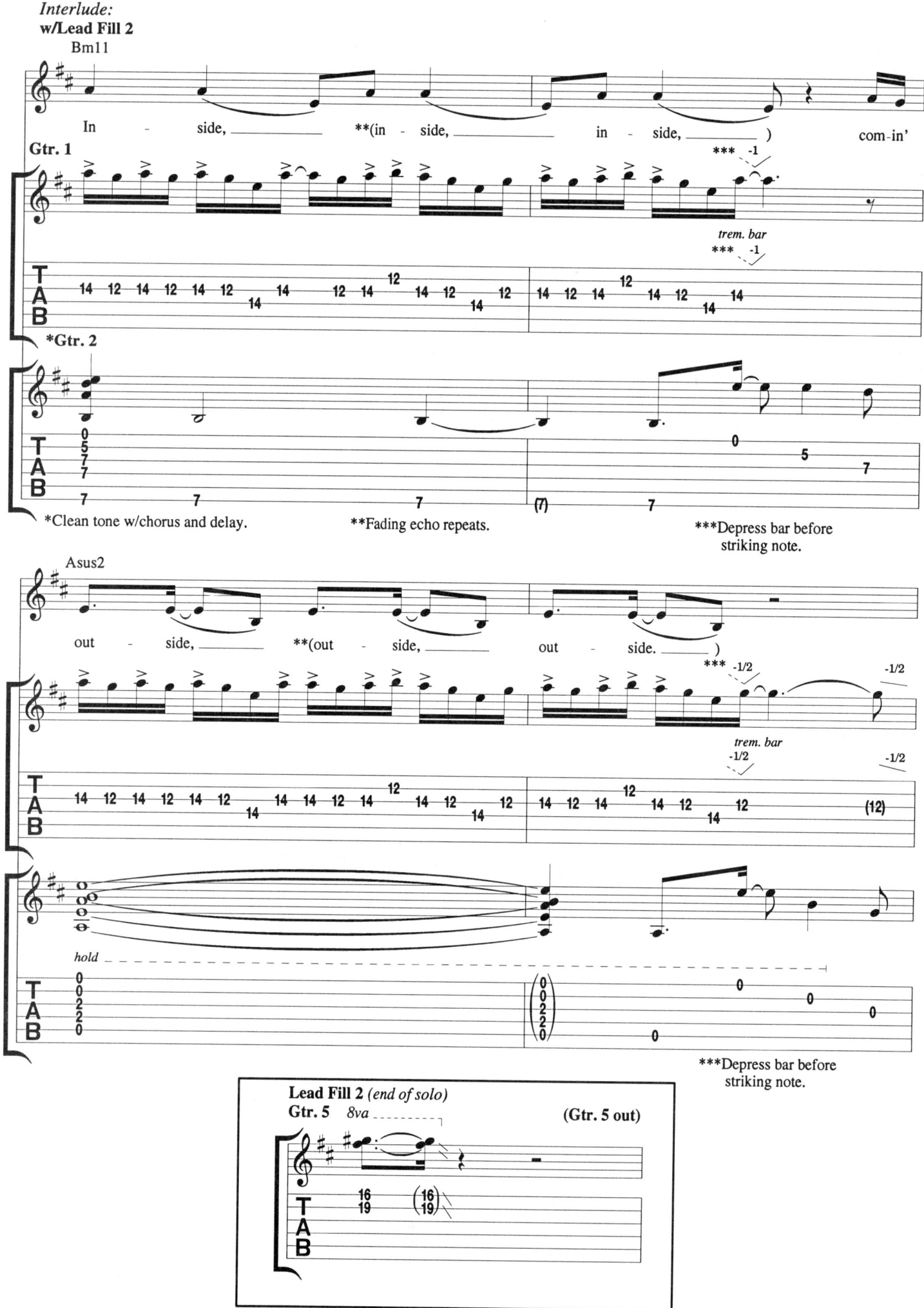

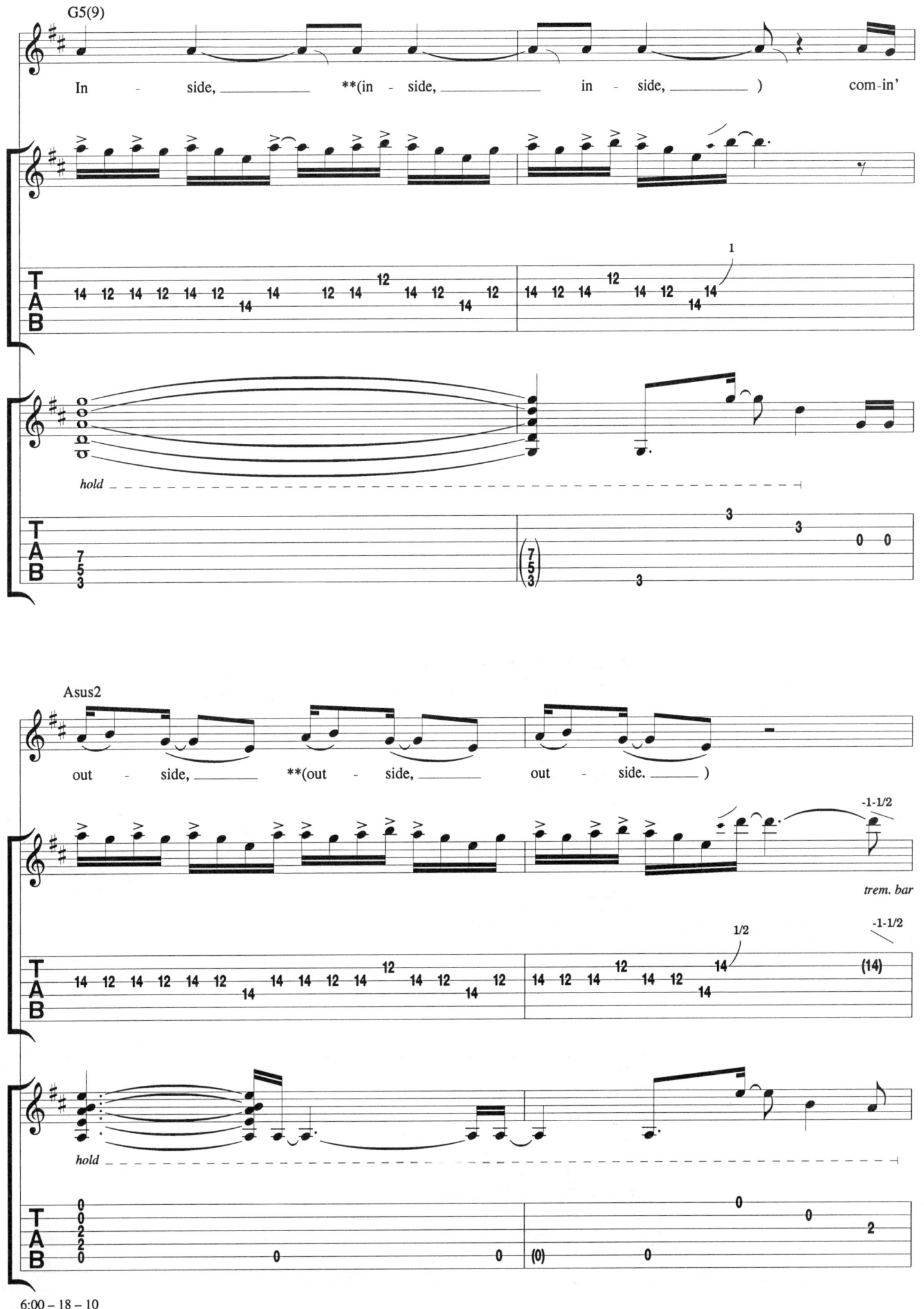

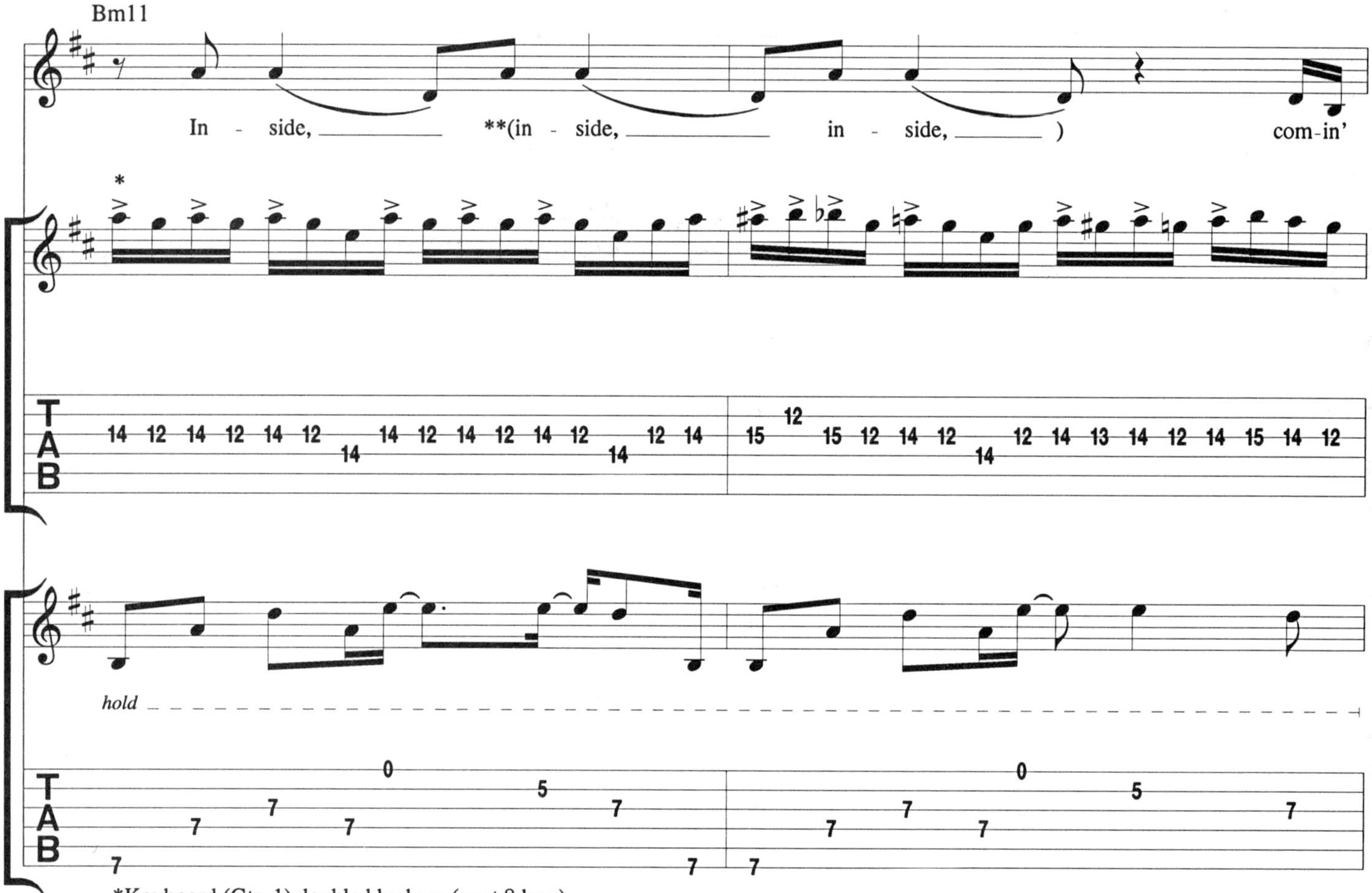

*Keyboard (Gtr. 1) doubled by bass (next 8 bars).

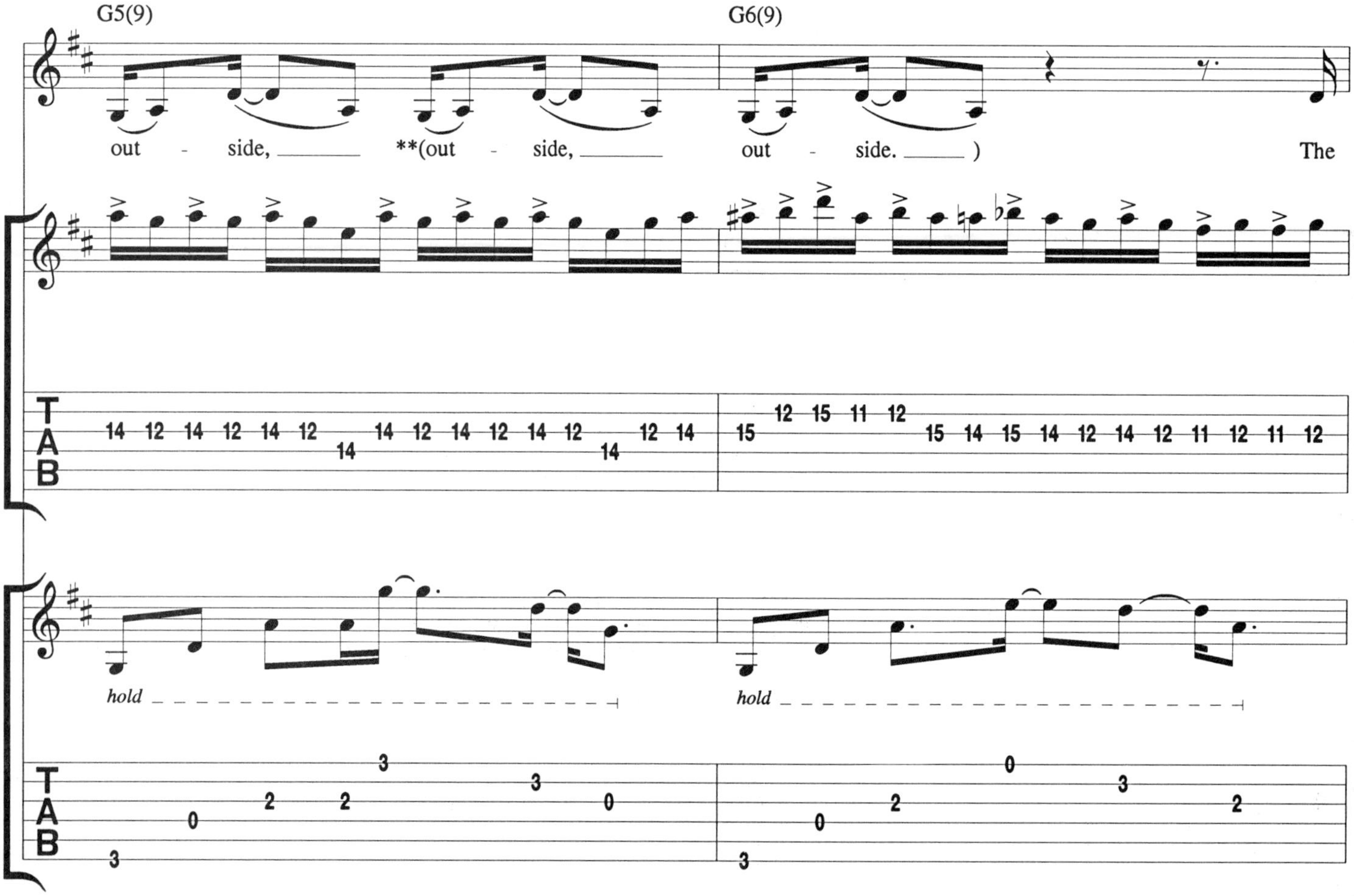

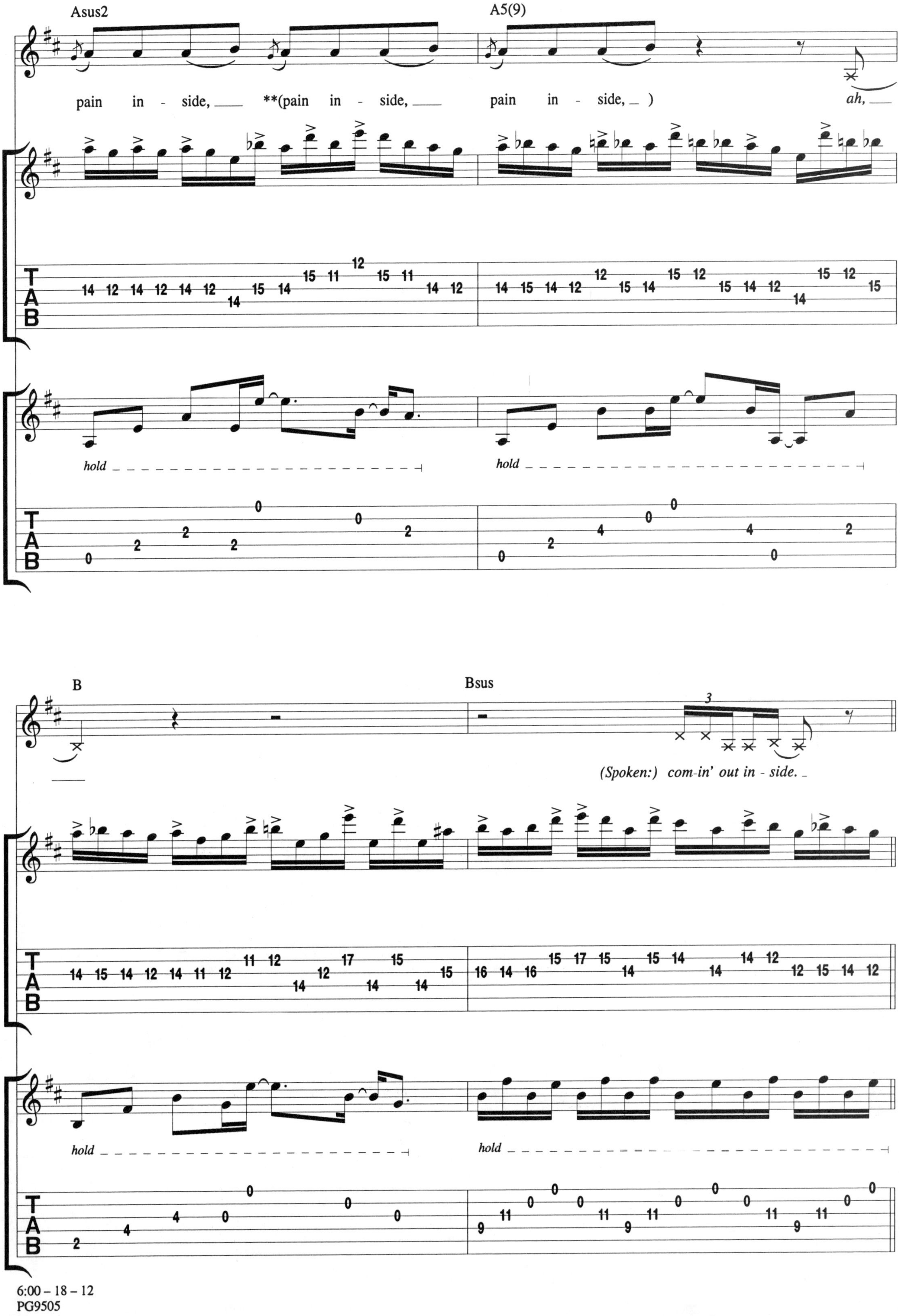
Asus2
A5(9)
pain in - side, **(pain in - side, pain in - side,)
ah,
hold
hold
B
Bsus
(Spoken:) com-in' out in - side.
hold
hold

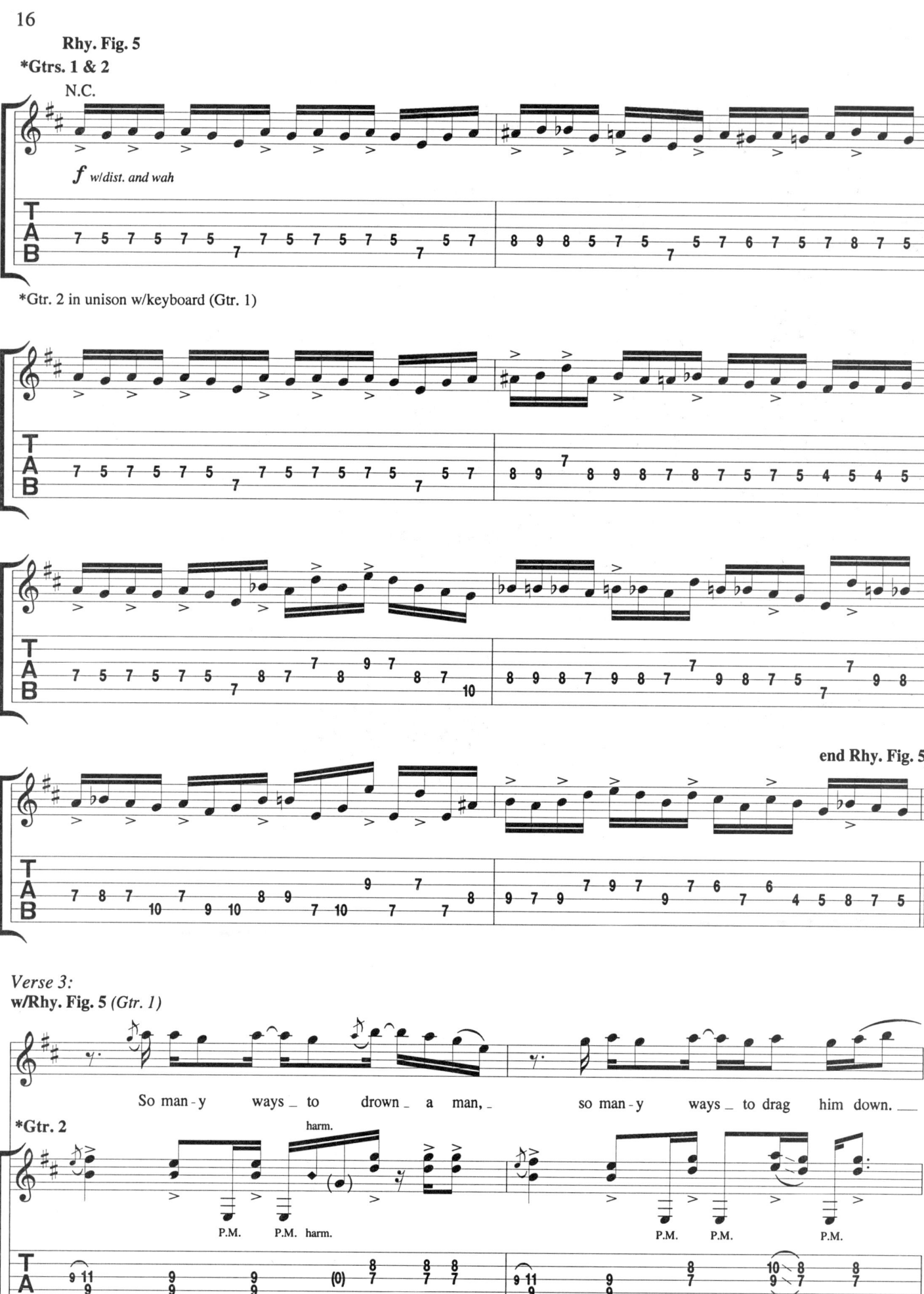

Double - time Feel
G#7sus
(Spoken:) know all a - bout the hon - or of God, Mar - y...
Gtr. 6
f
Gtrs. 1 & 2
P.M.
f
I know all a - bout the hon - or of God, Mar - y...
5:4
P.M.
hold

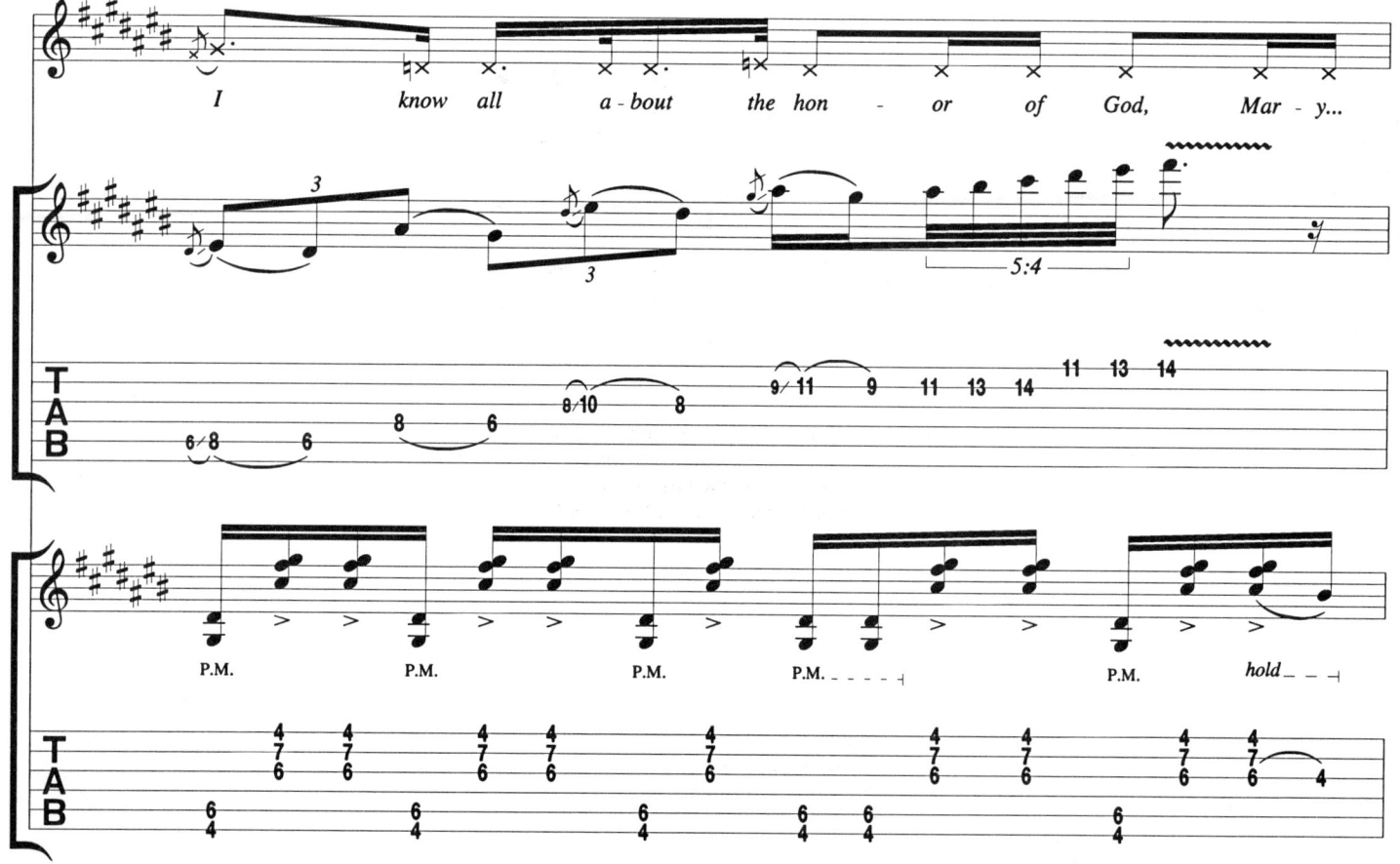

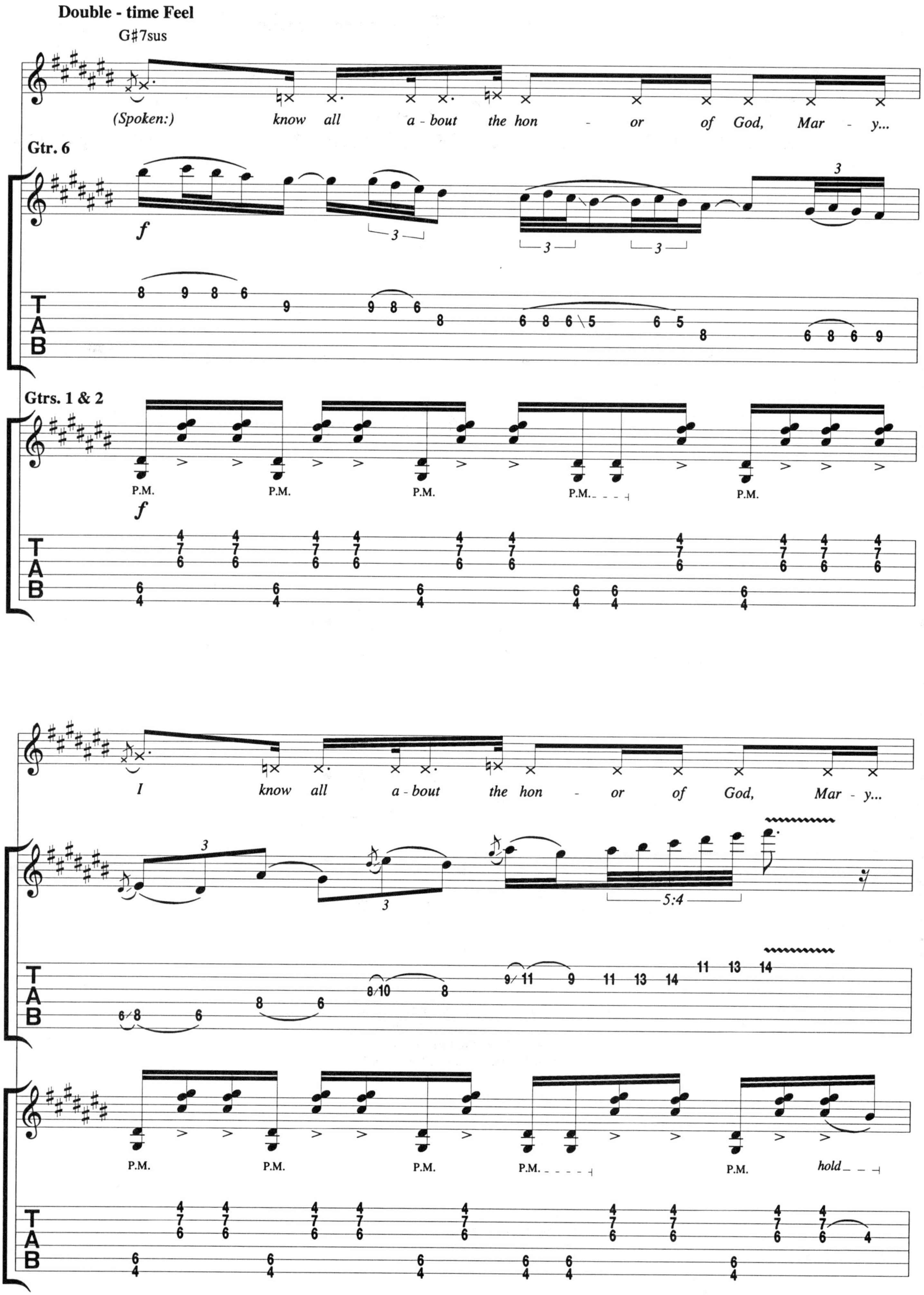

Verse 2:
He's in the parking lot just sitting in his car.
It's nine o'clock, but he can't get out.
He lights his cigarette and turns the music down,
but he just can't seem to shake that sound.

Bridge 2:
Once I thought I'd get over,
But it's too late for me now.
I've got bases to cover.
(To Chorus:)

Bridge 3:
I could never get over,
Is it too late for me now?
Feel like blowing my cover.
(To Chorus:)

CAUGHT IN A WEB

By JAMES LABRIE, KEVIN MOORE
JOHN MYUNG, JOHN PETRUCCI and MICHAEL PORTNOY

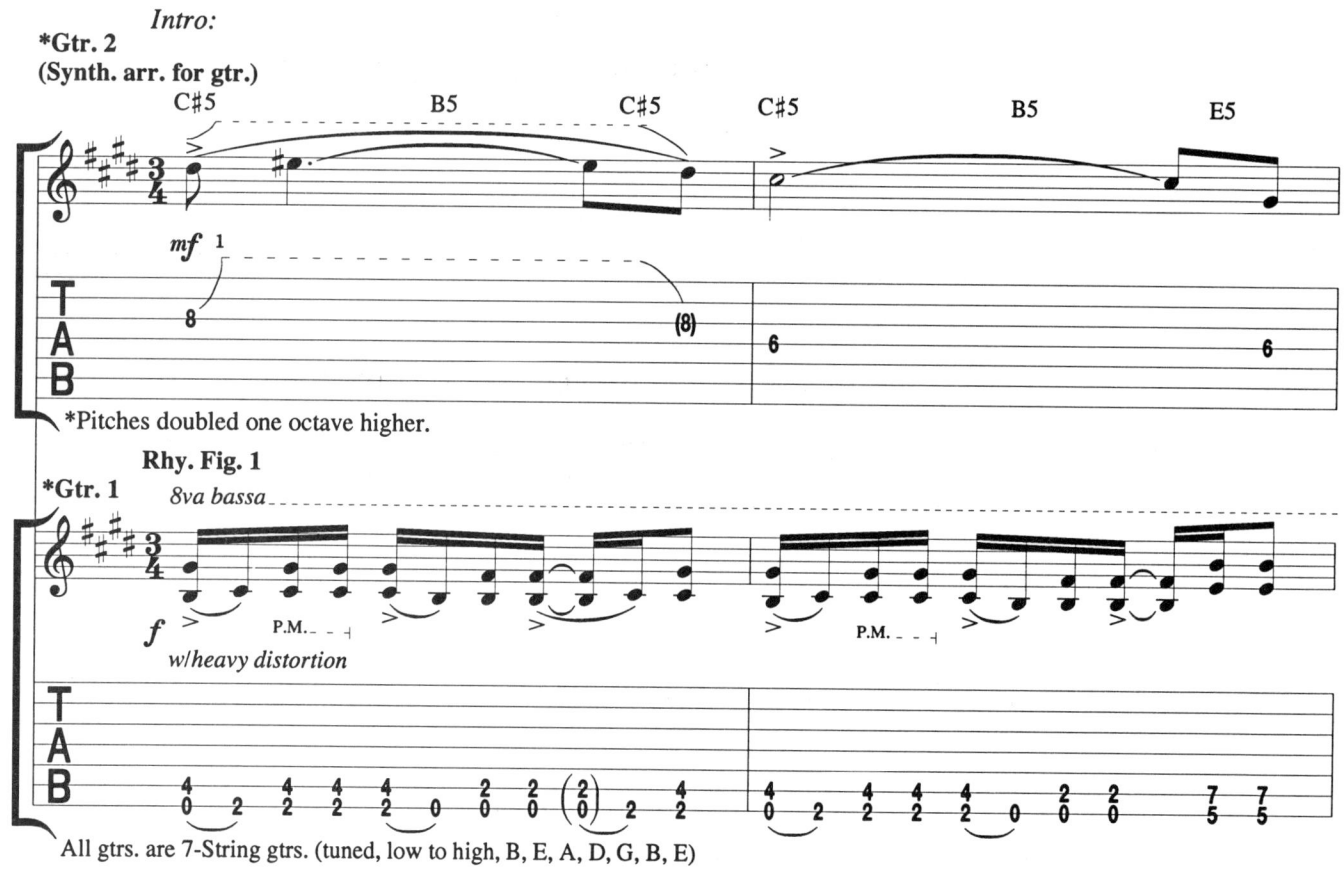

All gtrs. are 7-String gtrs. (tuned, low to high, B, E, A, D, G, B, E)

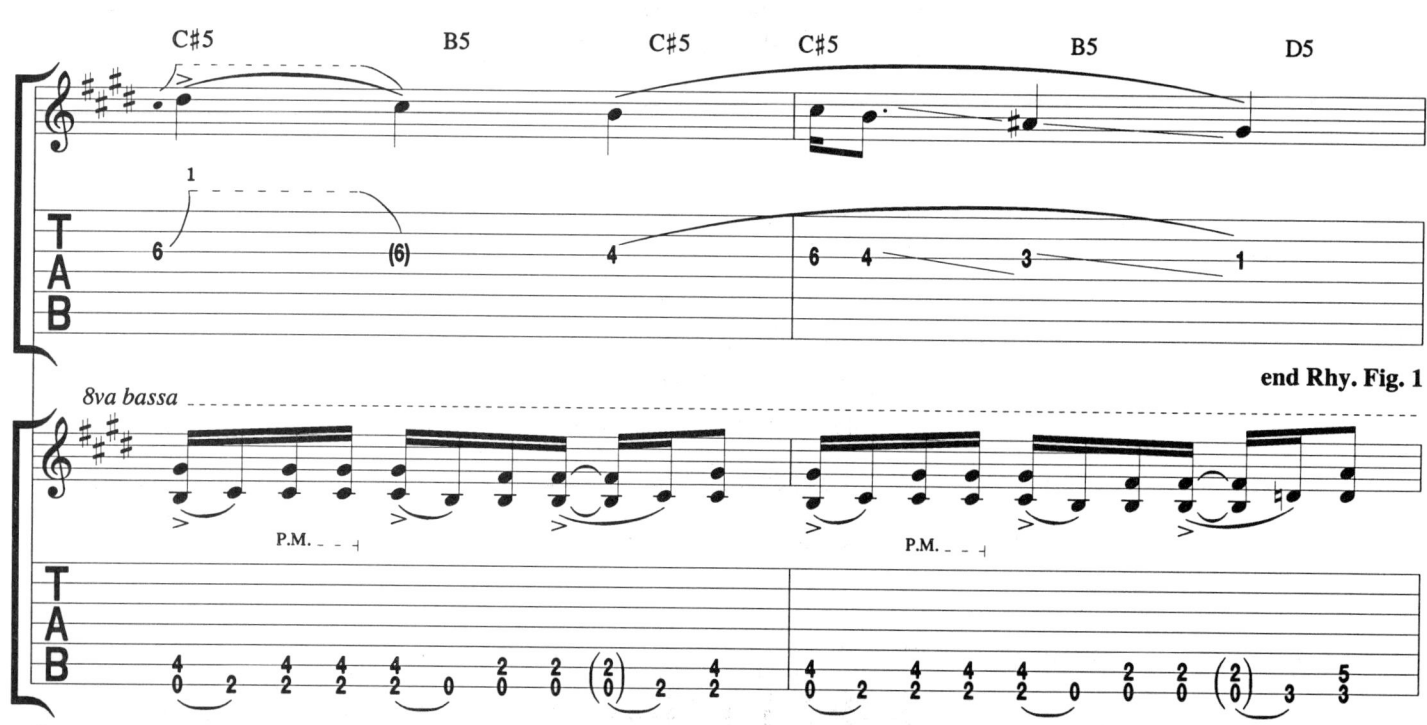

Caught In A Web – 14 – 1
PG9505

© 1994 OCTA MUSIC, INC. (ASCAP), YTSE JAMS, INC. (ASCAP)
All rights on behalf of OCTA MUSIC, INC. & YTSE JAMS, INC. administered by WB MUSIC CORP. (ASCAP)
All rights reserved

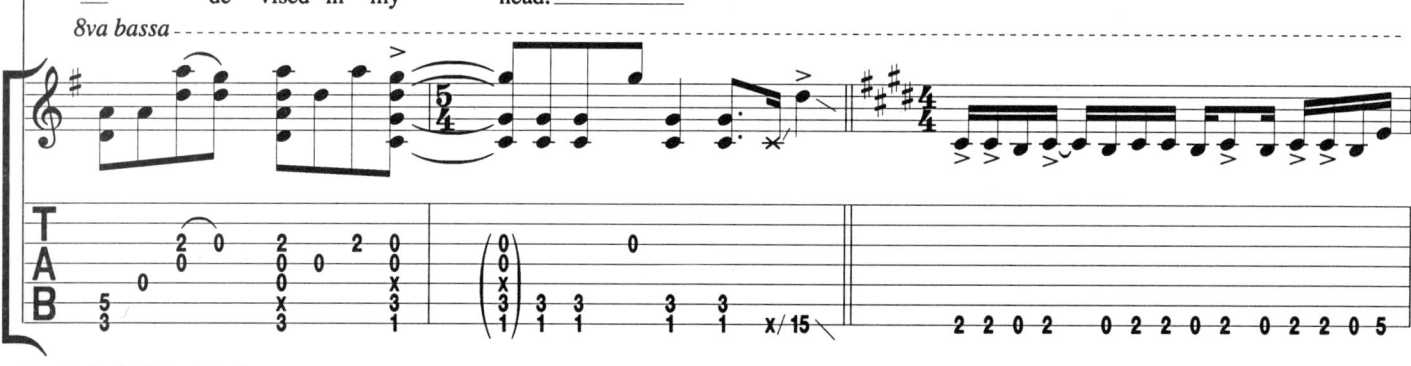

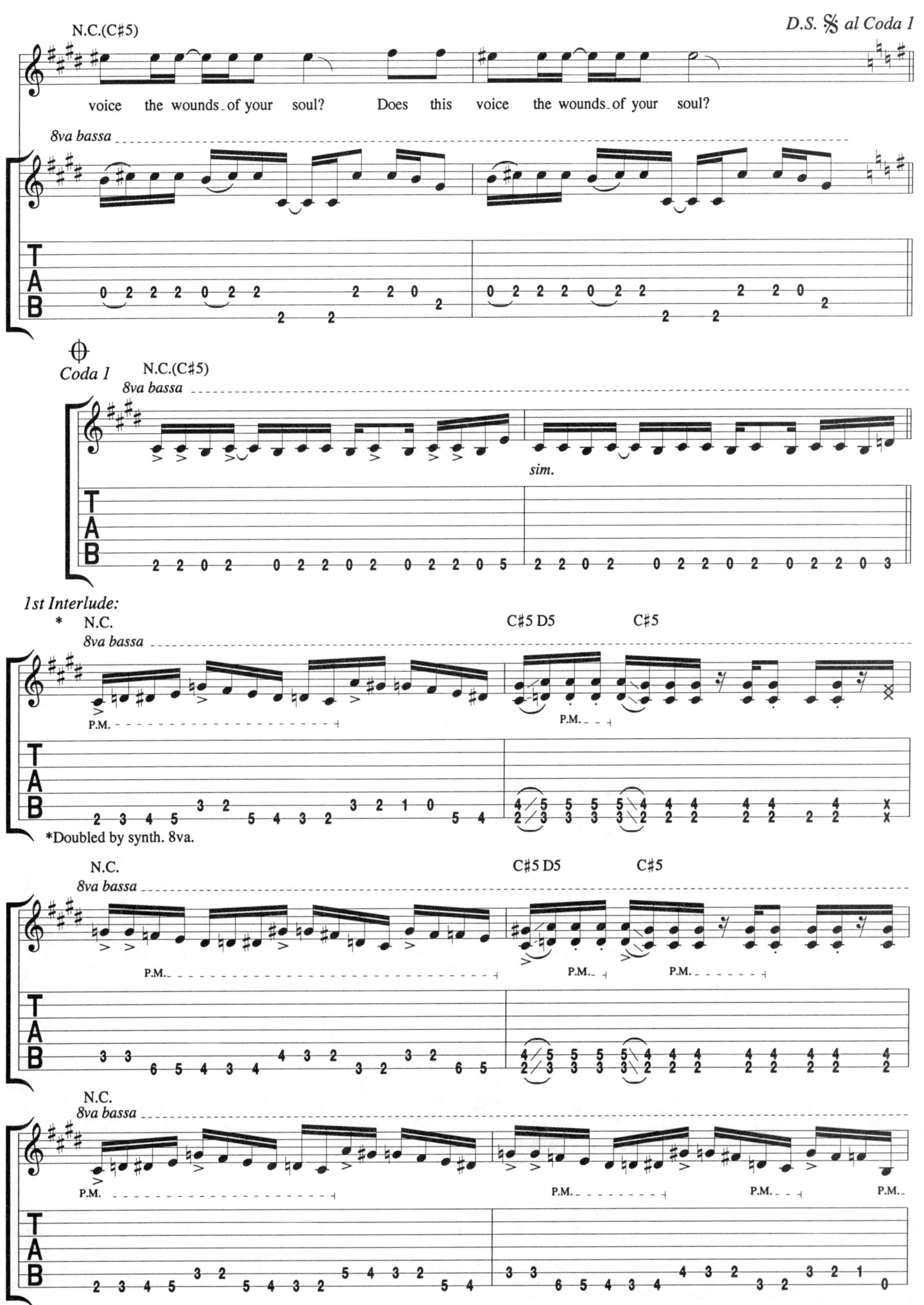

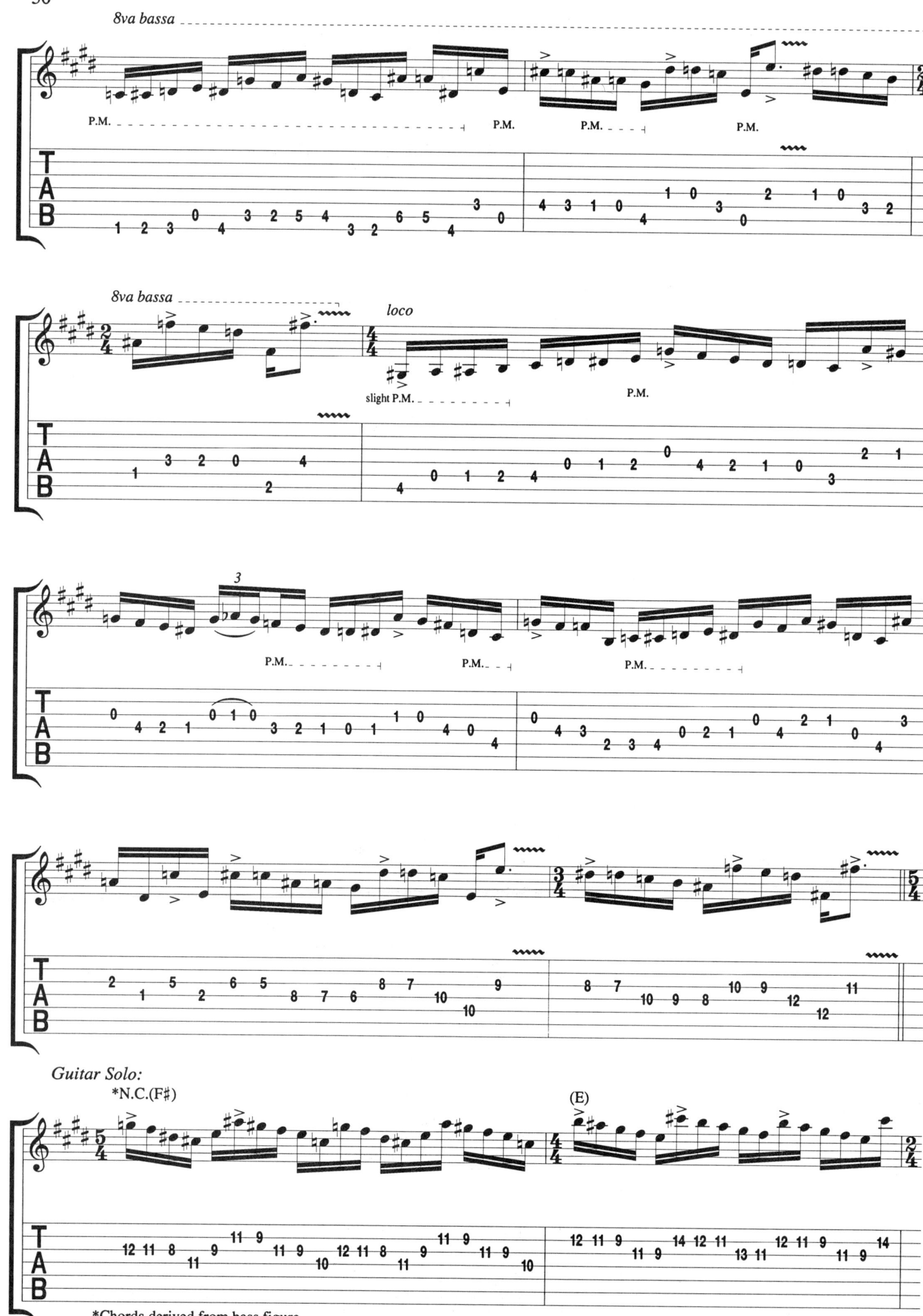

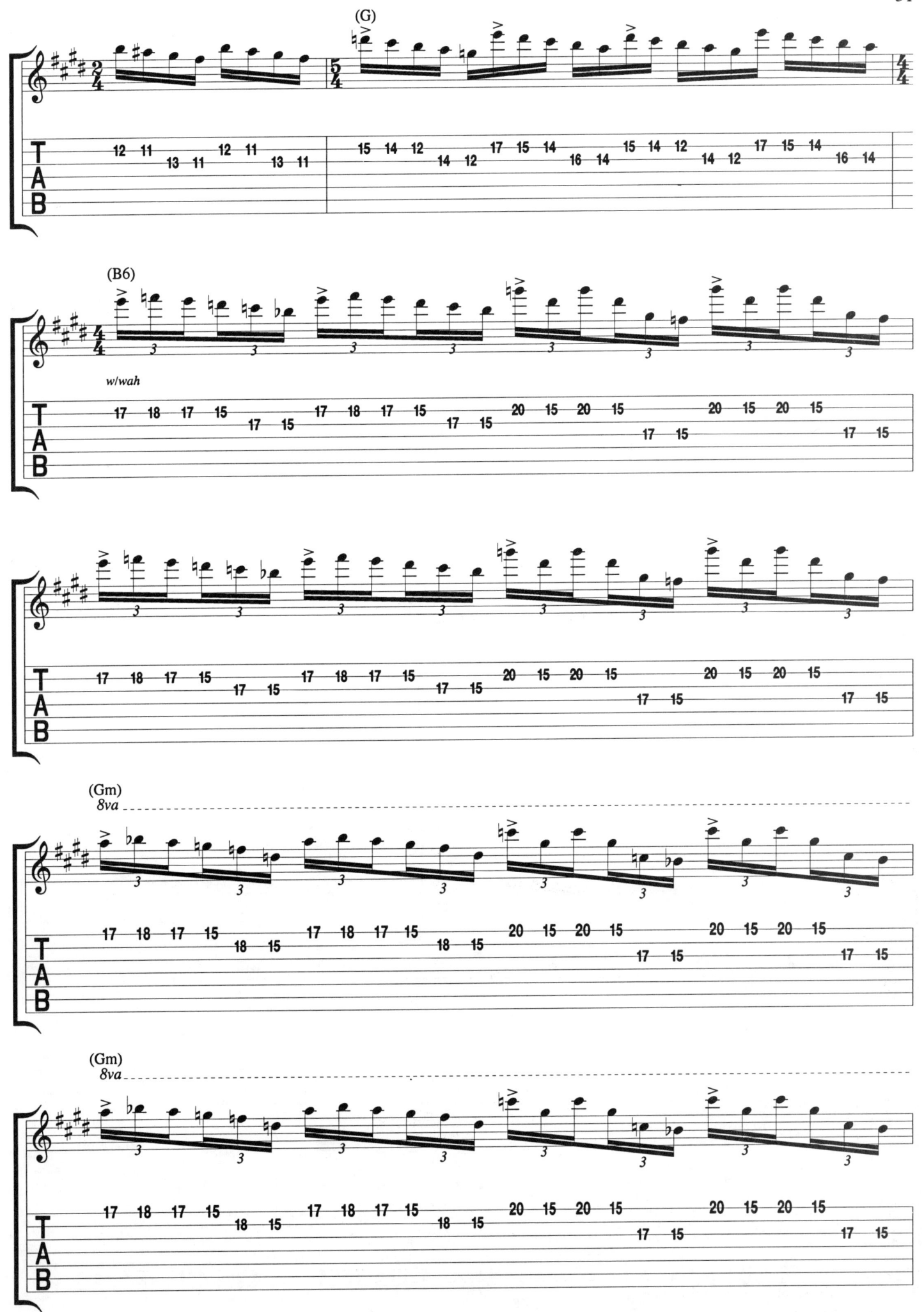

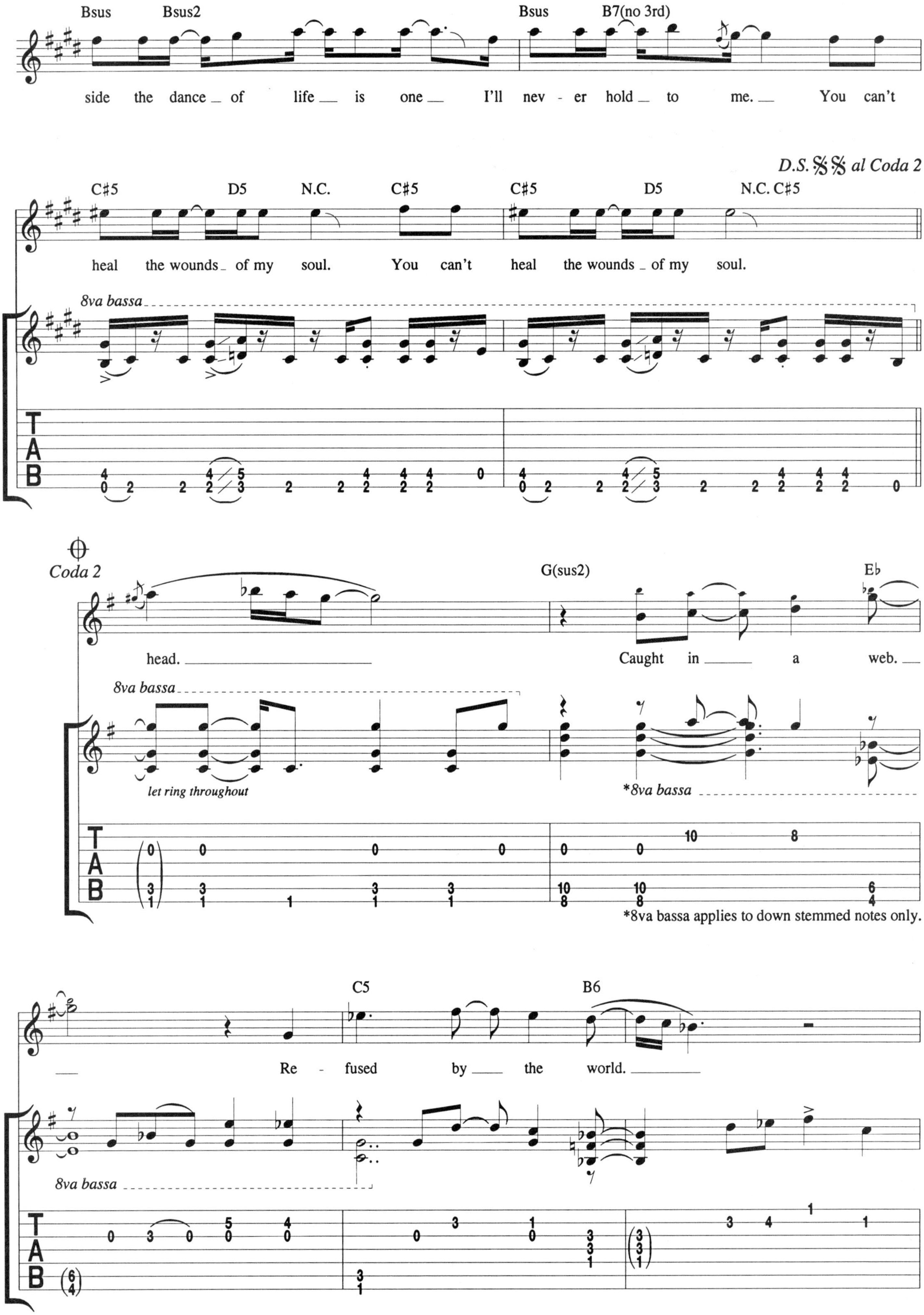
Bsus
Bsus2
Bsus
B7(no 3rd)
side the dance of life is one I'll nev - er hold to me. You can't
D.S. 𝄋𝄋 al Coda 2
C♯5
D5
N.C.
C♯5
C♯5
D5
N.C. C♯5
heal the wounds of my soul. You can't heal the wounds of my soul.
8va bassa
Coda 2
G(sus2)
E♭
head. Caught in a web.
8va bassa
let ring throughout
*8va bassa
*8va bassa applies to down stemmed notes only.
C5
B6
Re - fused by the world.
8va bassa

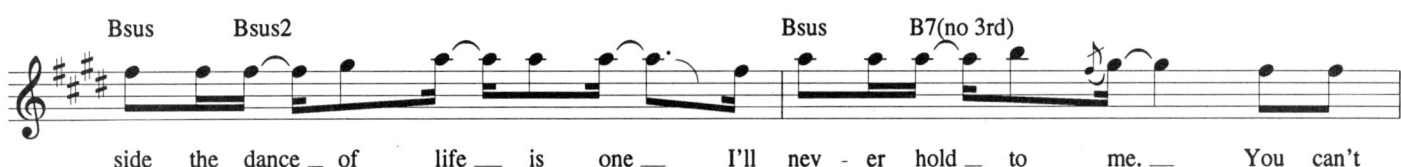

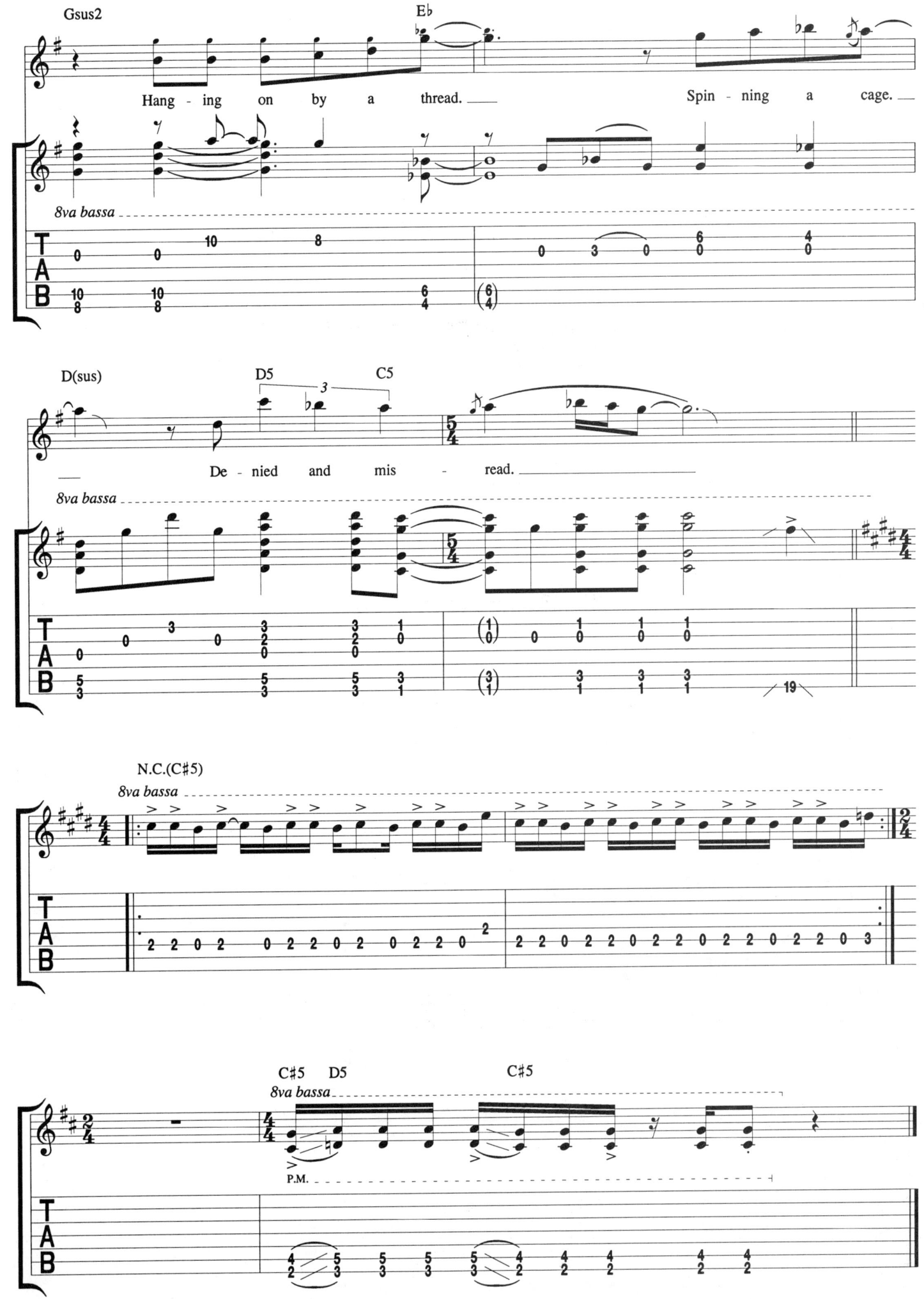

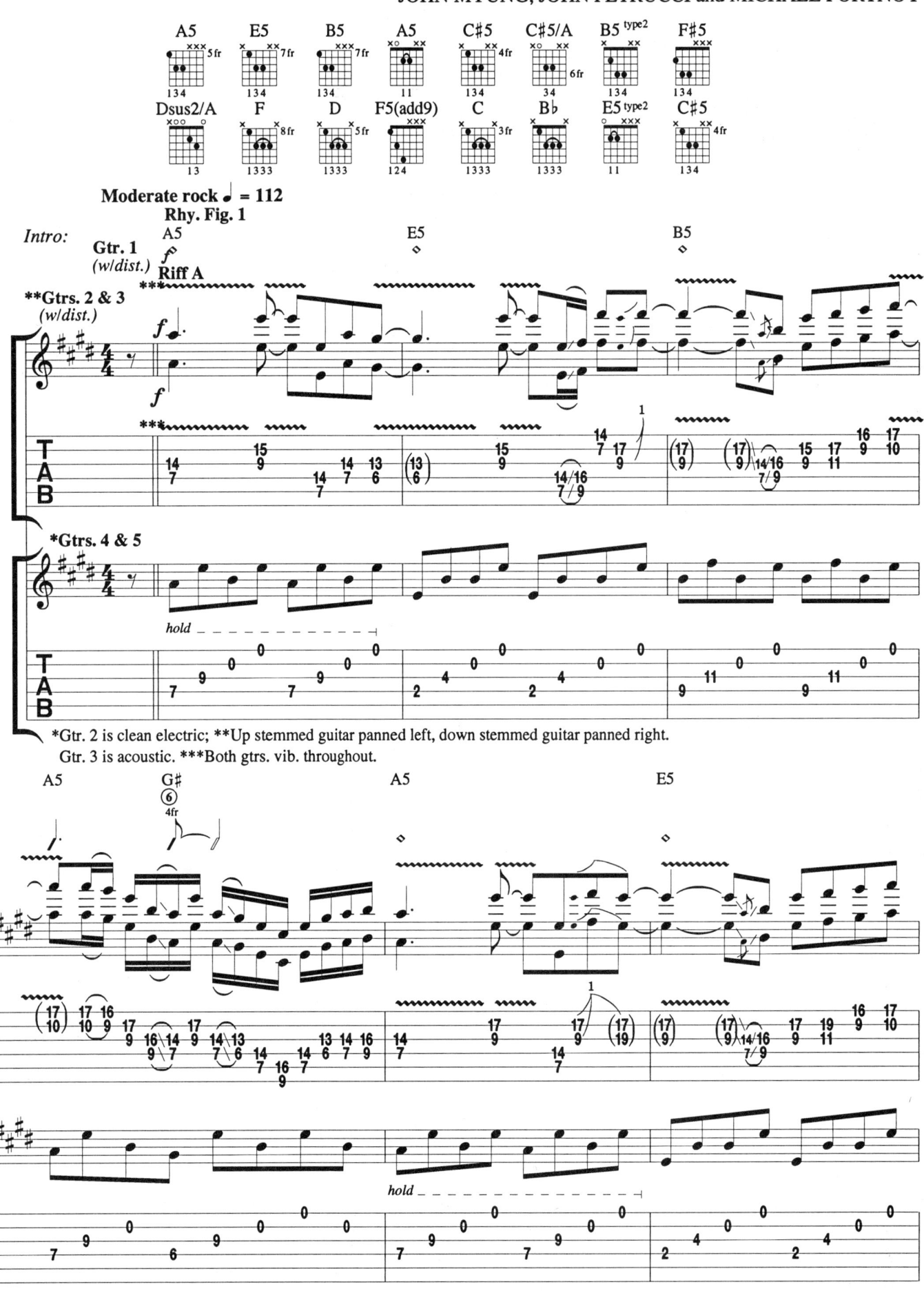

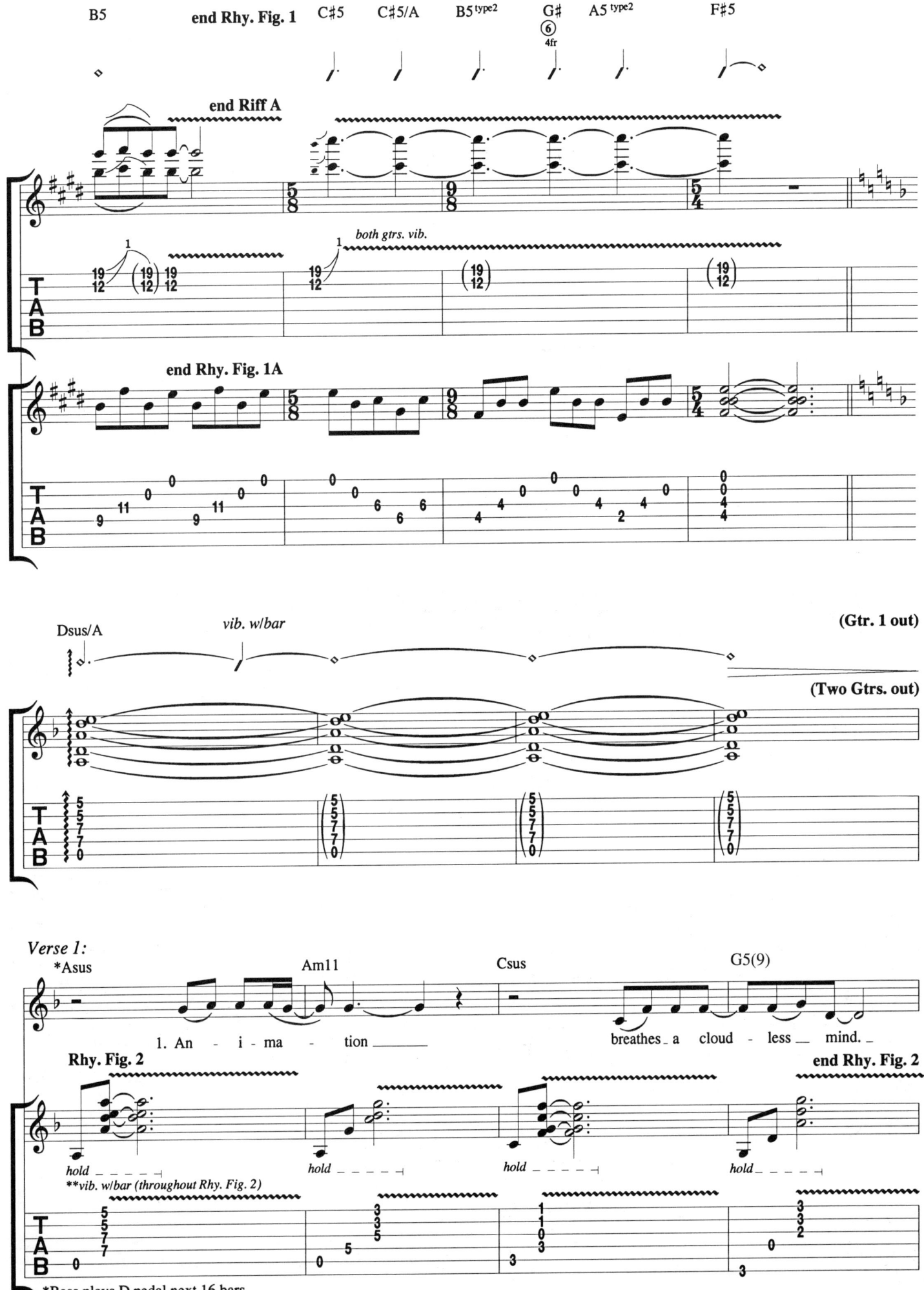

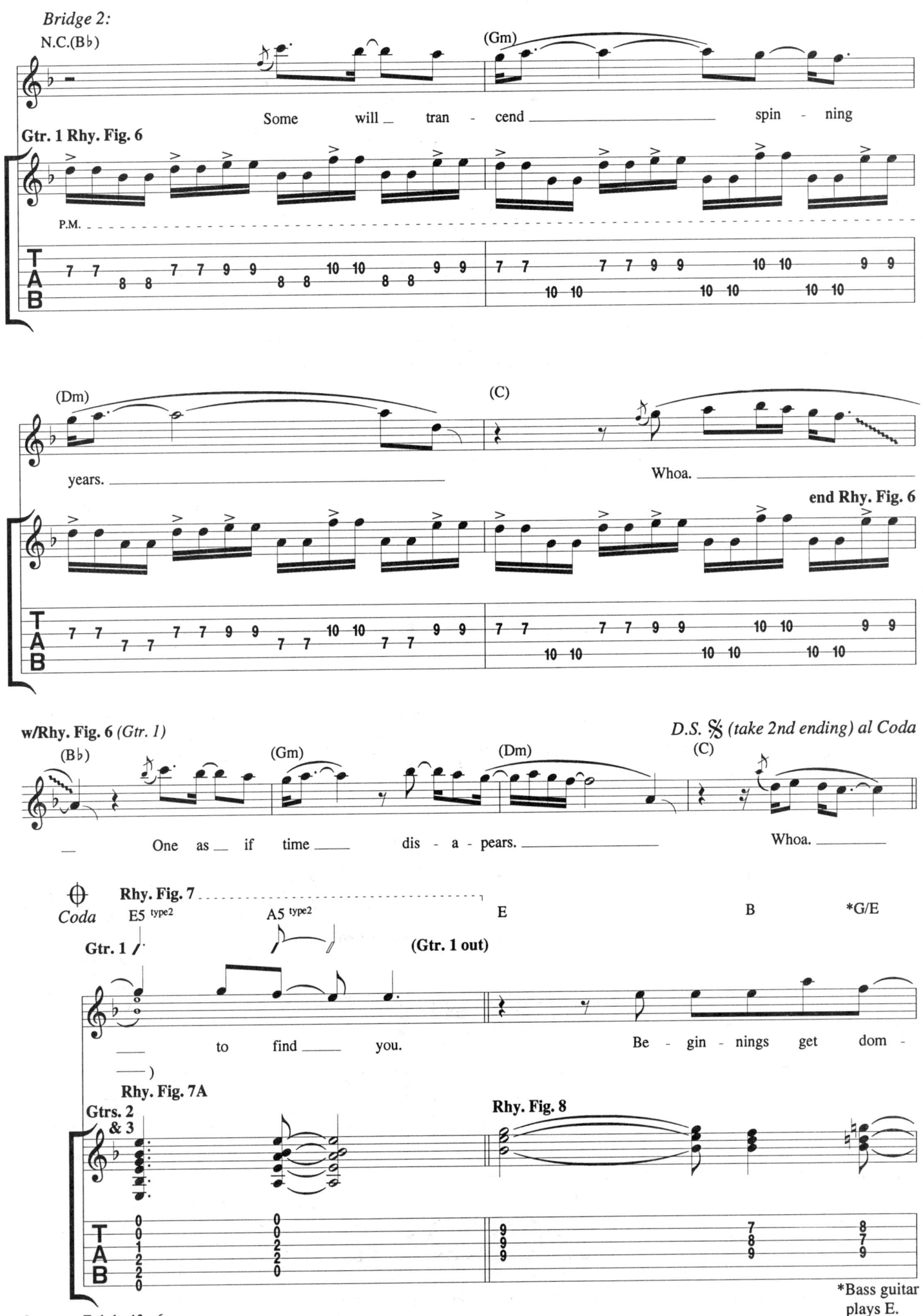

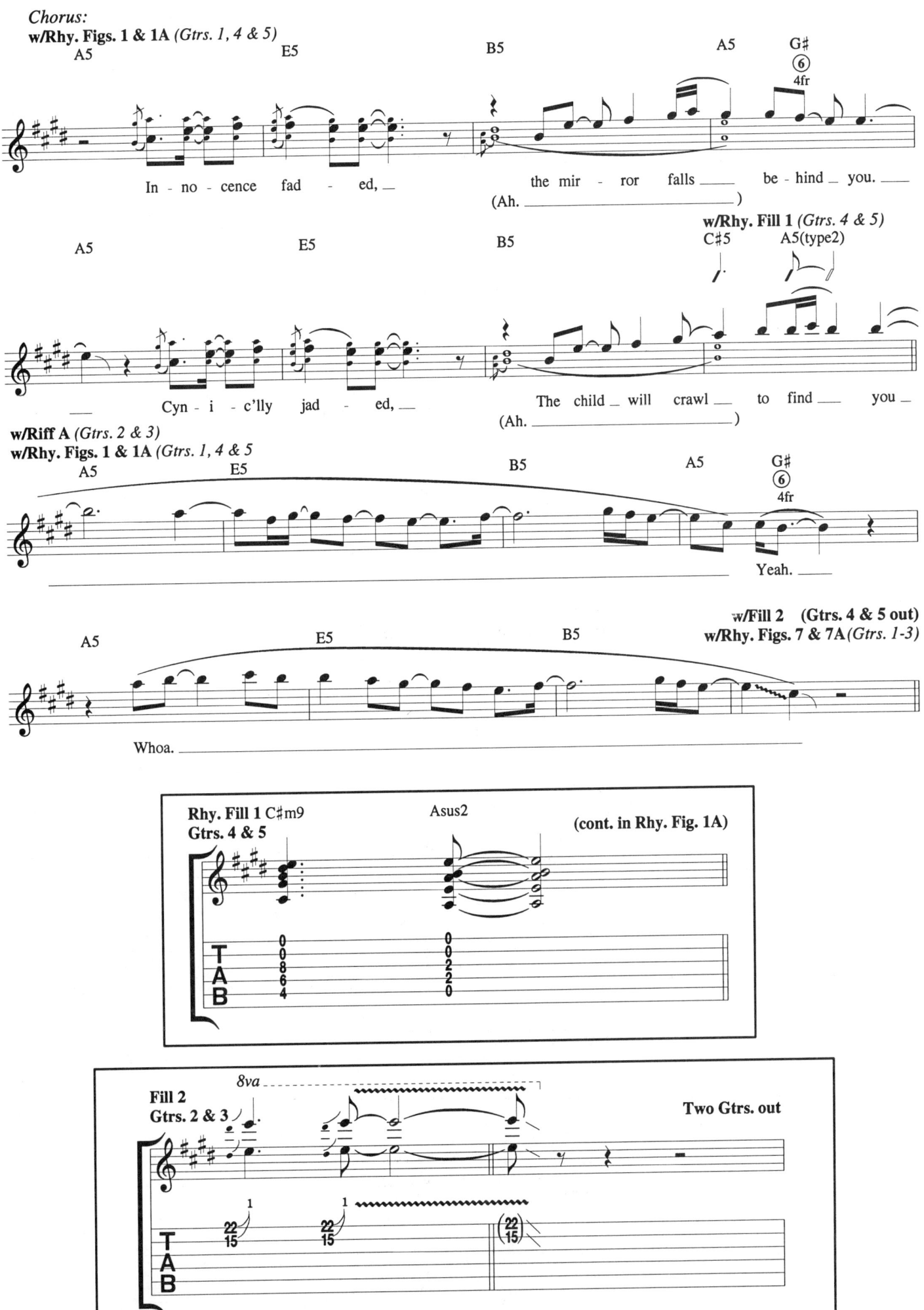

46

Innocence Faded – 13 – 11
PG9505

Innocence Faded – 13 – 12
PG9505

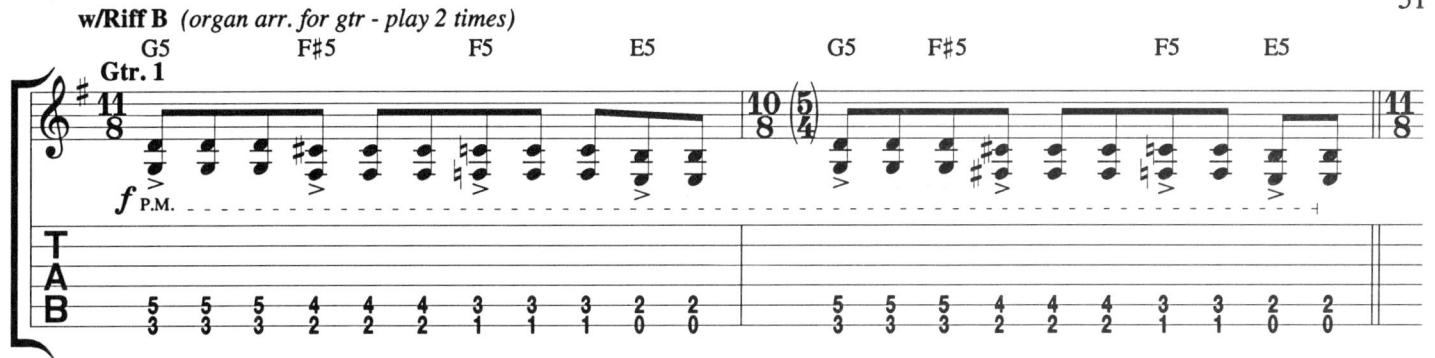
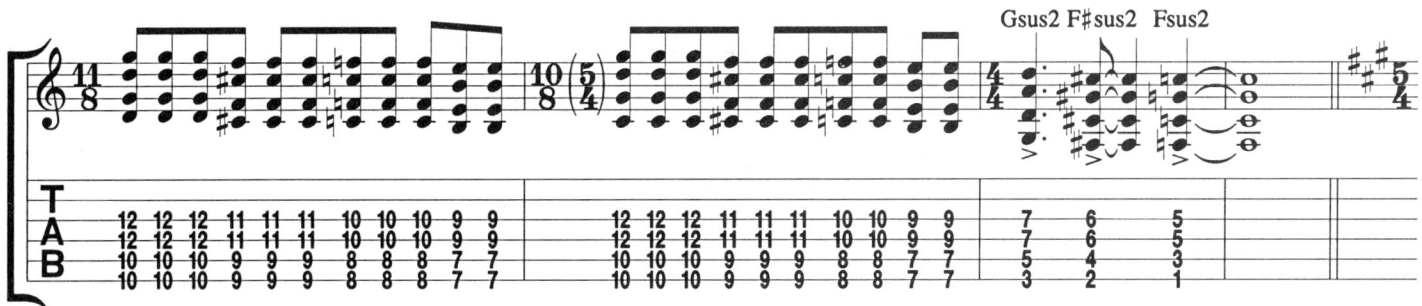

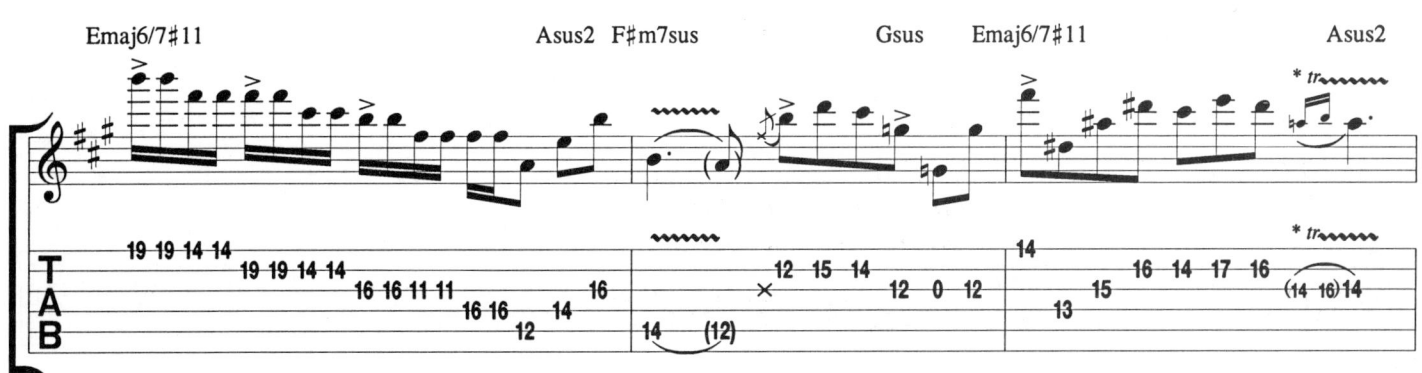
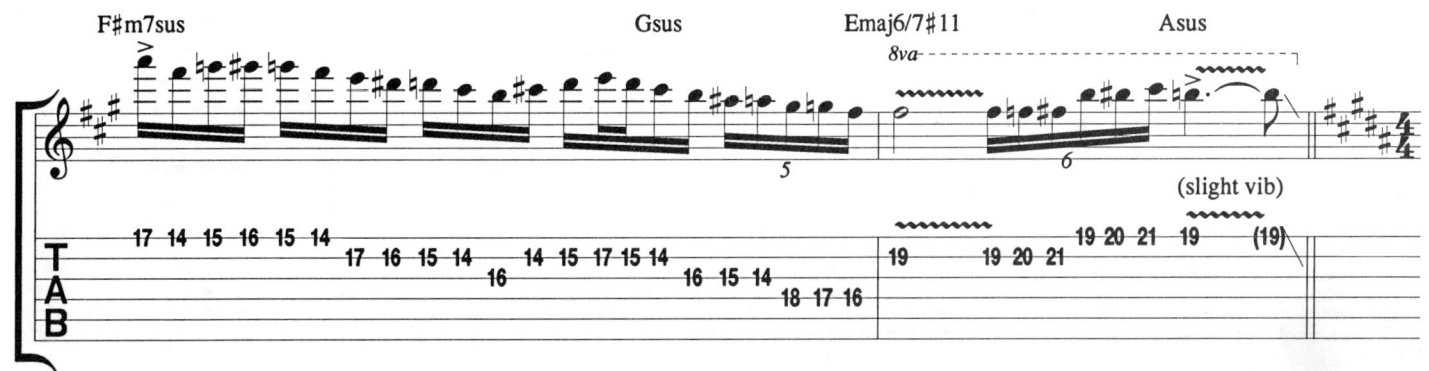

Erotomania – 12 – 3
PG9505

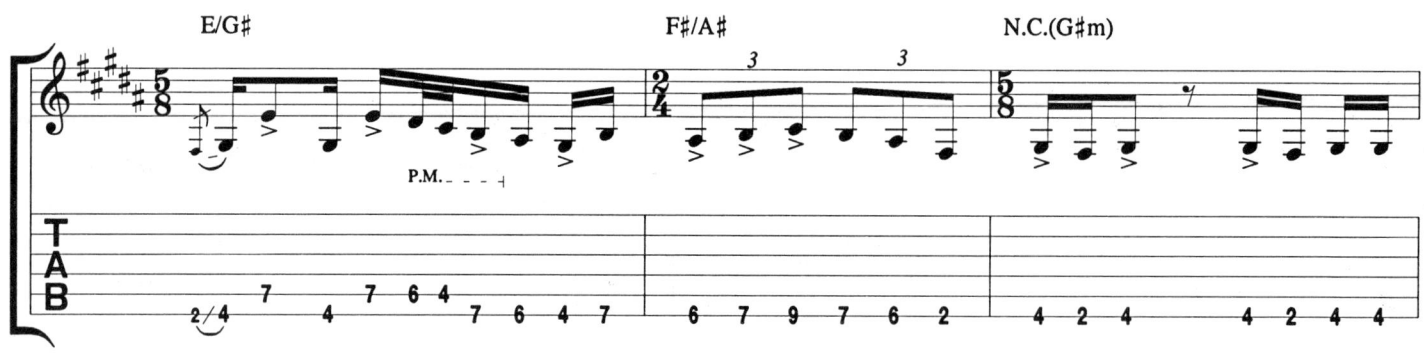

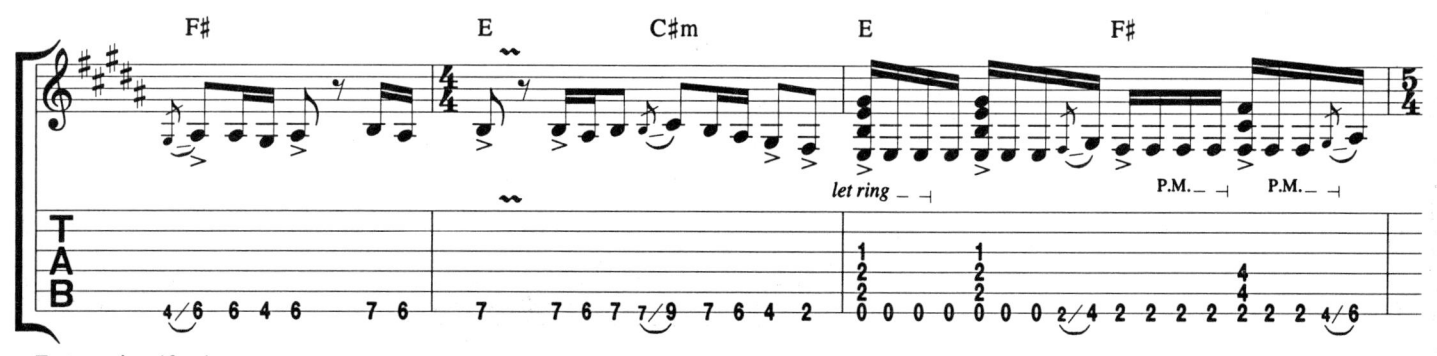

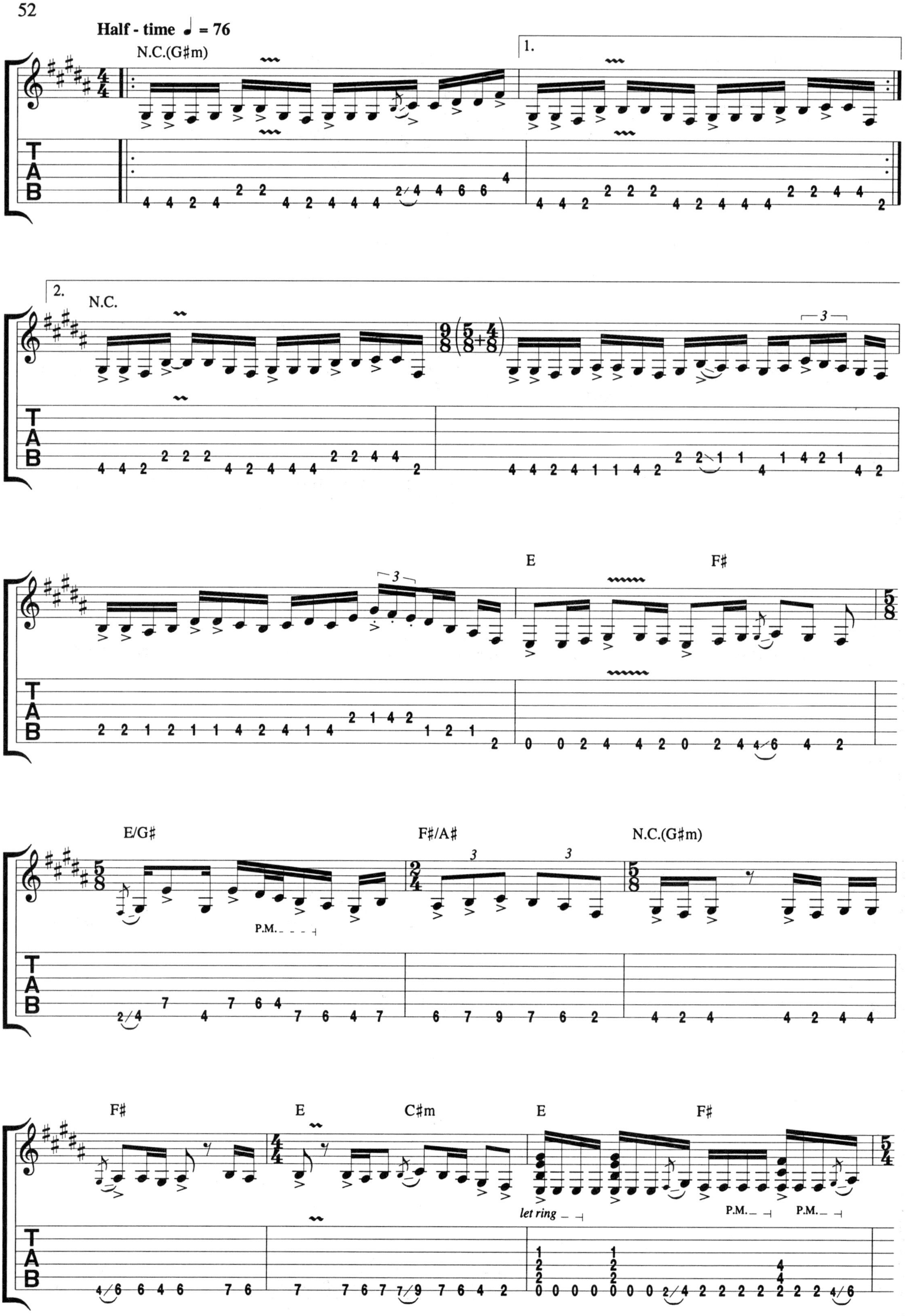
Half - time ♩ = 76
N.C.(G♯m)
1.
2.
N.C.
E
F♯
E/G♯
P.M.
F♯/A♯
N.C.(G♯m)
F♯
E
C♯m
E
let ring
F♯
P.M.
P.M.

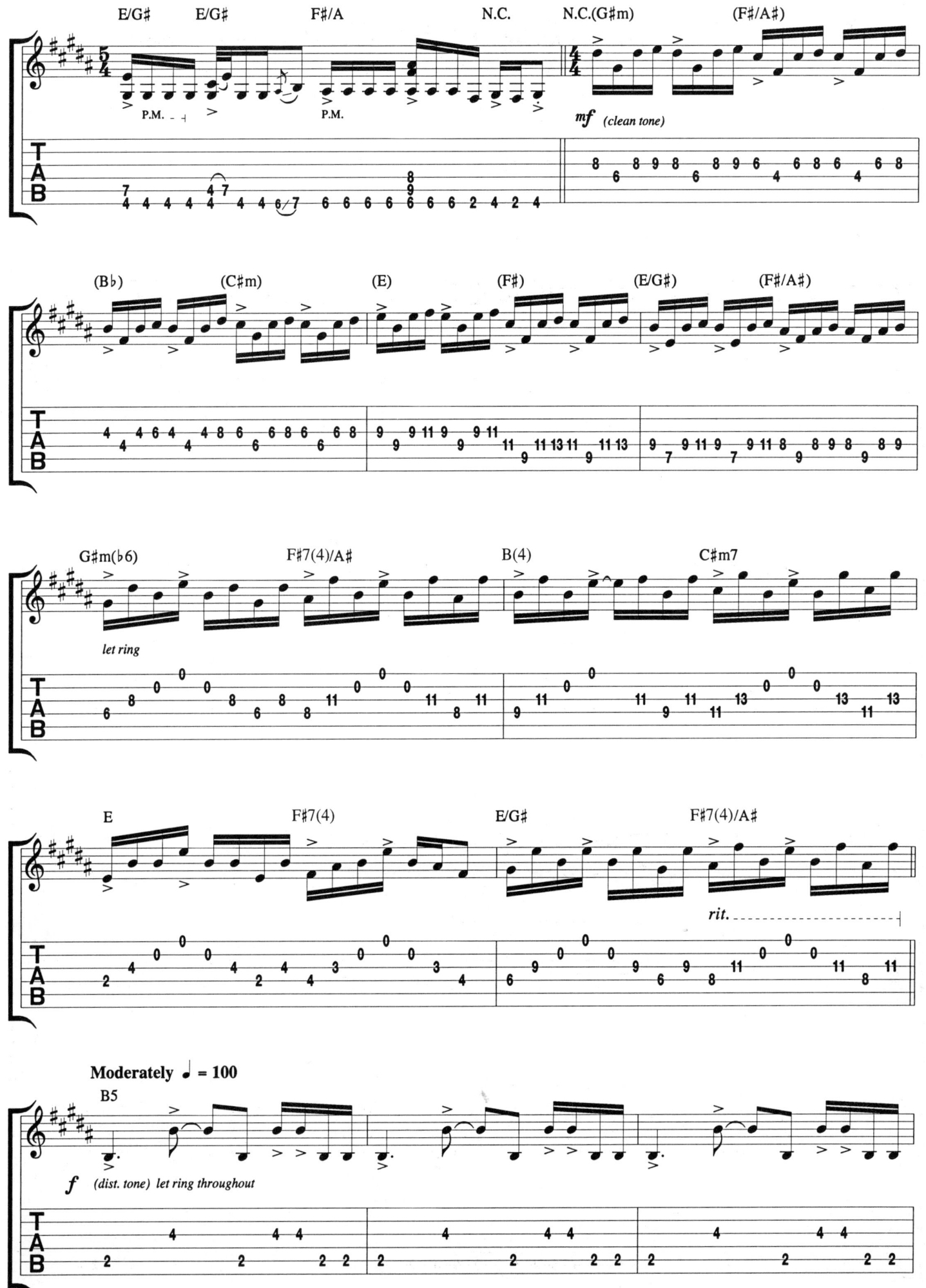

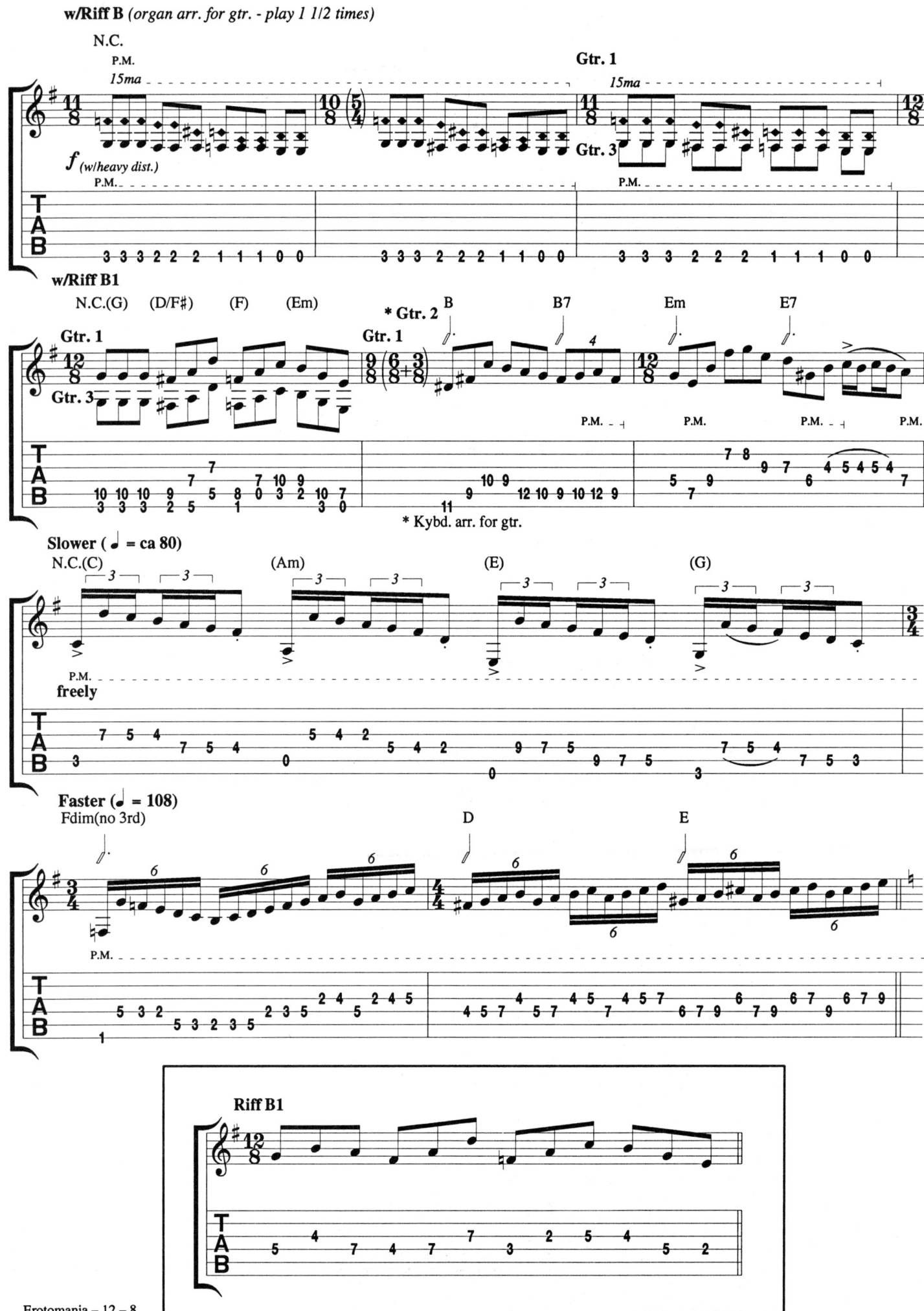

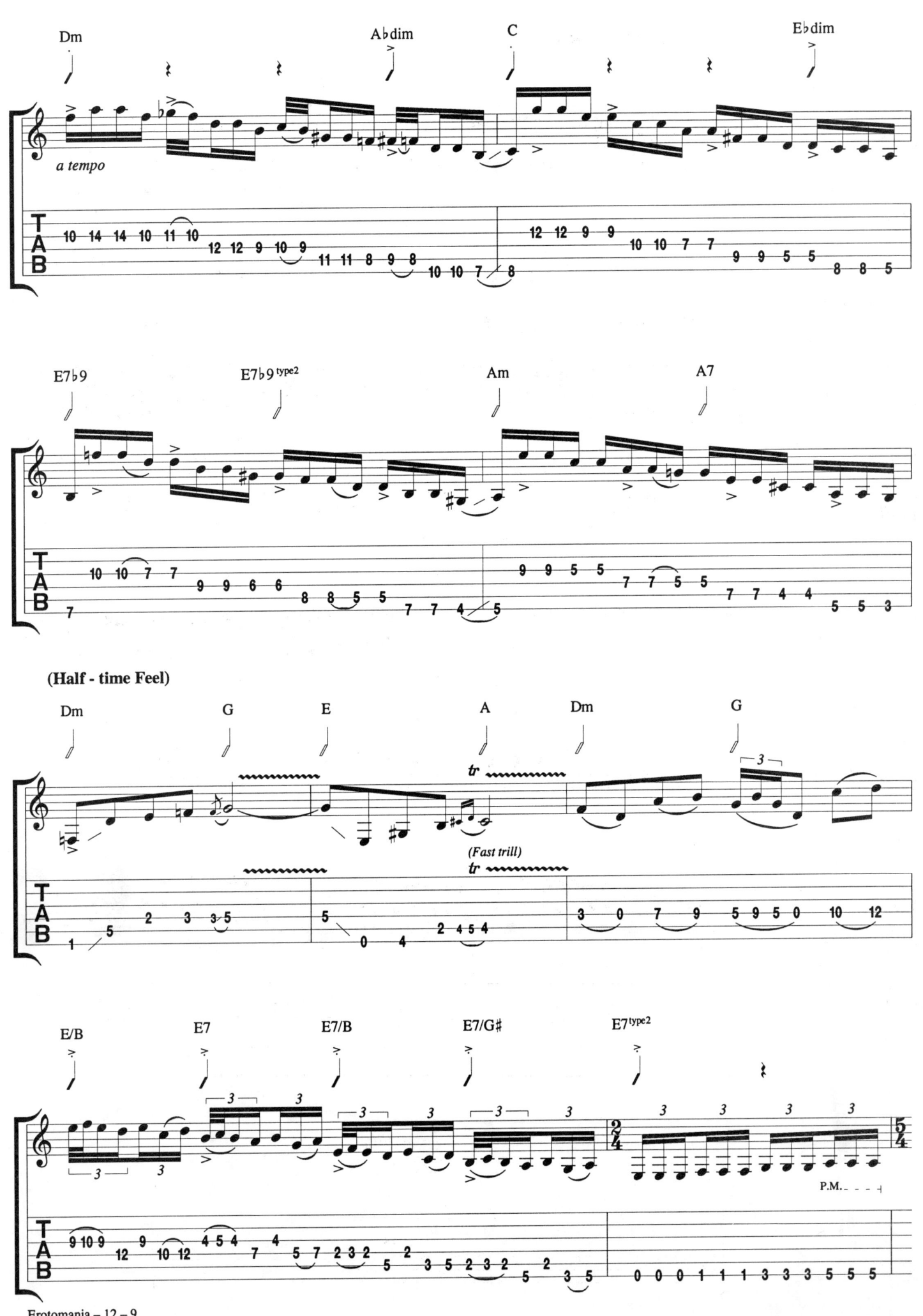

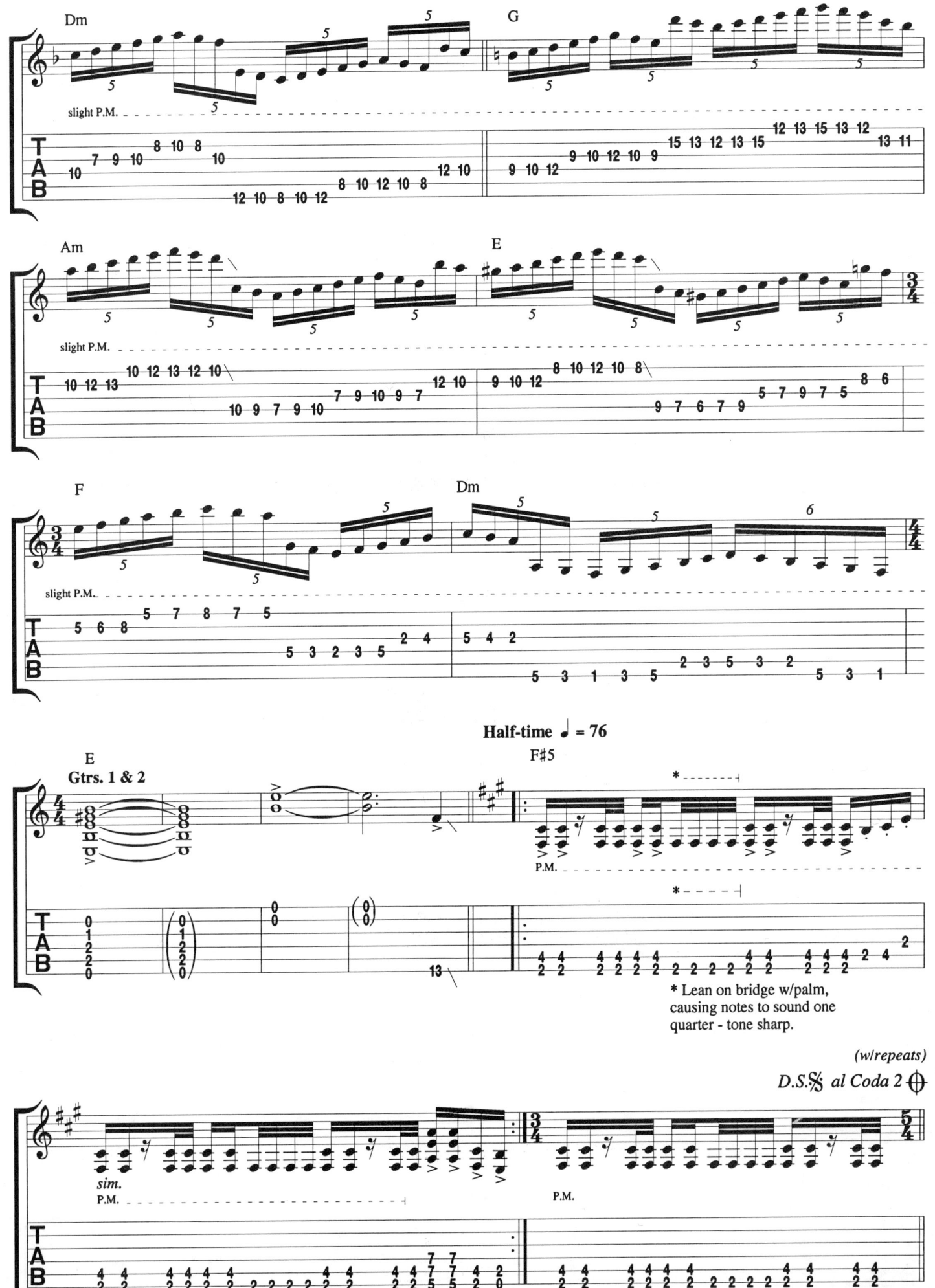

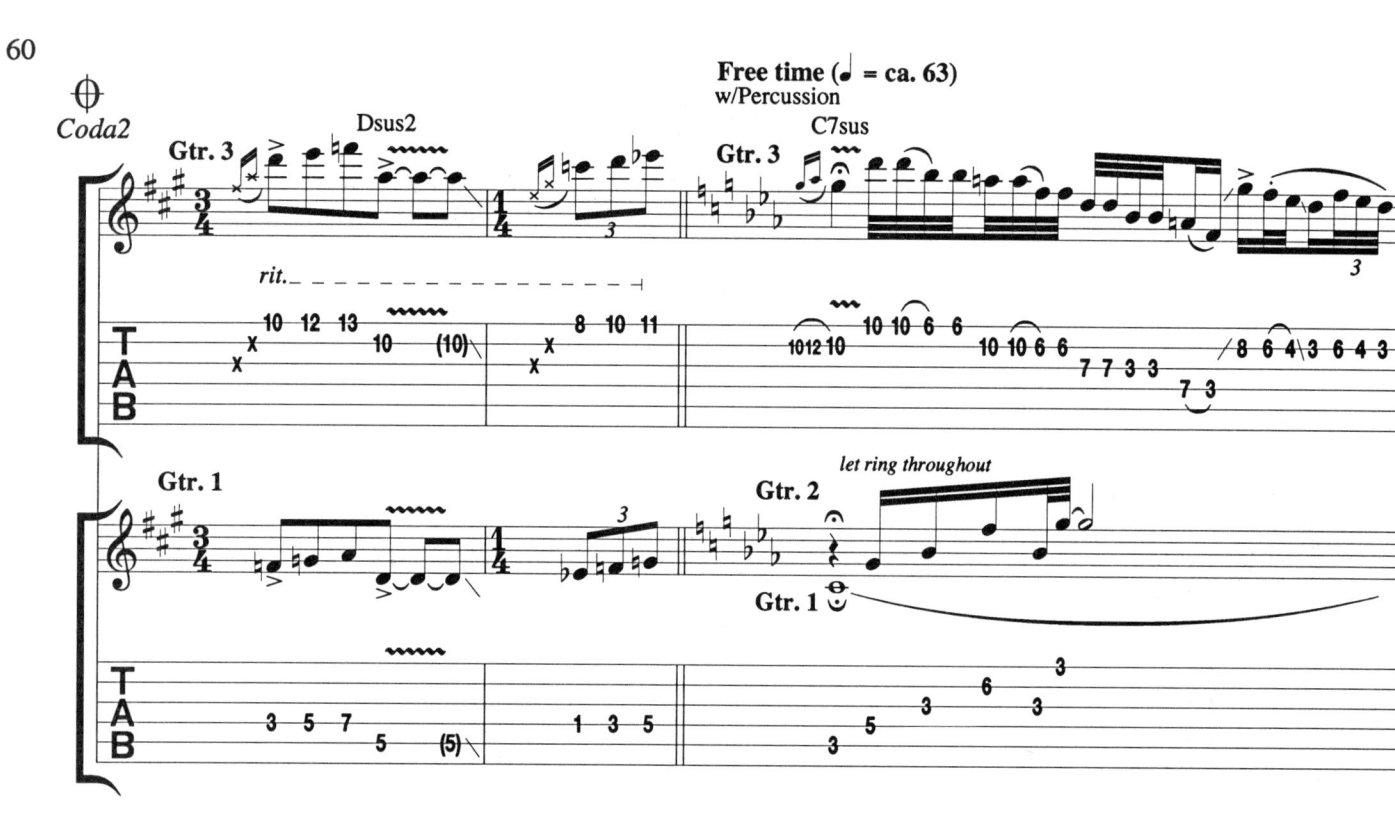
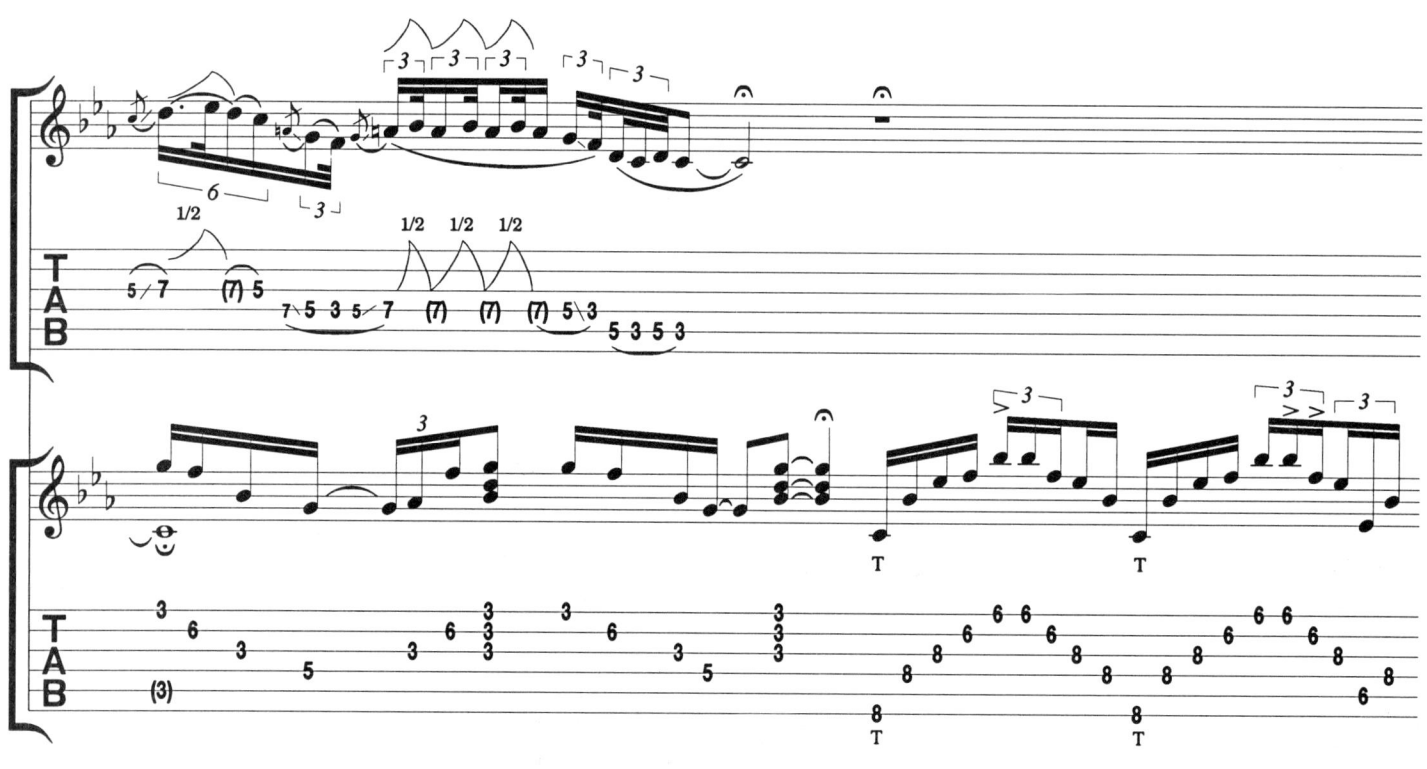
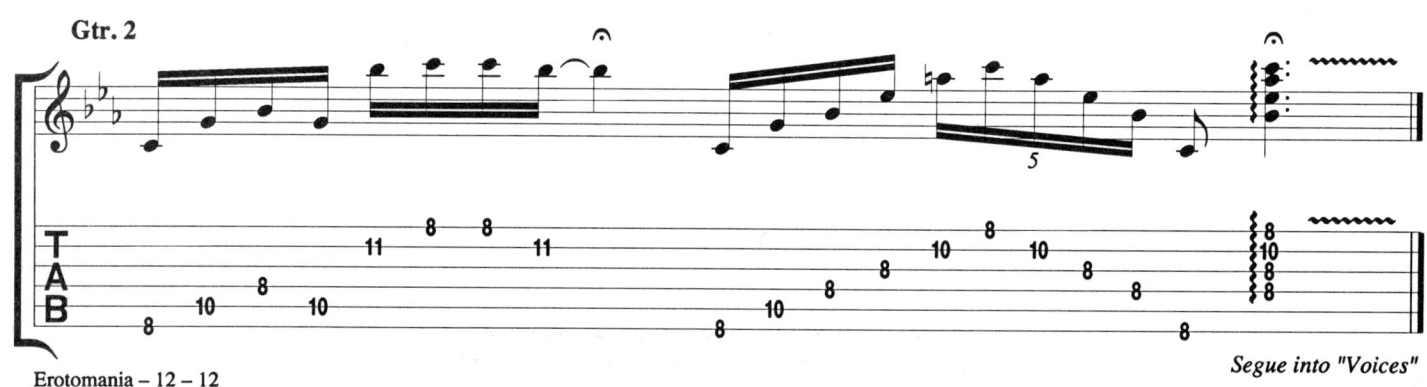

Segue into "Voices"

VOICES

By JAMES LABRIE, KEVIN MOORE,
JOHN MYUNG, JOHN PETRUCCI and MICHAEL PORTNOY

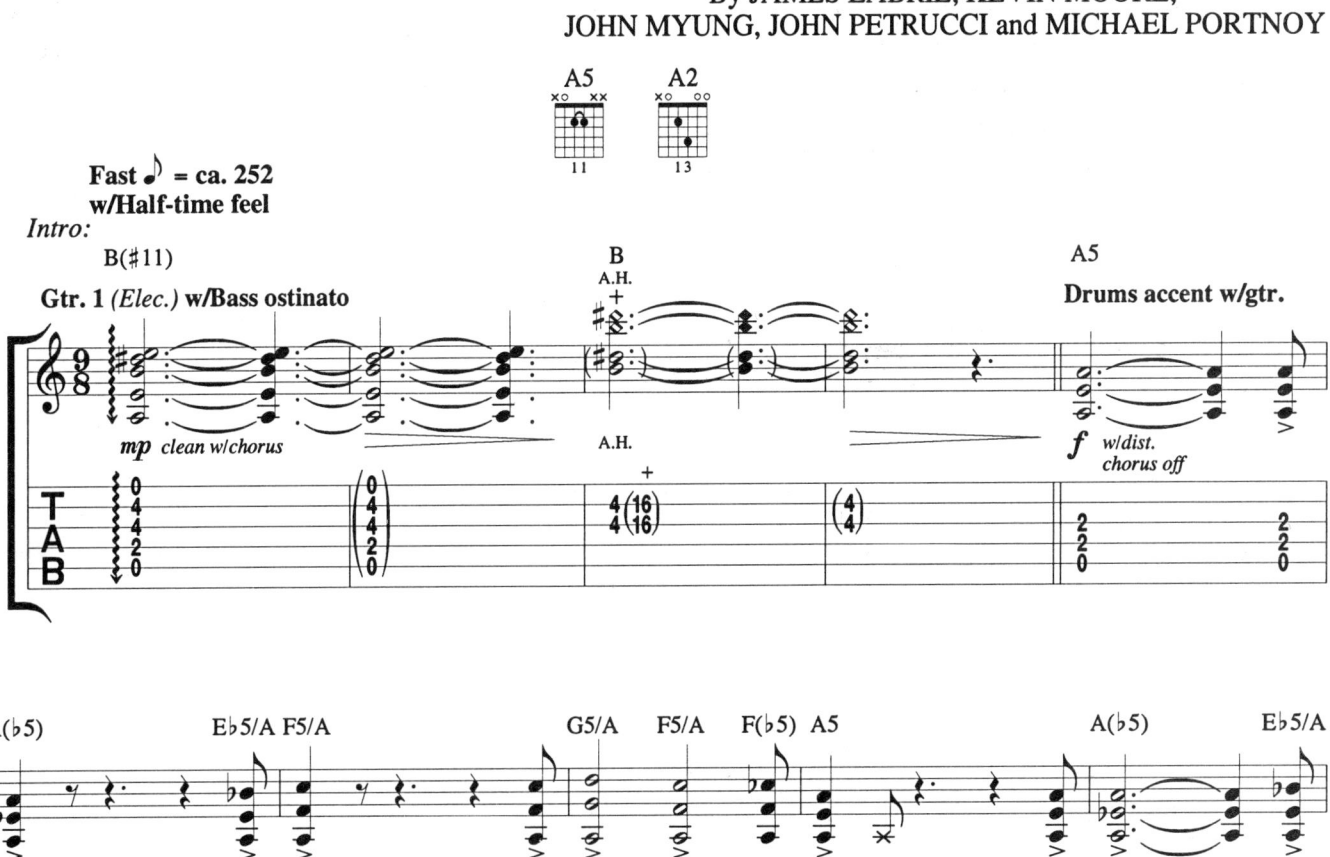

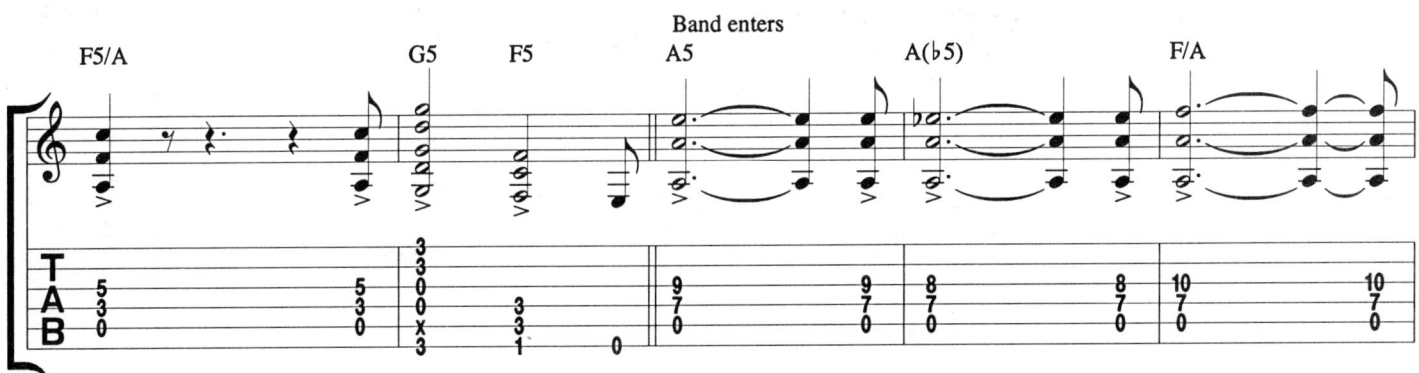

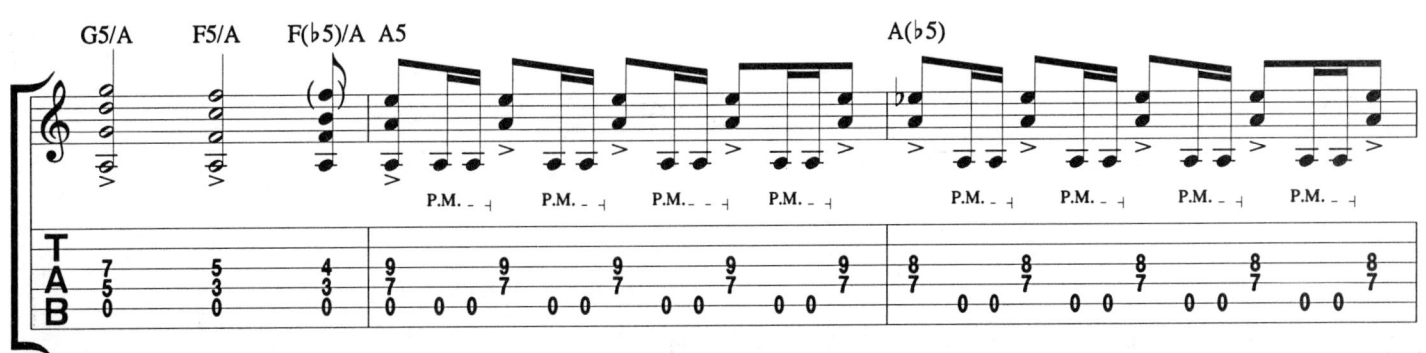

© 1994 OCTA MUSIC, INC. (ASCAP), YTSE JAMS, INC. (ASCAP)
All Rights on behalf of OCTA MUSIC, INC. & YTSE JAMS, INC. administered by WB MUSIC CORP. (ASCAP)
All rights reserved

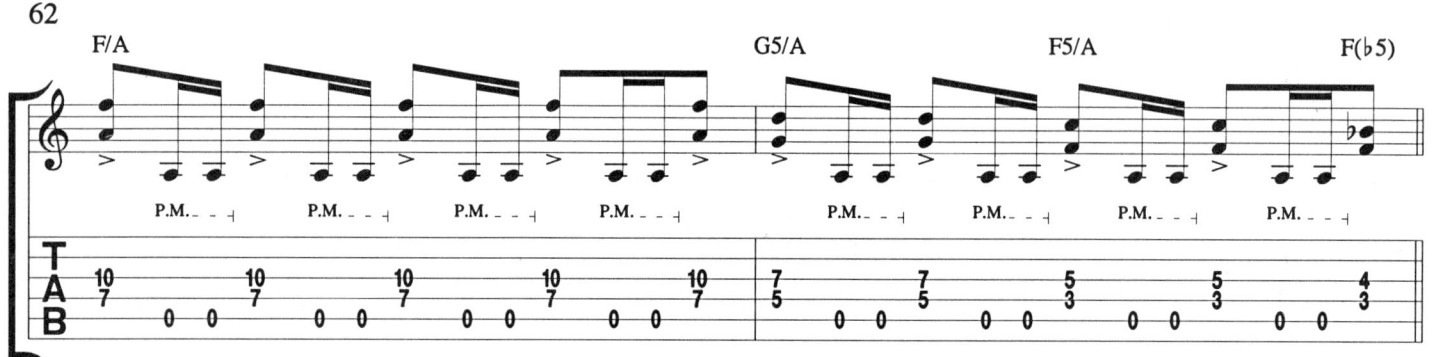

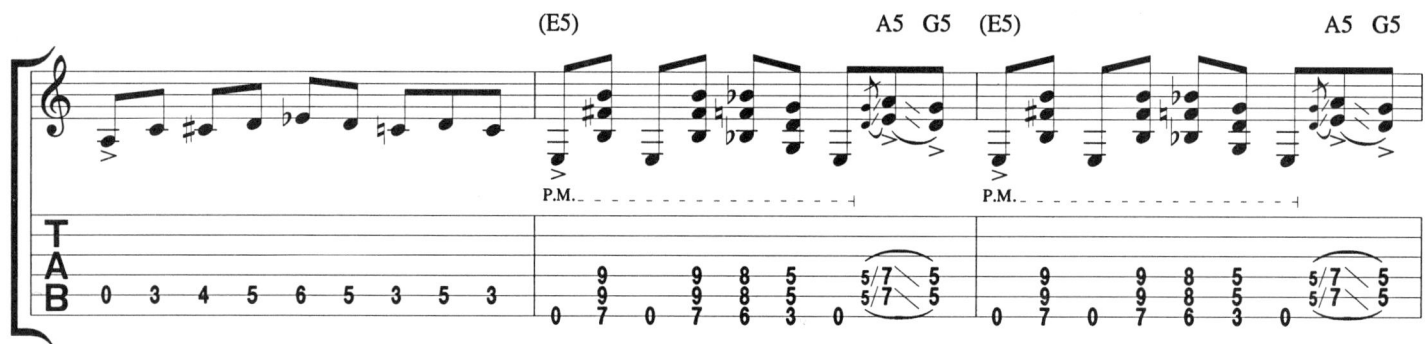
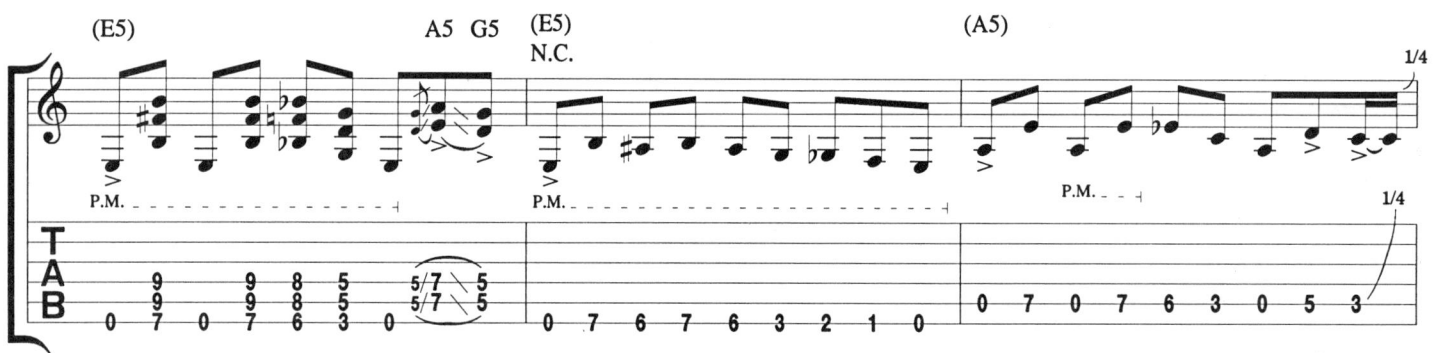

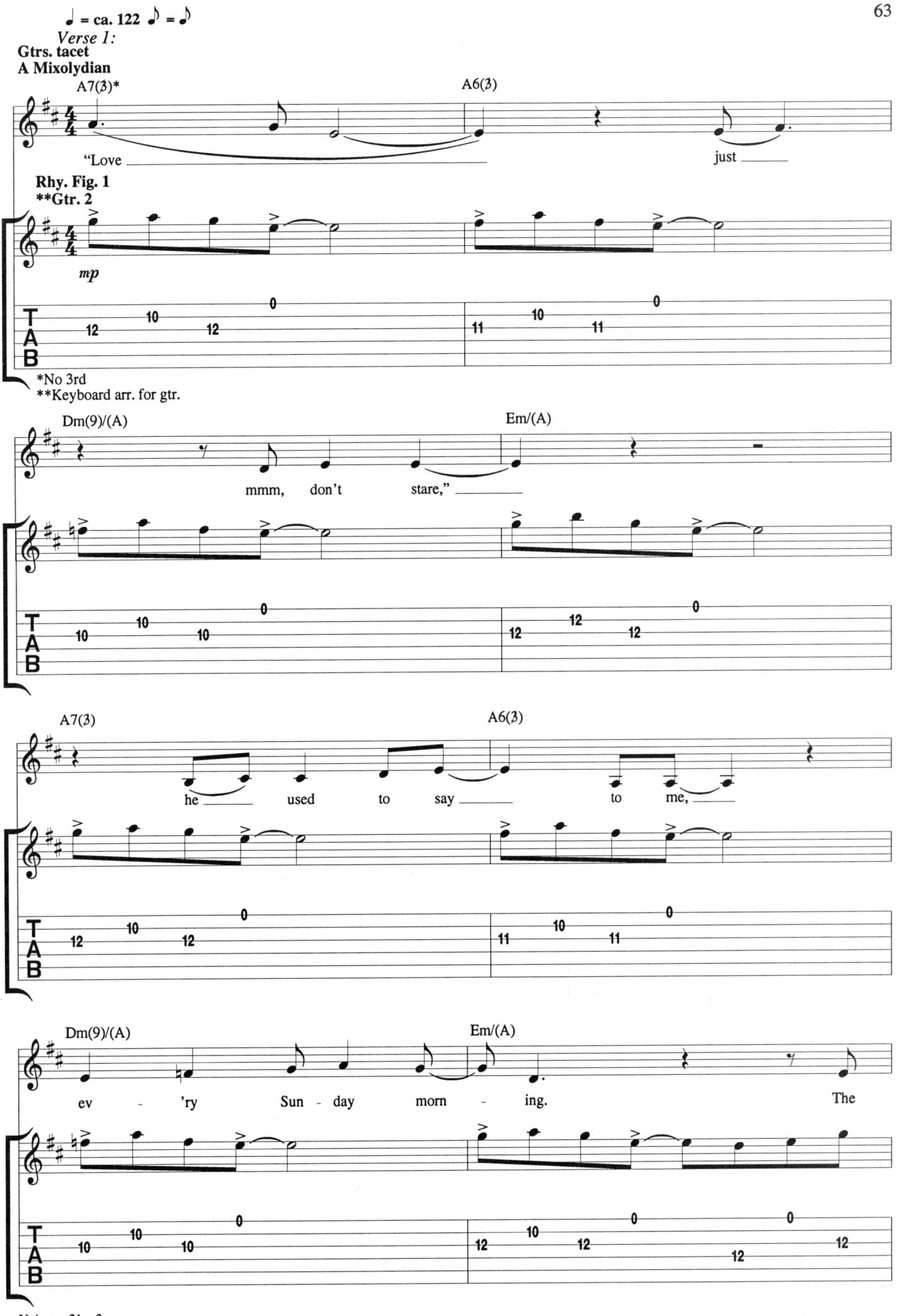

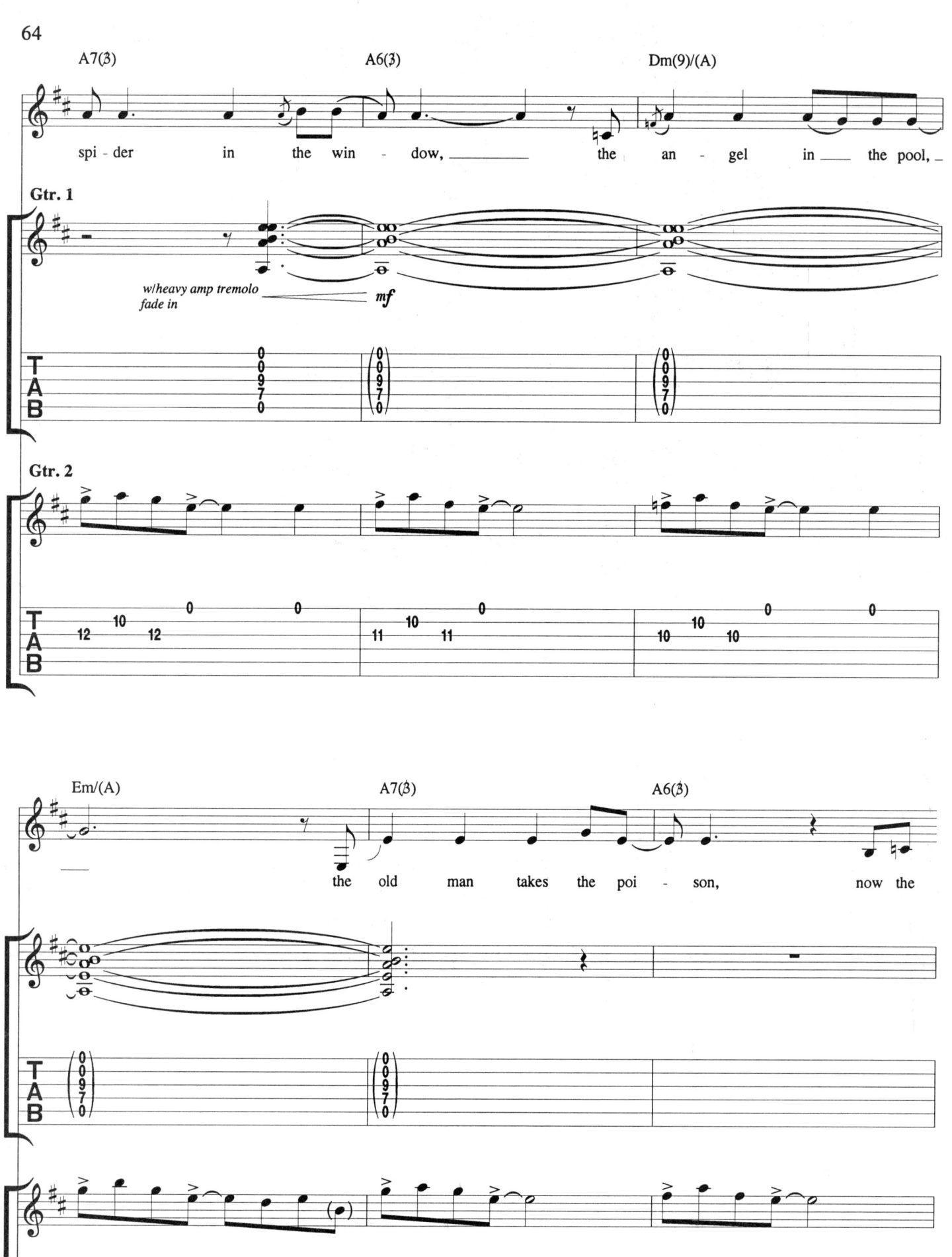

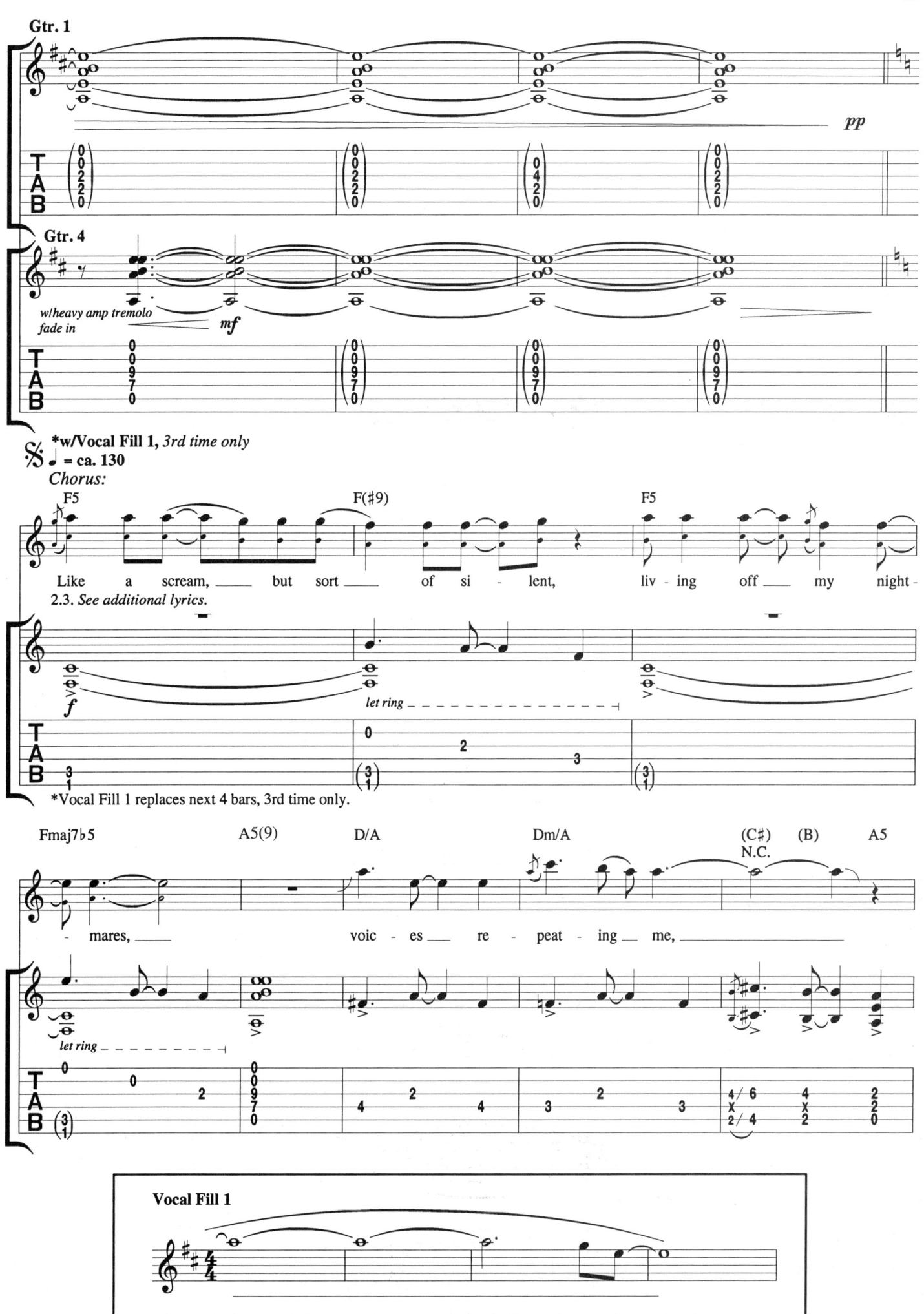

68

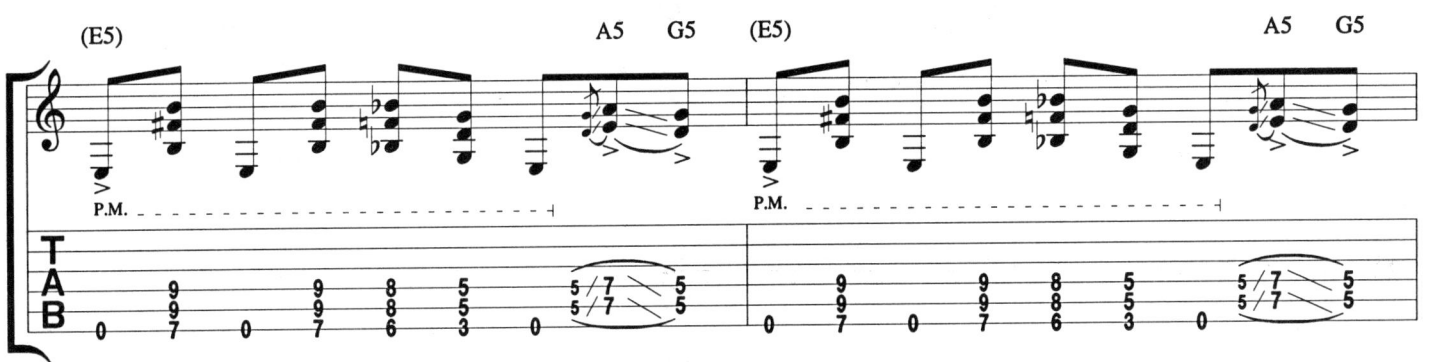

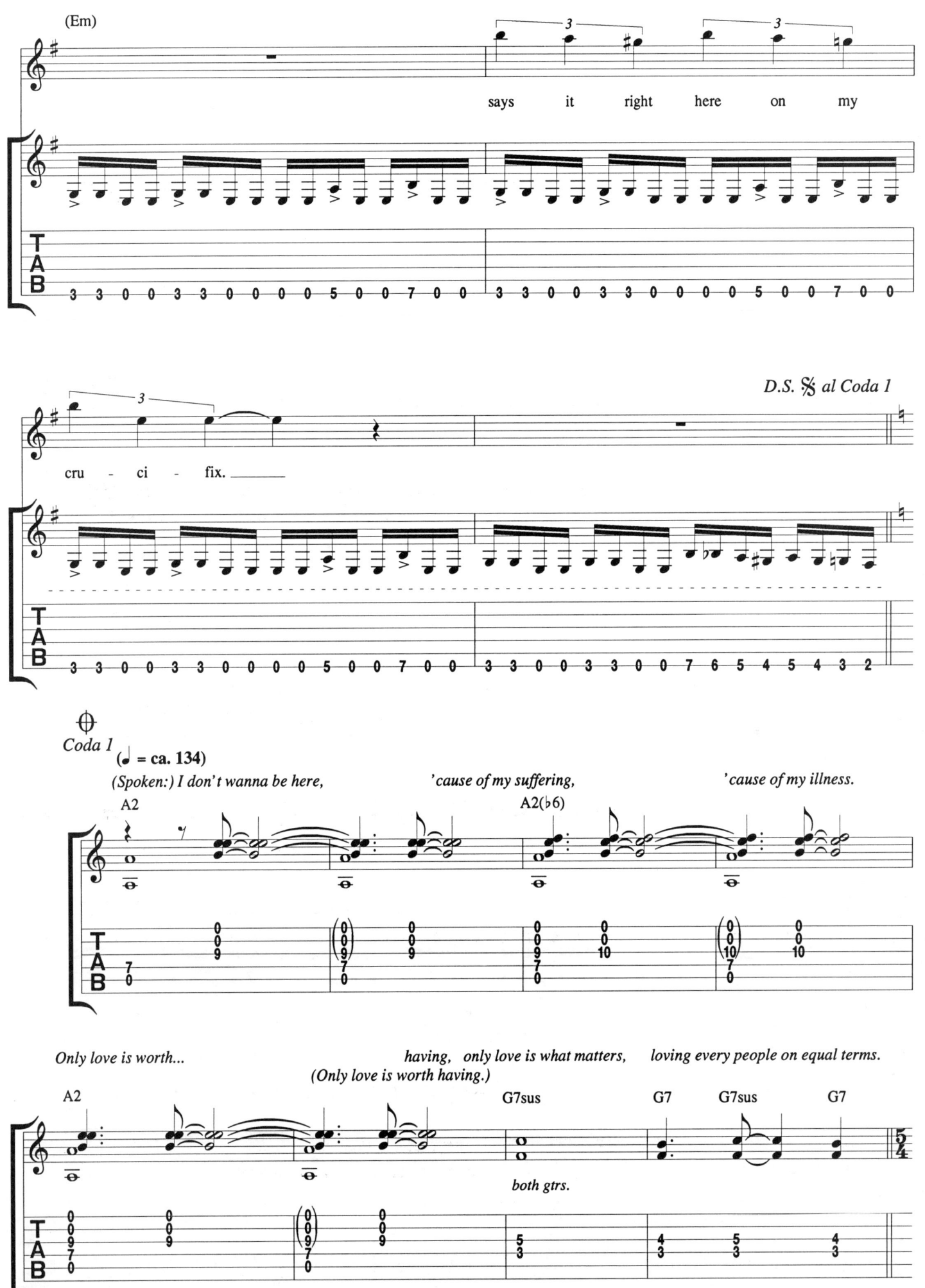

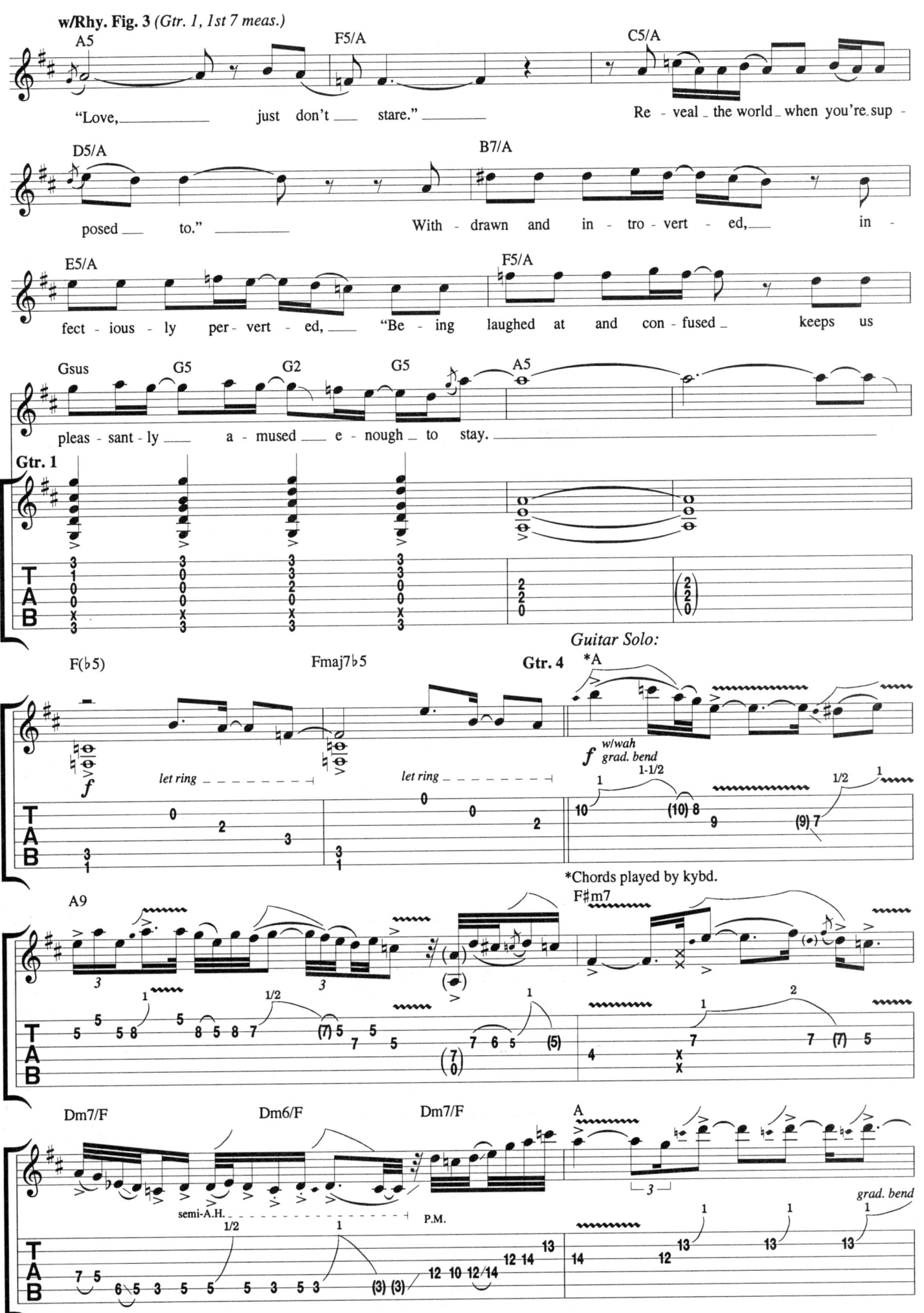

78

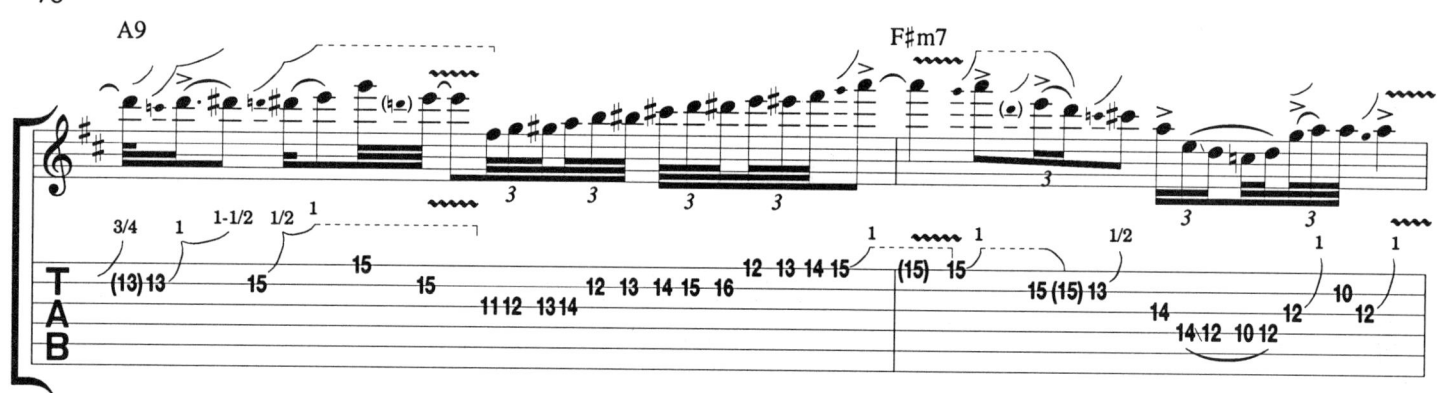

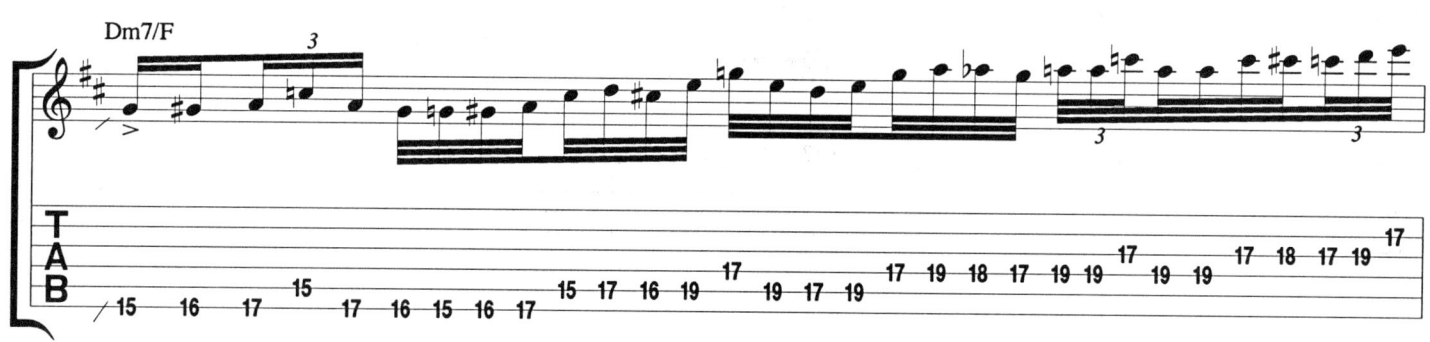

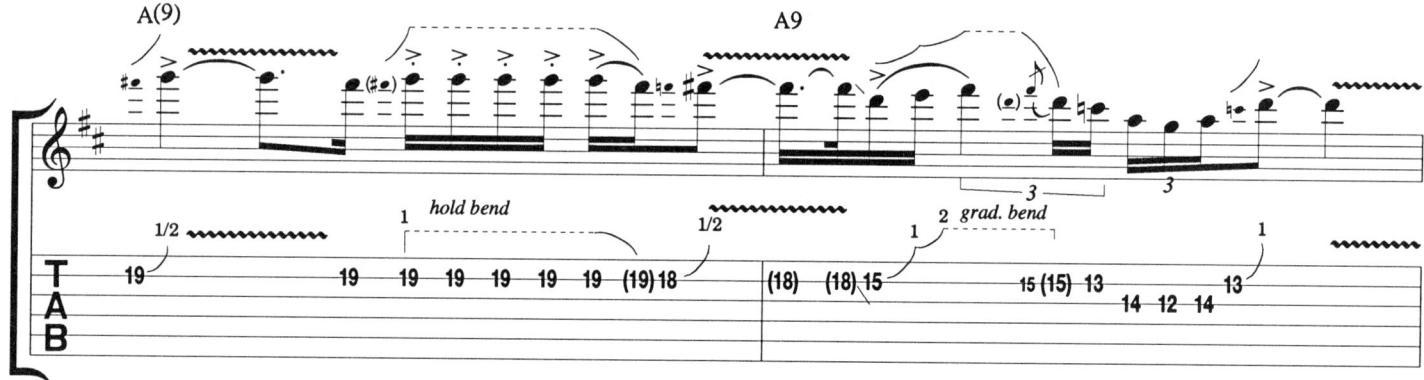

Chorus 2:
Like a scream, but sort of silent,
Living off my nightmares,
Voices protecting me.
Good behavior brings the Savior to his knees.
Voices rejecting me.
Others steal your thoughts.
They're not confined to your mind.

Chorus 3:
Voices repeating me.
"Feeling threatened?
We reflect your hopes and fears."
Voices discussing me.
Don't expect your own Messiah.
This never world which you desire
Is only in your mind.

THE SILENT MAN

By JOHN PETRUCCI

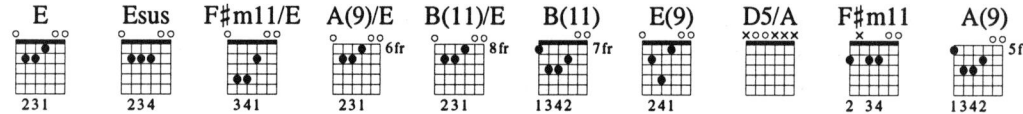

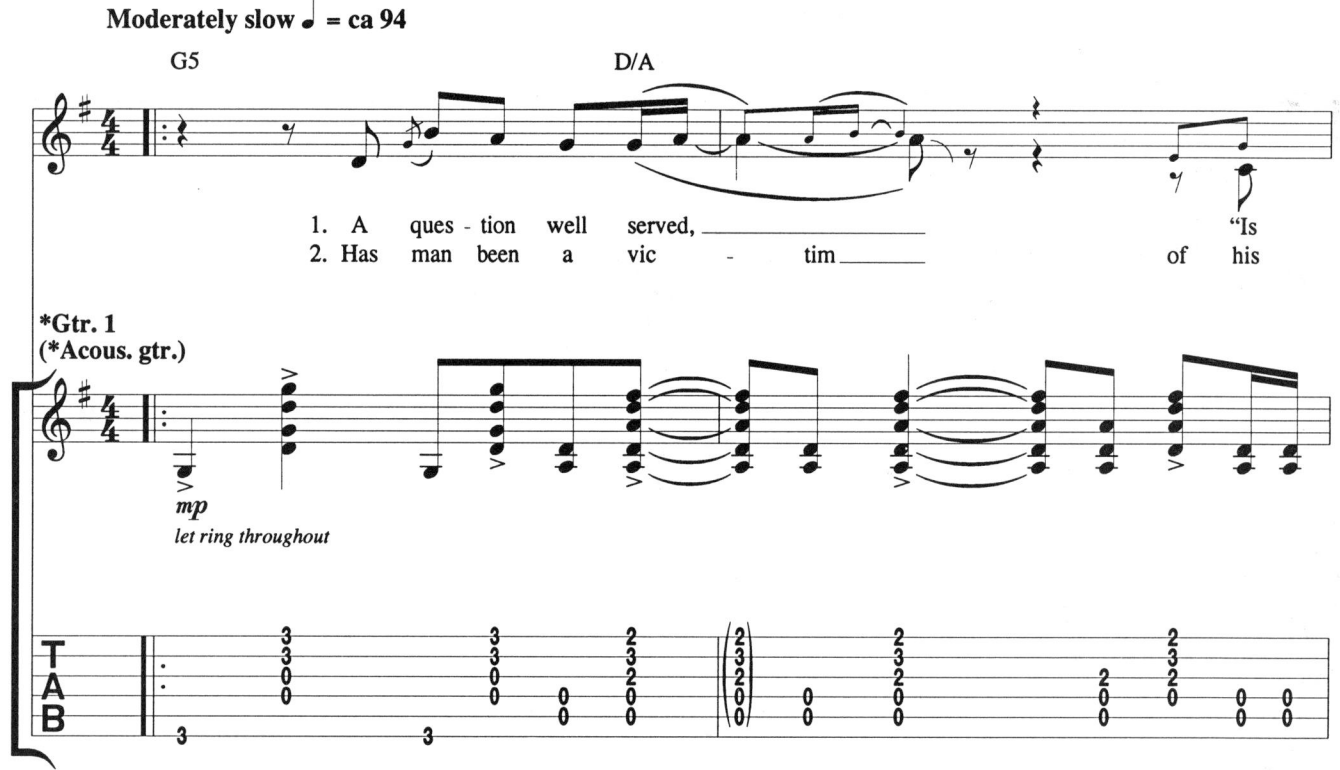

1. A question well served, "Is
2. Has man been a victim of his

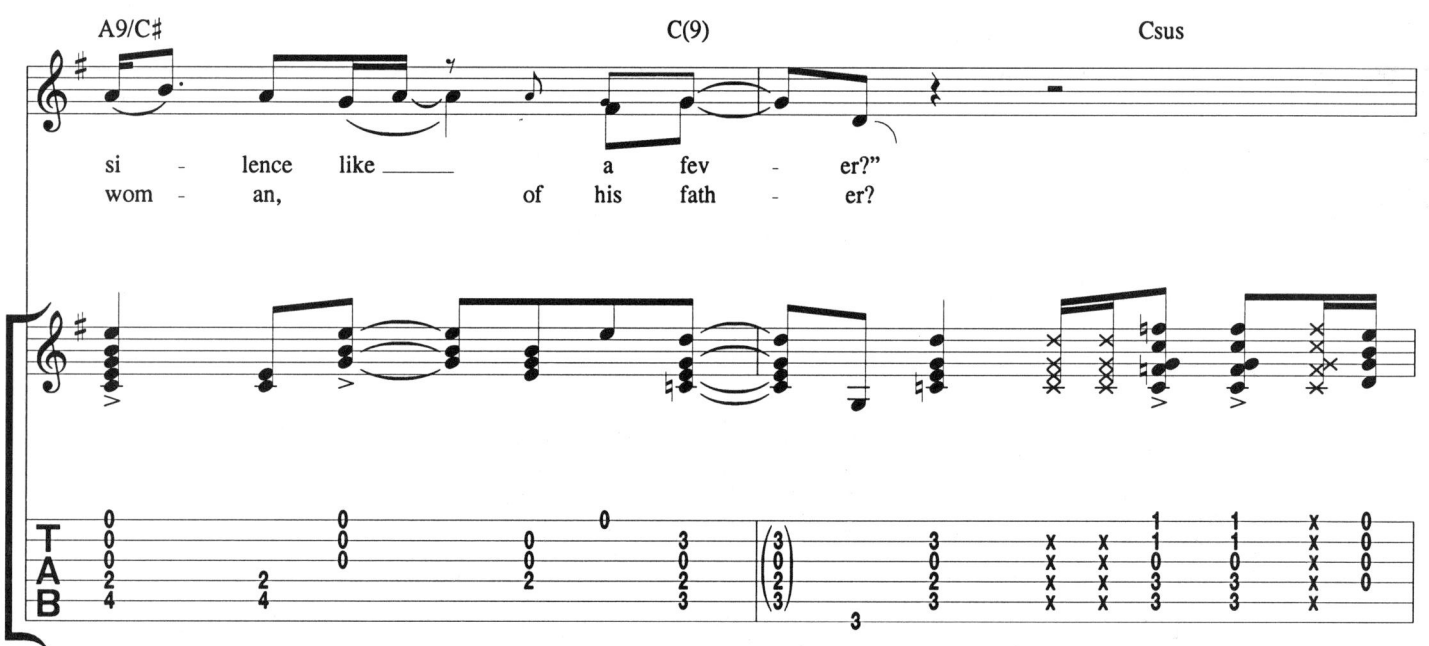

si- lence like a fev- er?"
wom- an, of his fath- er?

© 1994 OCTA MUSIC, INC. (ASCAP), YTSE JAMS, INC. (ASCAP)
All rights on behalf of OCTA MUSIC, INC. & YTSE JAMS, INC. administered by WB MUSIC CORP. (ASCAP)
All rights reserved

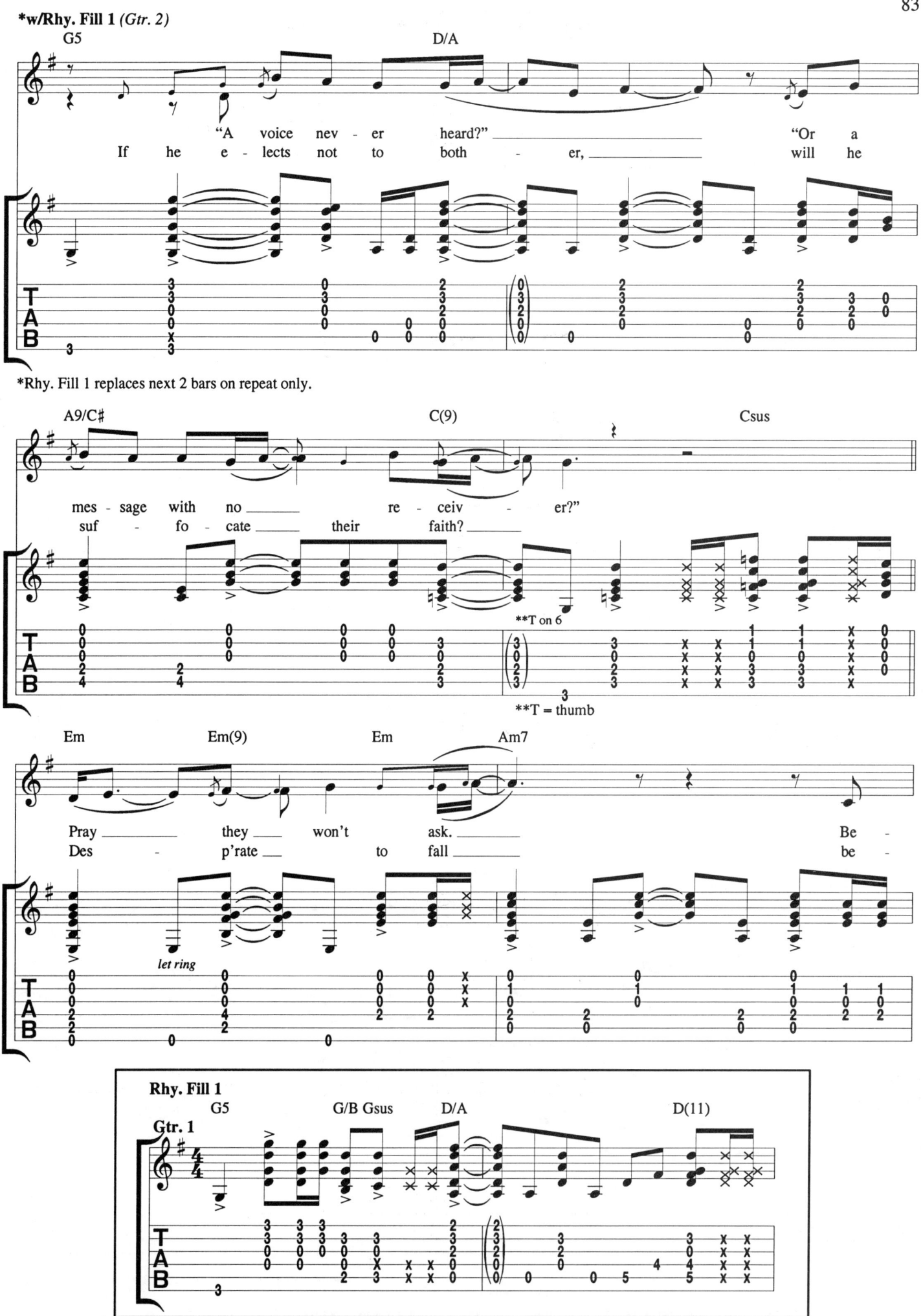

84

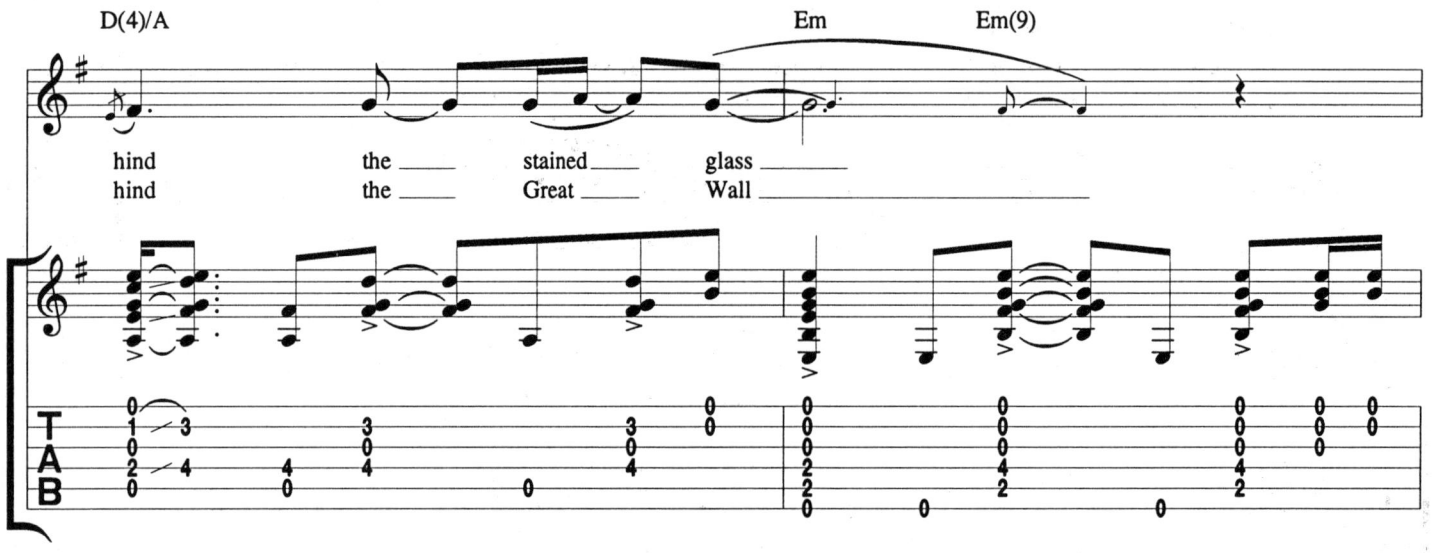

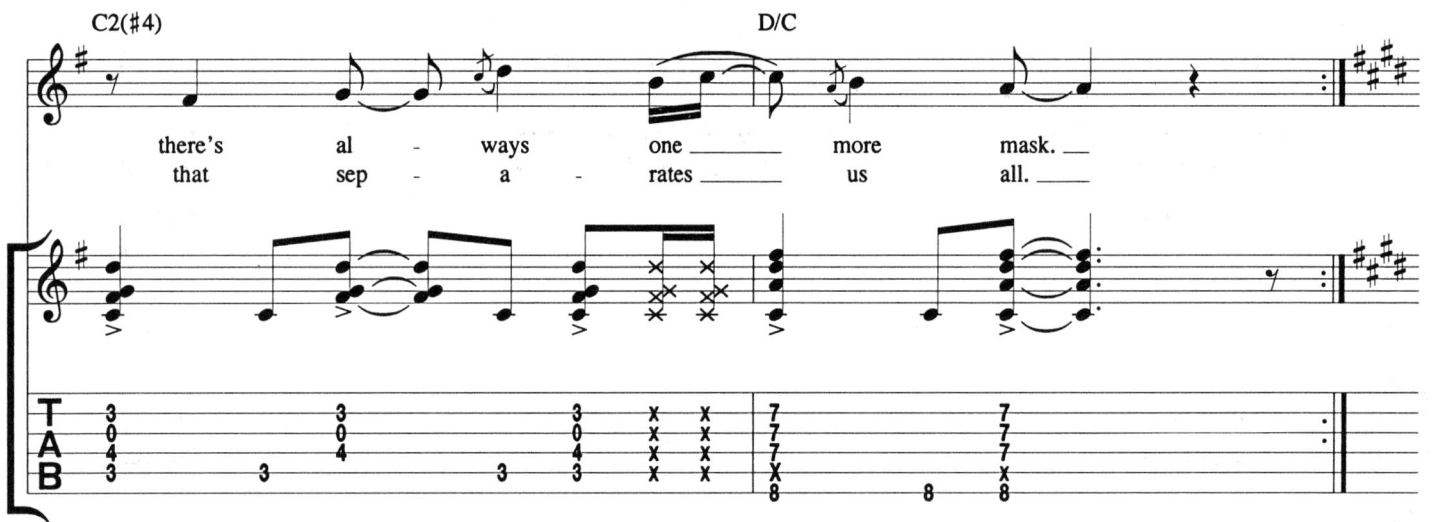

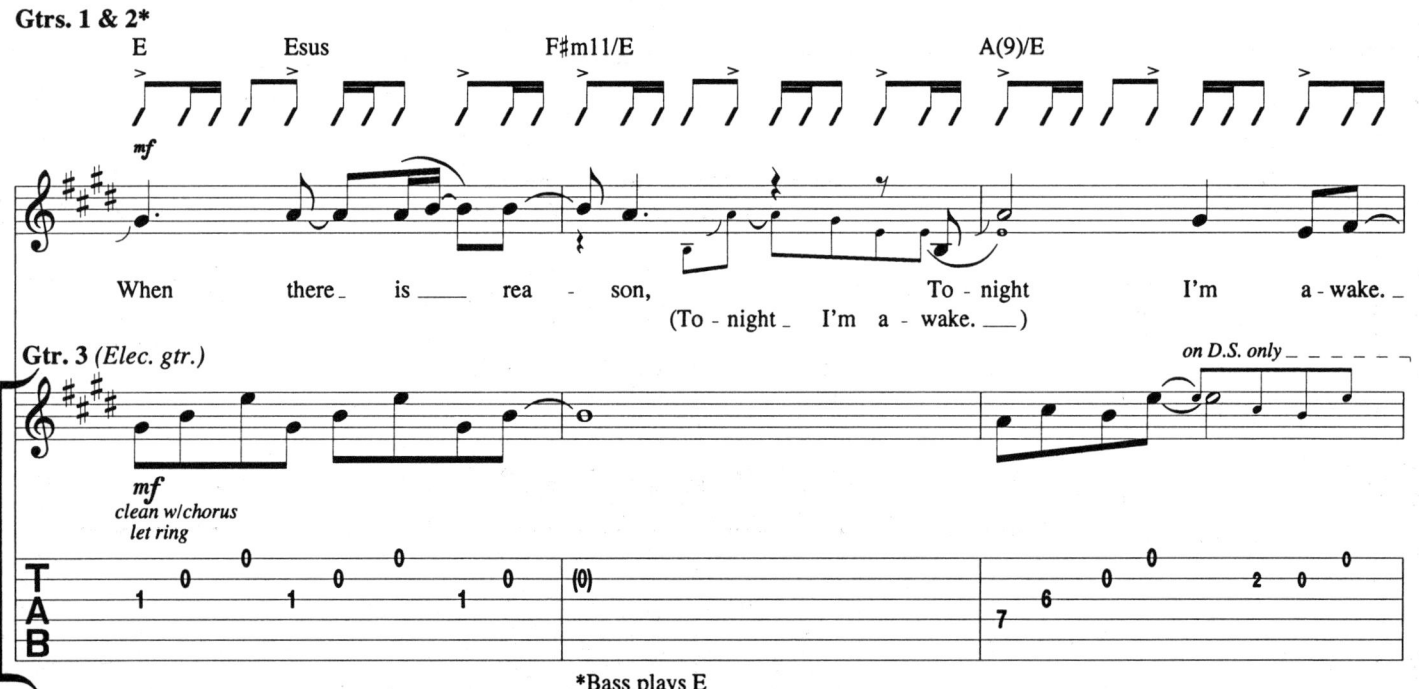

*Bass plays E

*Gtr. 2 is "Nashville" tuned acoustic. Strings ④ to ⑥ are tuned 8va like 12 string w/o lower octave strings.

Silent Man – 9 – 3
PG9505

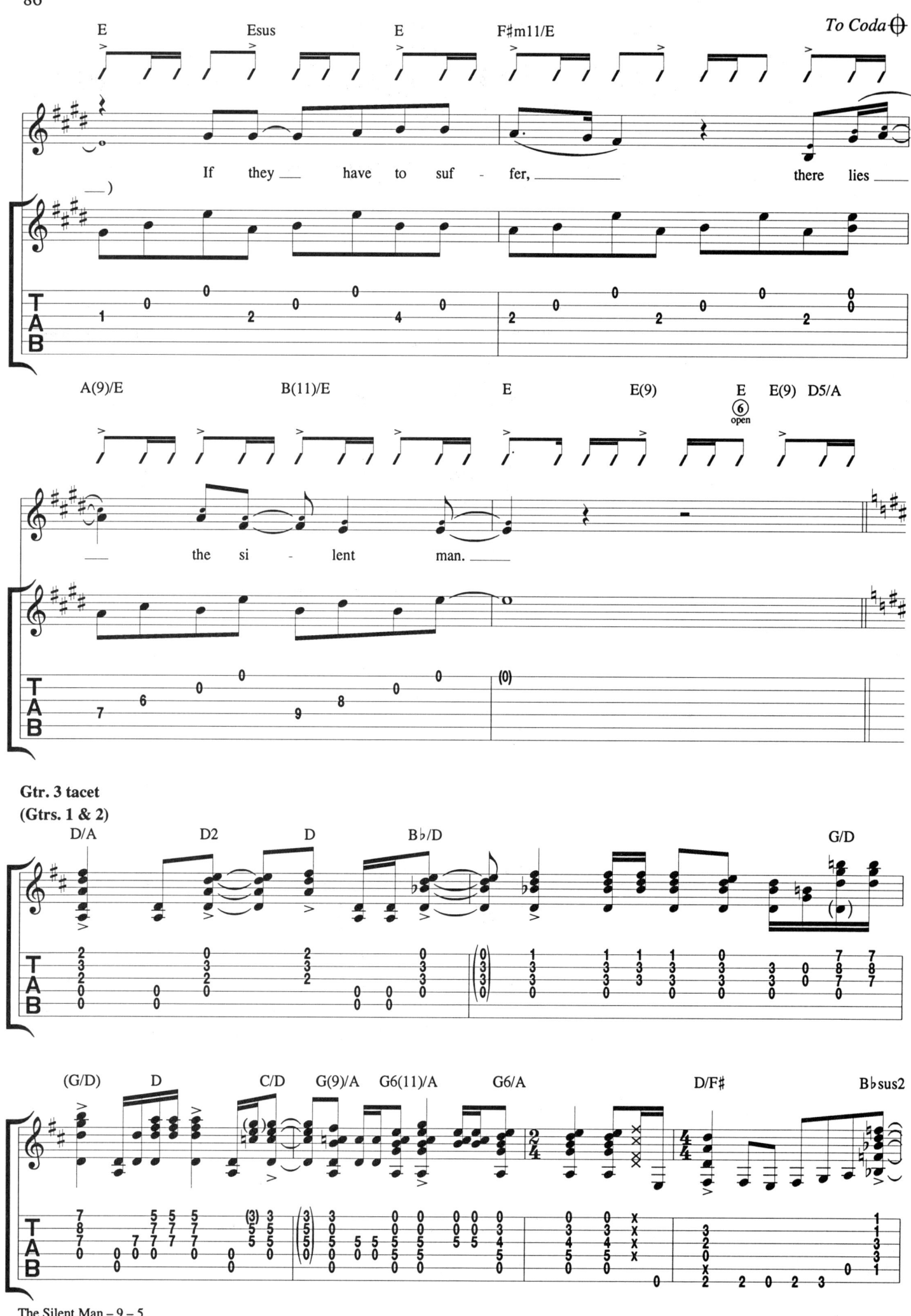

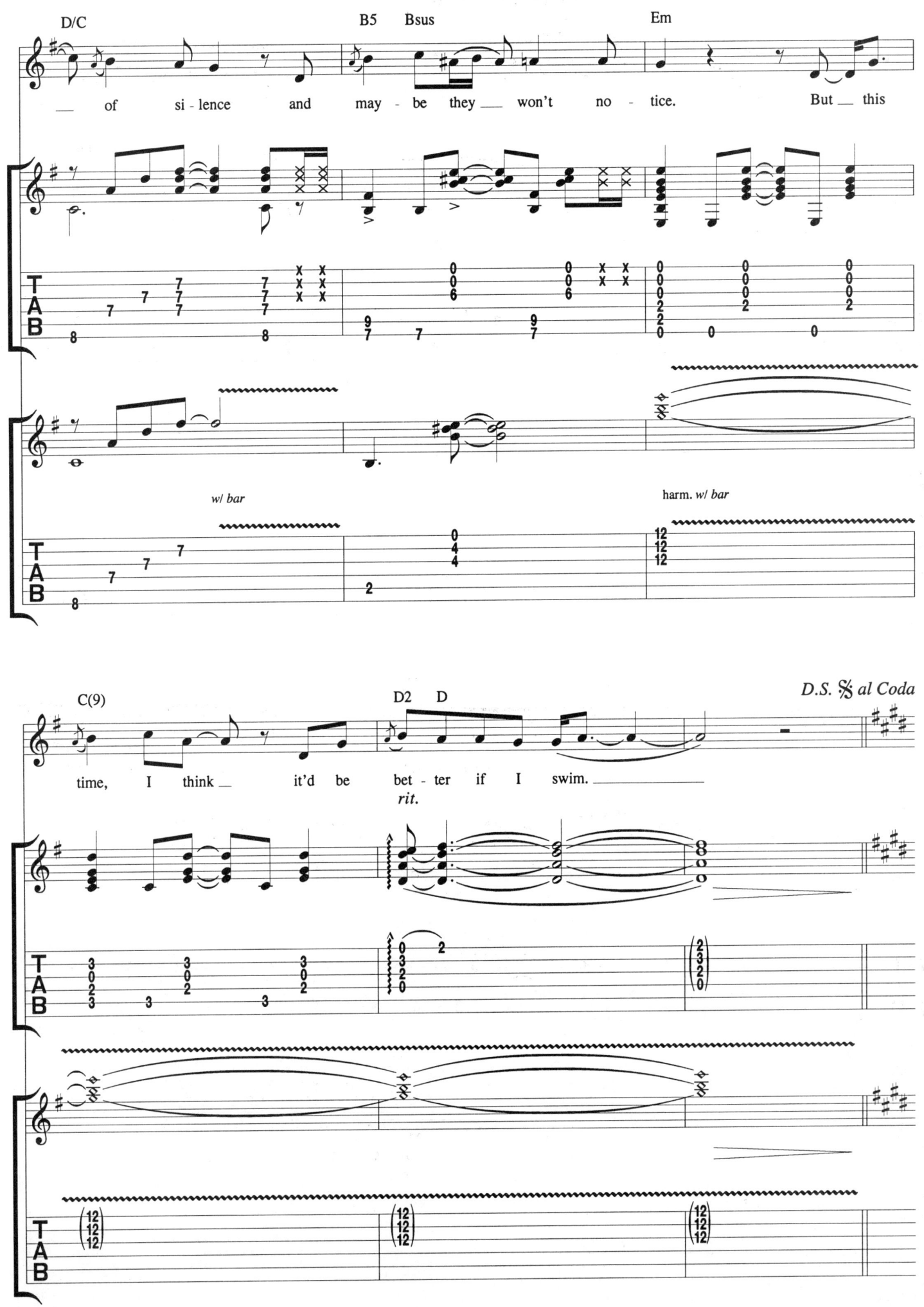

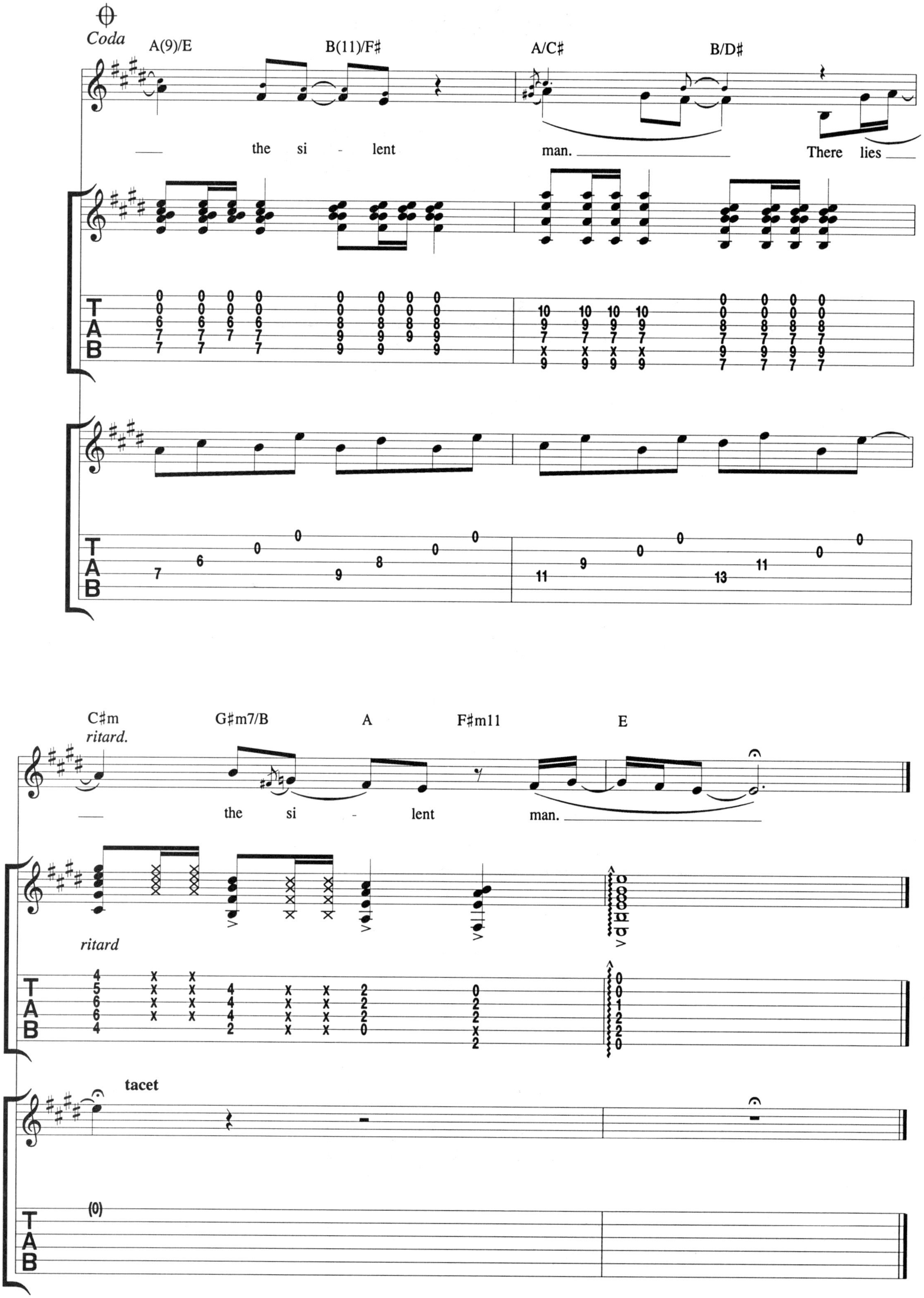

Coda

the si - lent man. There lies

the si - lent man.

ritard.

tacet

The Silent Man – 9 – 9
PG9505

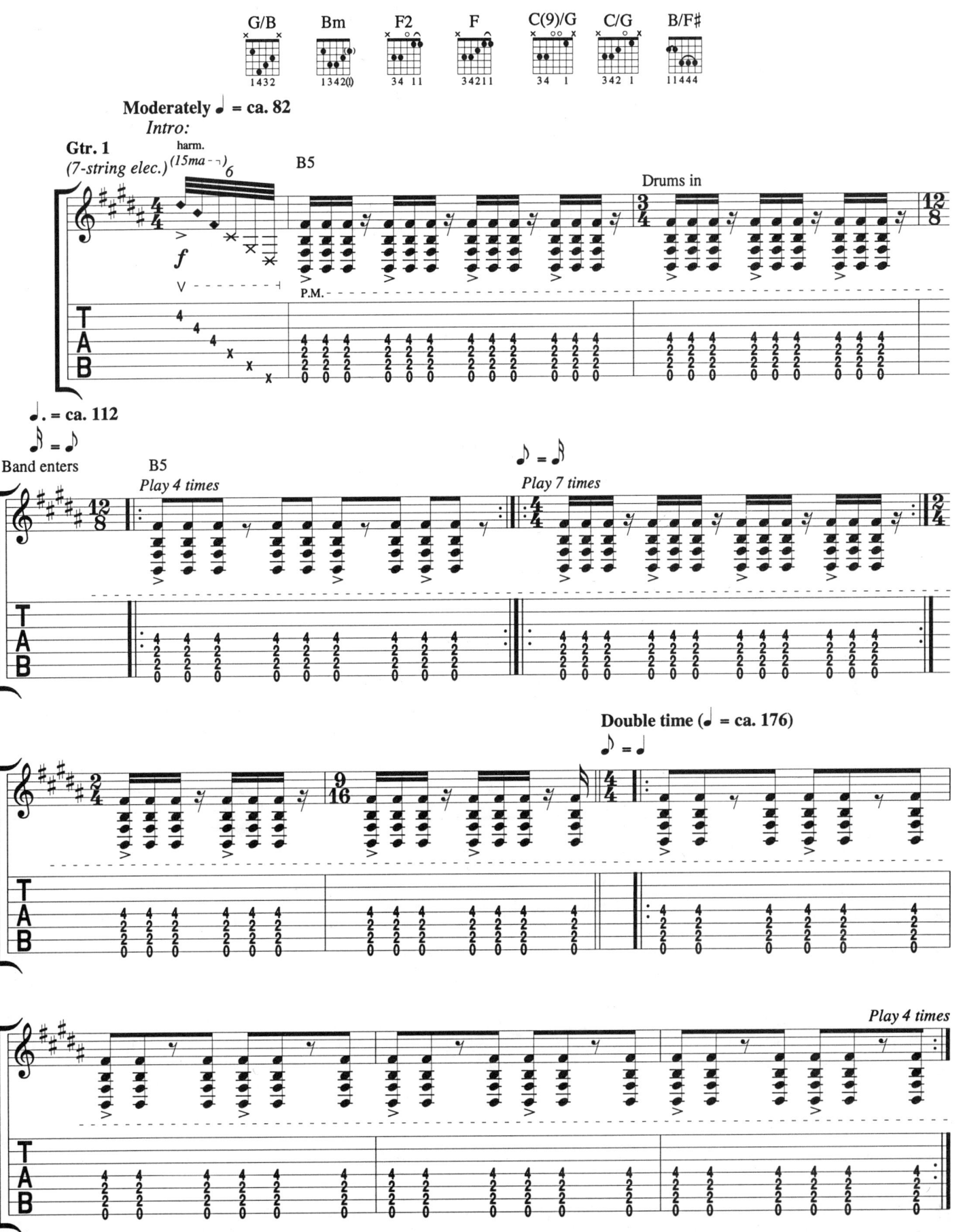

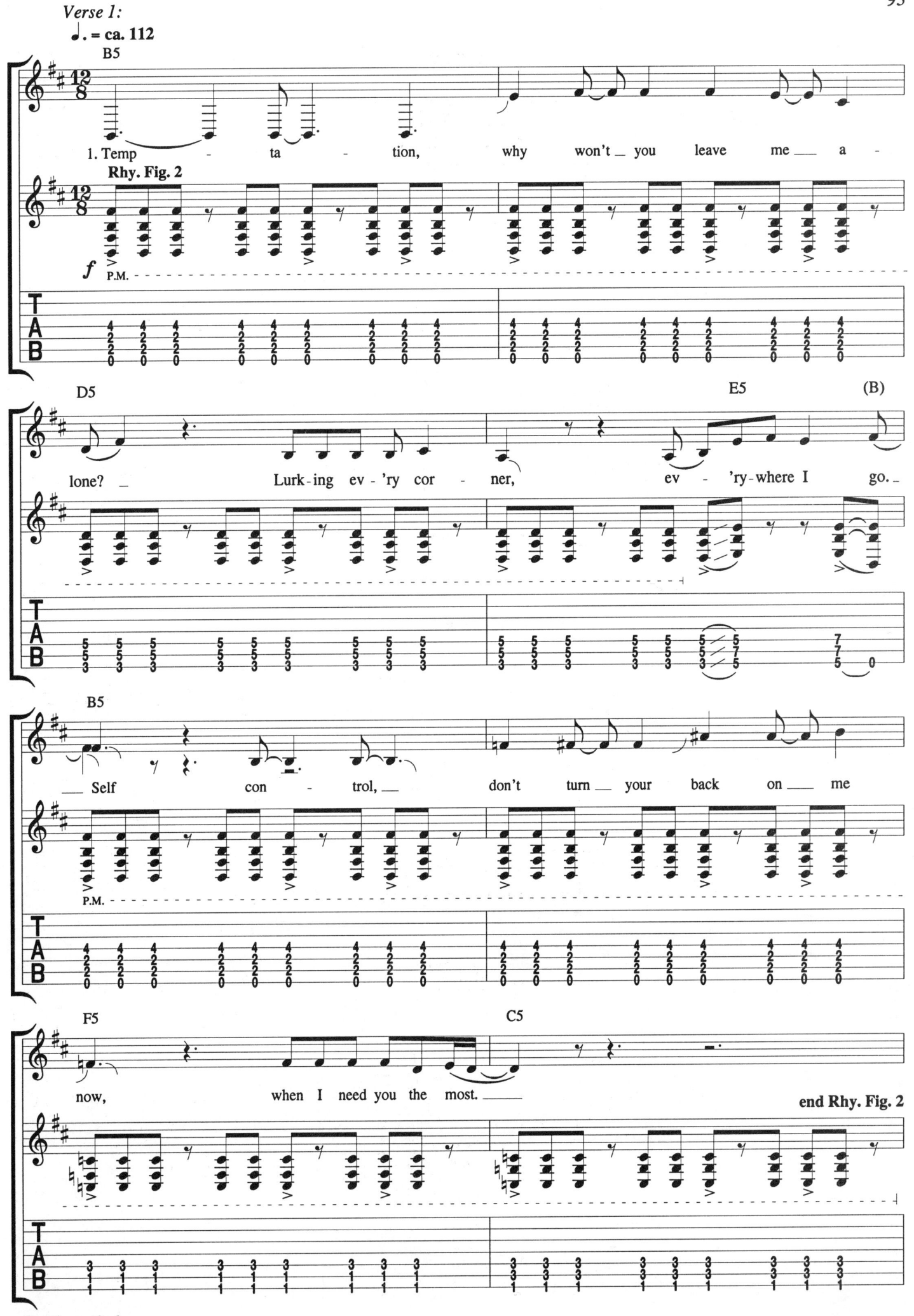

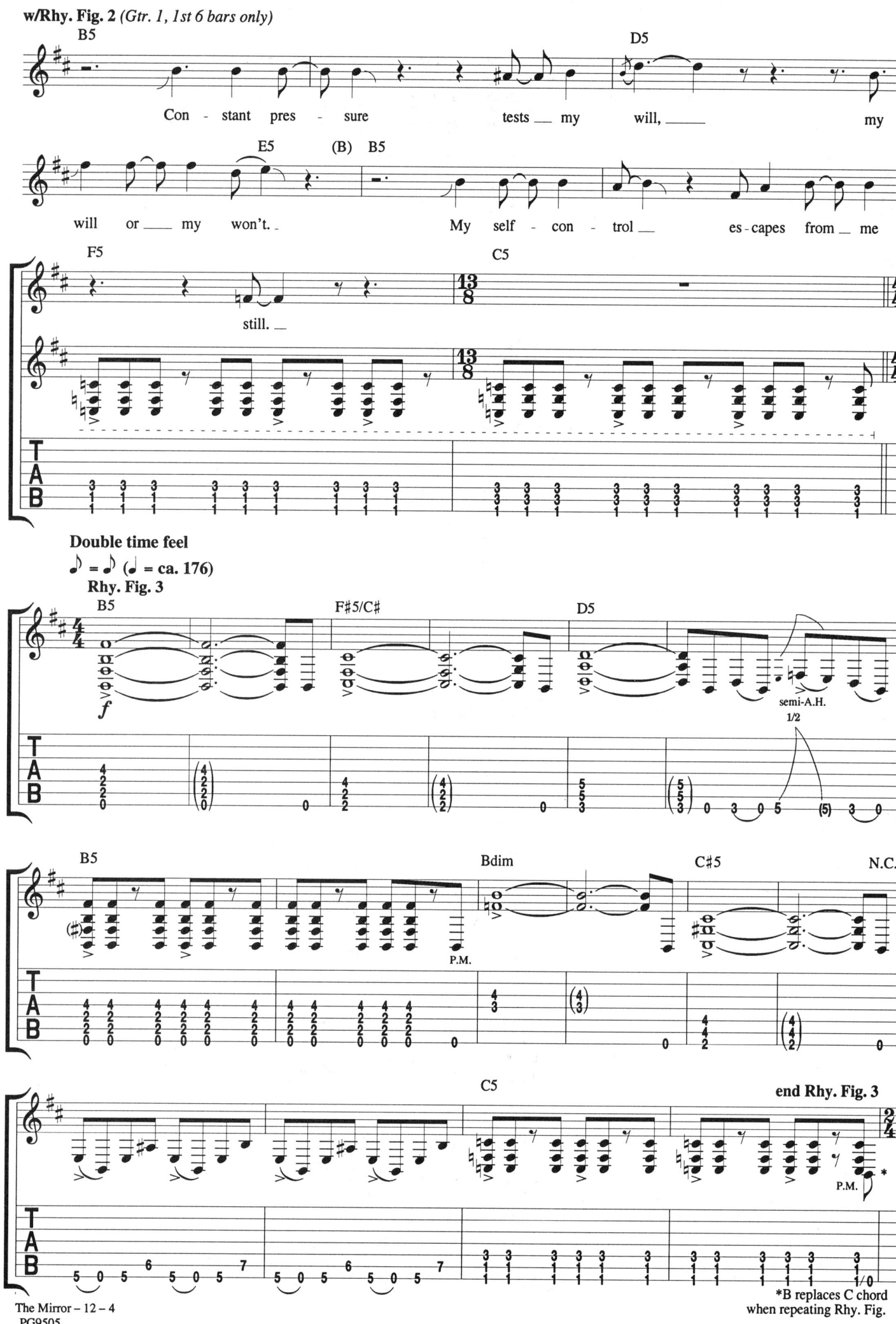

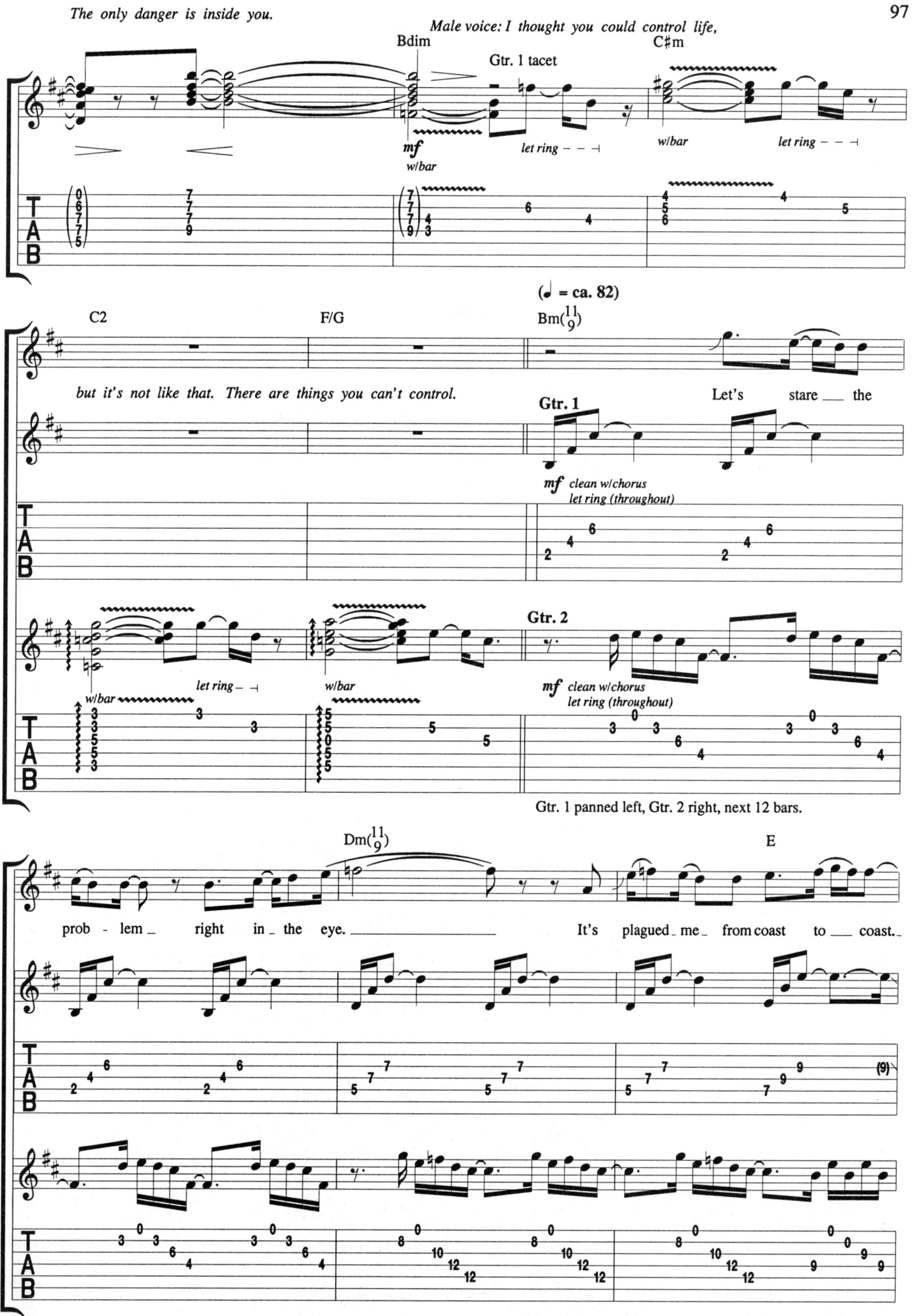

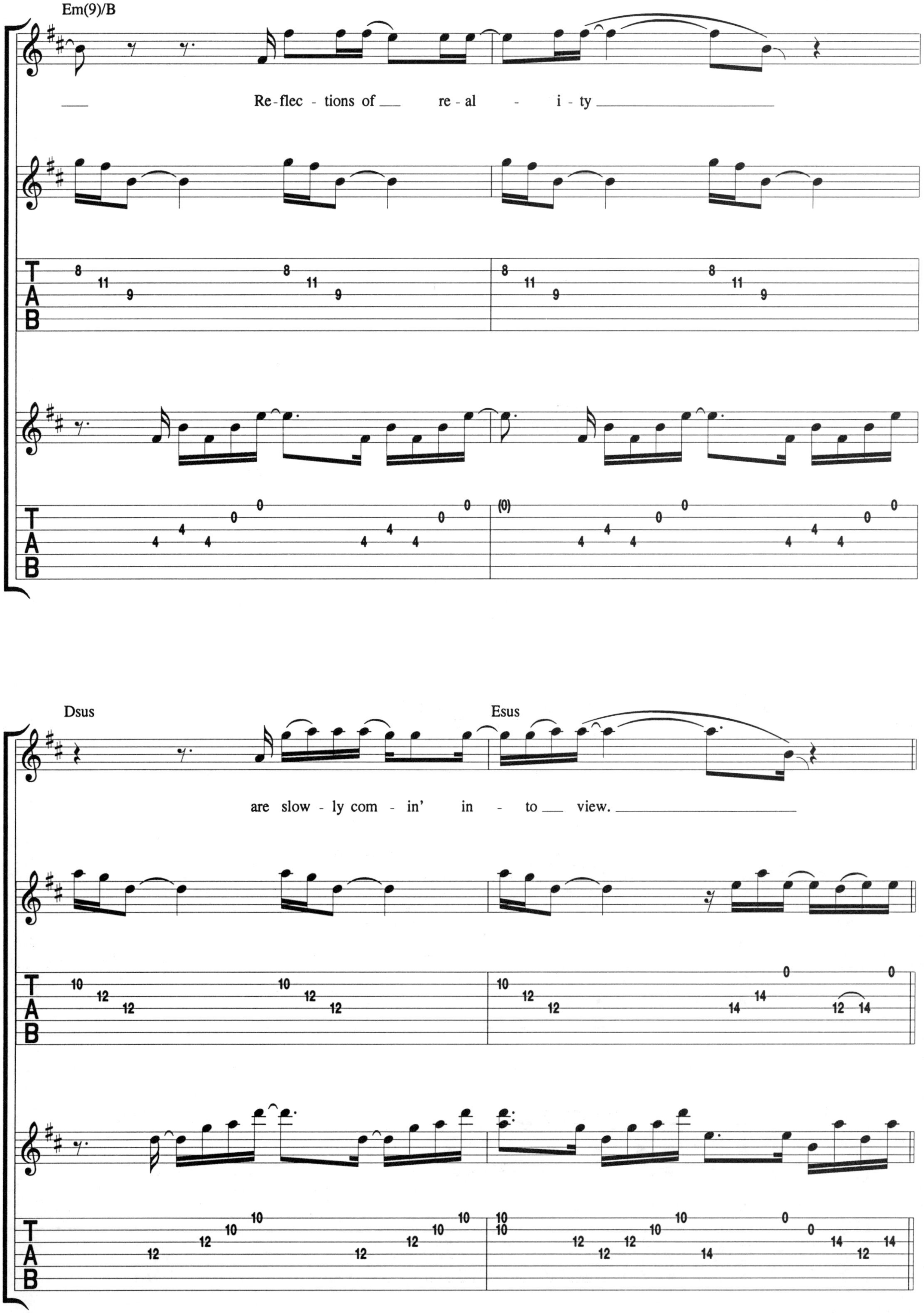
Em(9)/B
Re-flec - tions of ___ re - al - i - ty ___
Dsus
Esus
are slow - ly com - in' in - to ___ view. ___

Gtrs. 1 & 2 tacet
G/B
Bm
Gtr. 3
How in the hell could you pos - sib - ly for - give
*2 gtrs. arr. for 1. Gtr. 3 acoustic 6 string.
Gtr. 4 acoustic 12 string.
F(2)
F
F2
me
af - ter all the hell
Double-time (♩ = ca. 172)
w/Rhy. Fig. 3 (Gtr. 1)
D.S. 𝄋 al Coda
C(9)/G
C/G
B/F♯
Acous. gtrs.
Acous. gtrs. tacet
15
I put you through?
Gtr. 1
16
Coda
♩ = ca. 122
E5
D5
B5
I'll nev - er hurt you a - gain.
P.M.

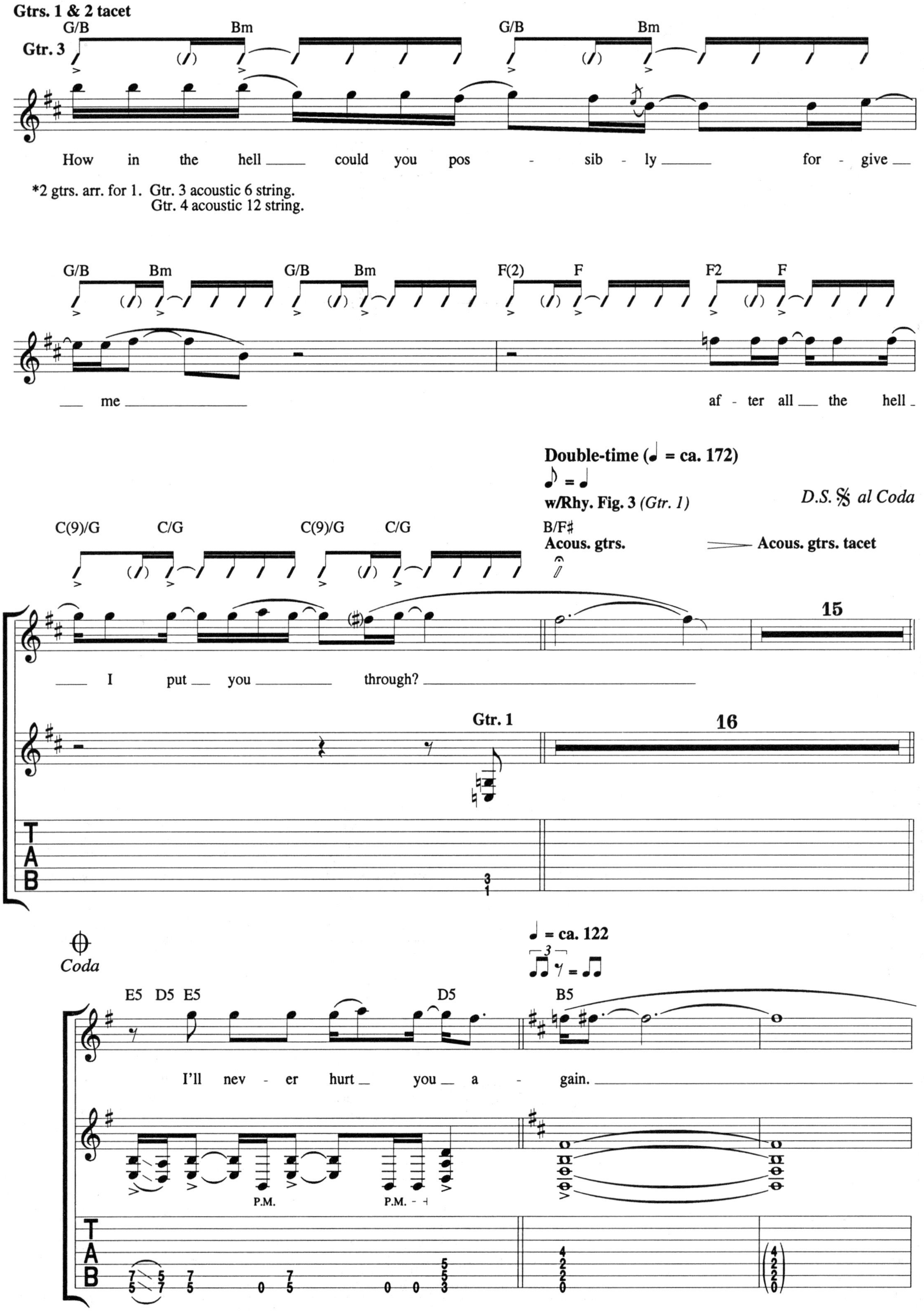

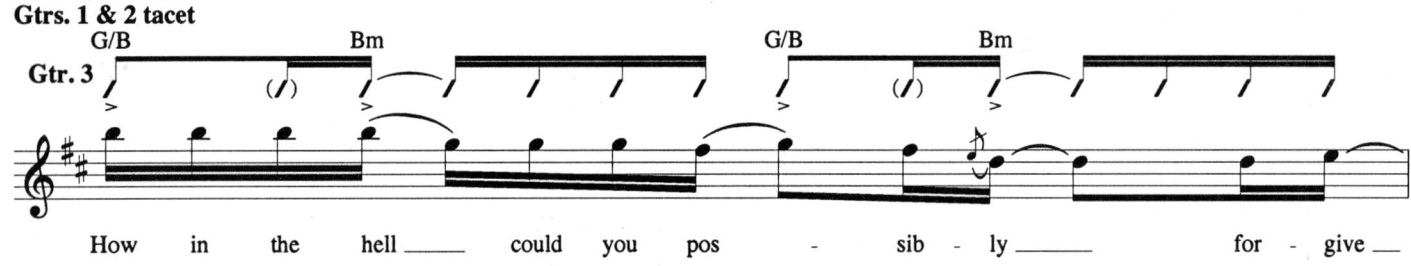

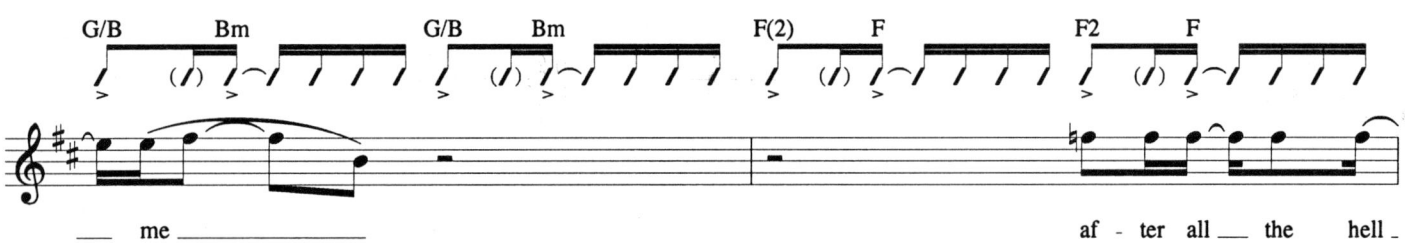

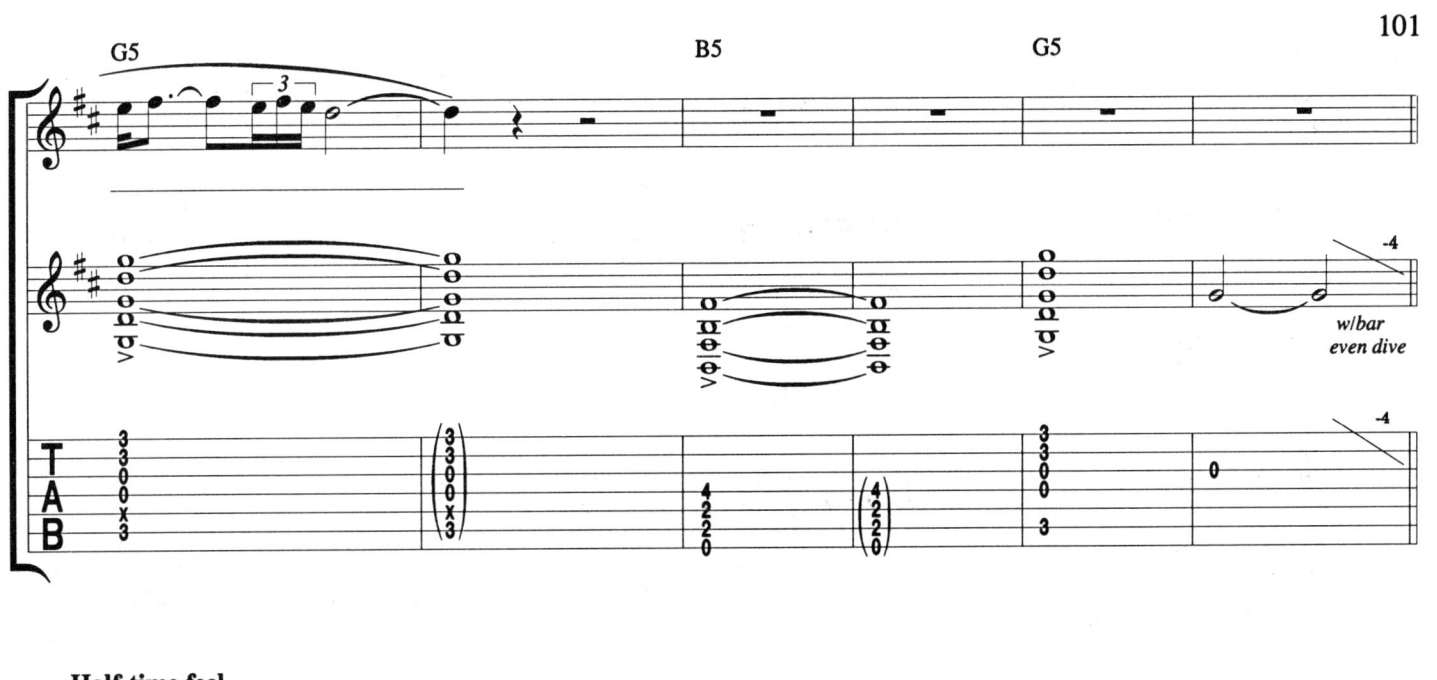
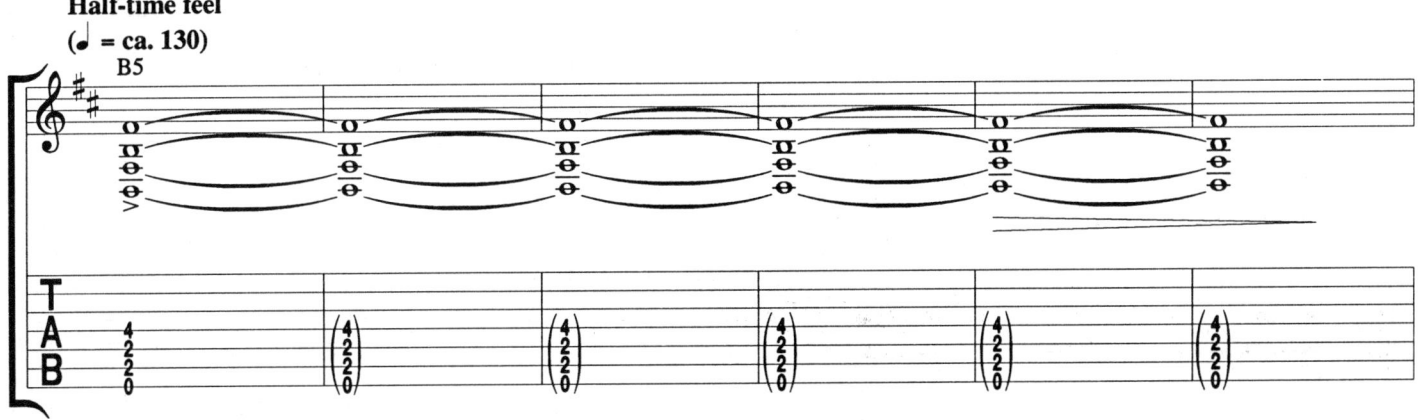
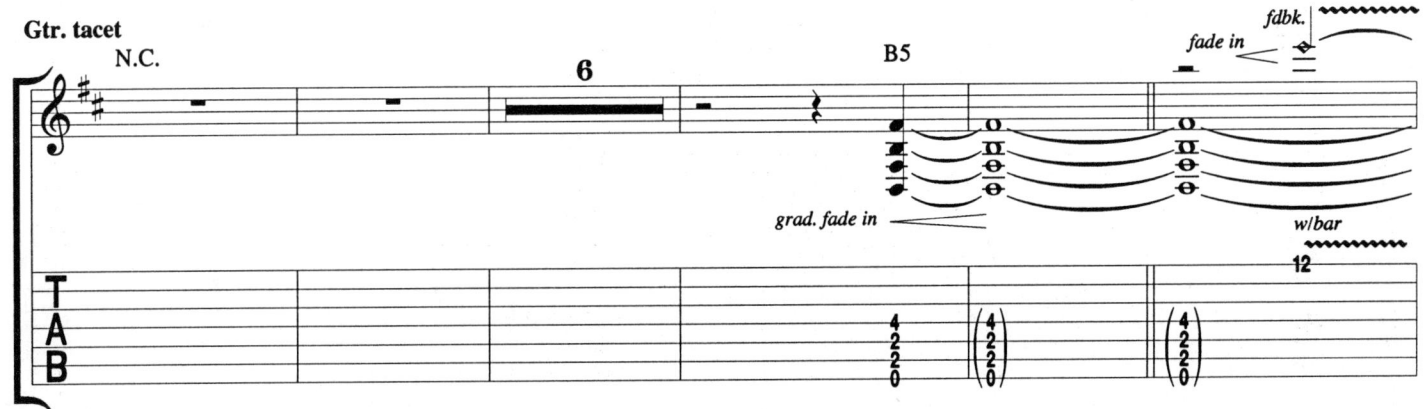
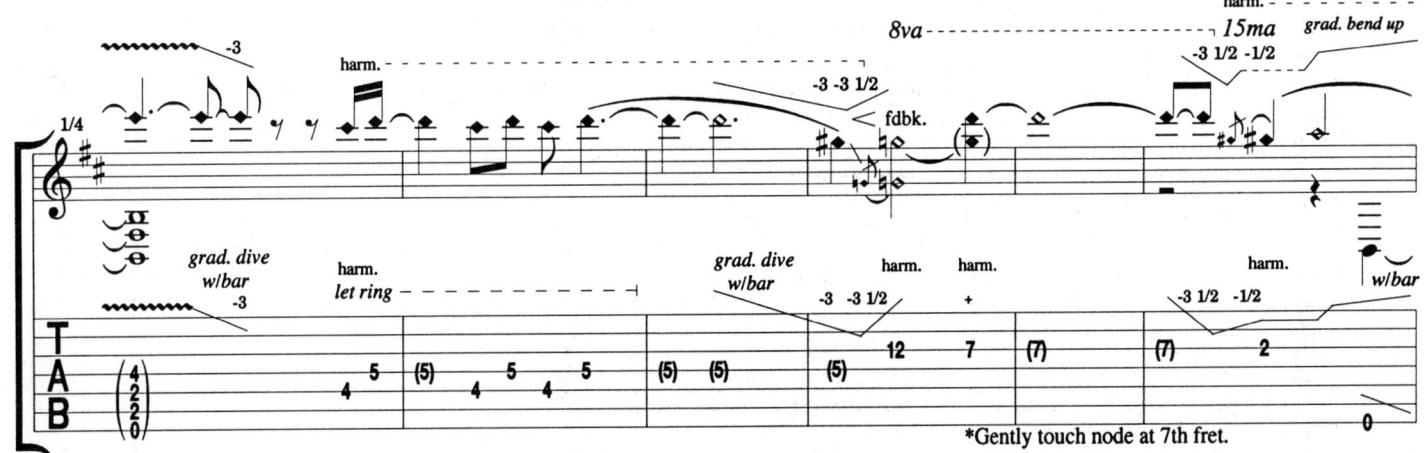

*Gently touch node at 7th fret.

The Mirror – 12 – 11
PG9505

102

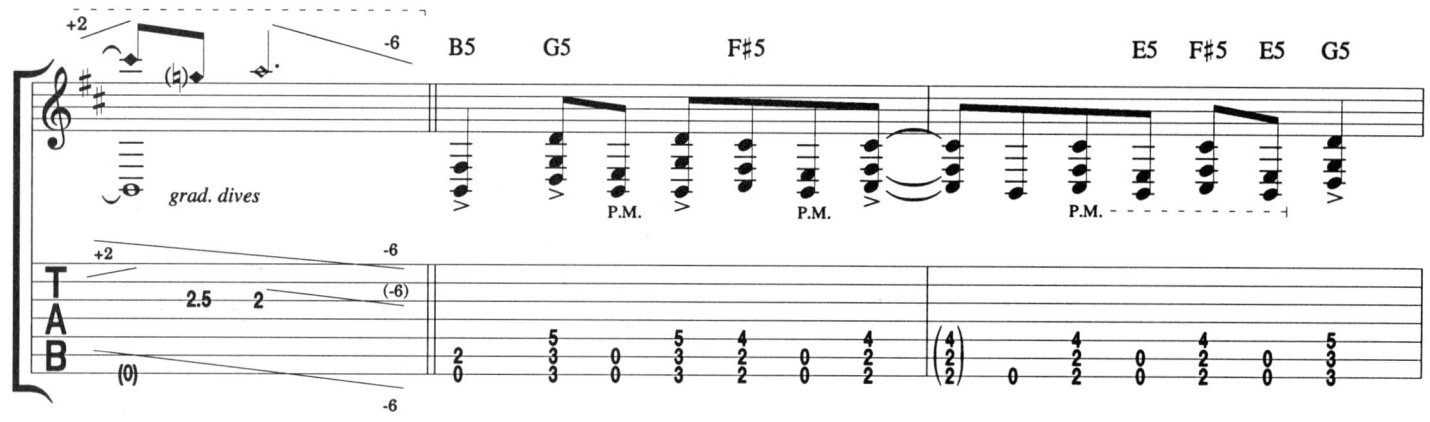

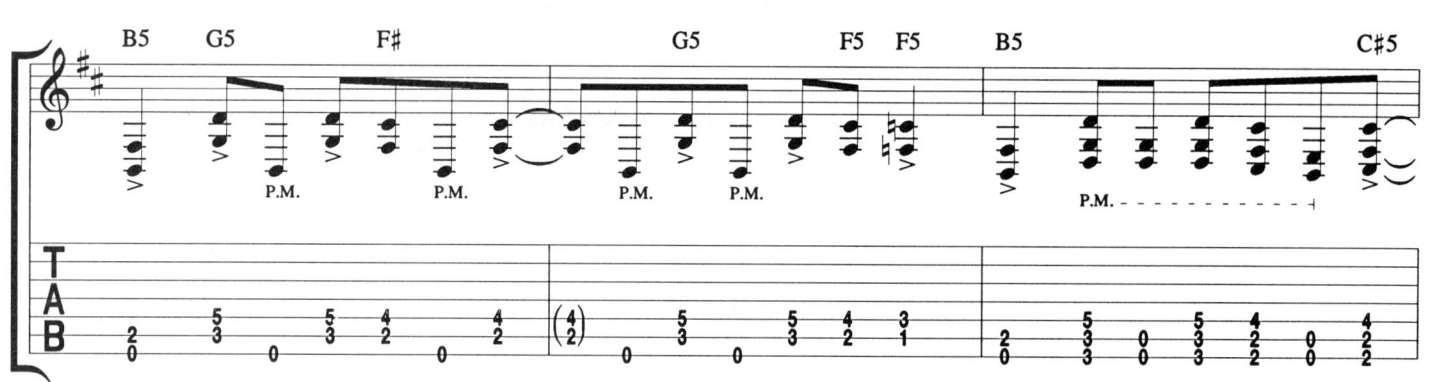

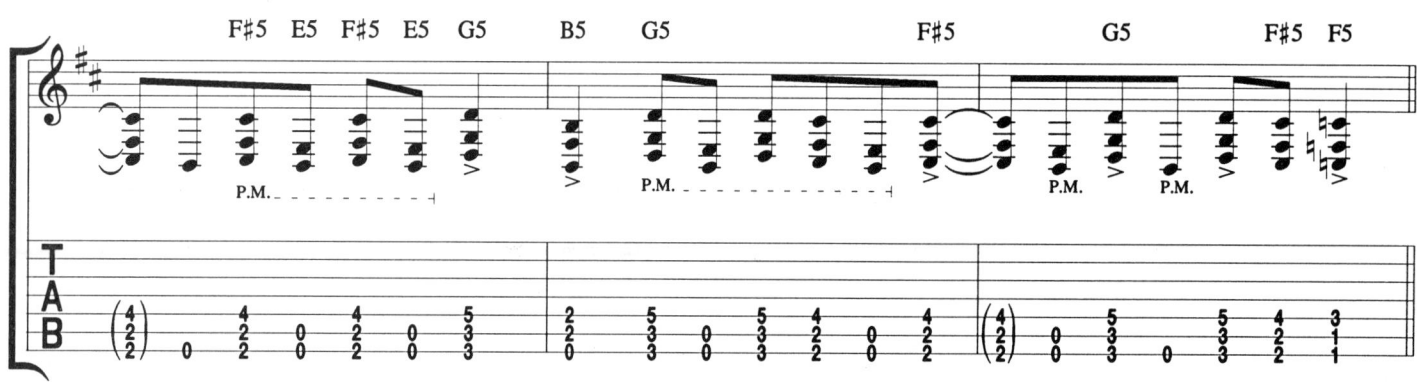

Play 4 times then segue to "LIE"

The Mirror – 12 – 12
PG9505

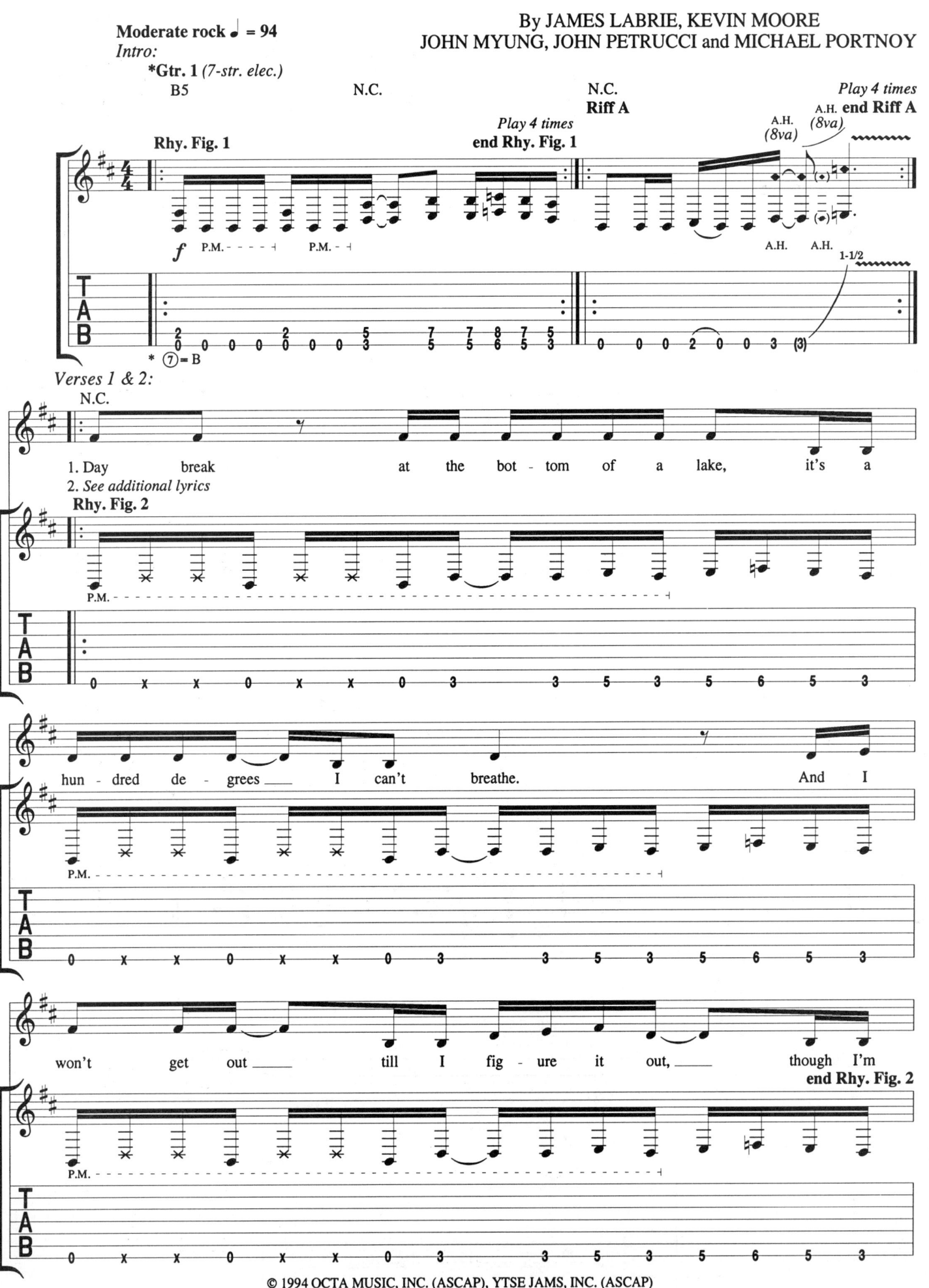

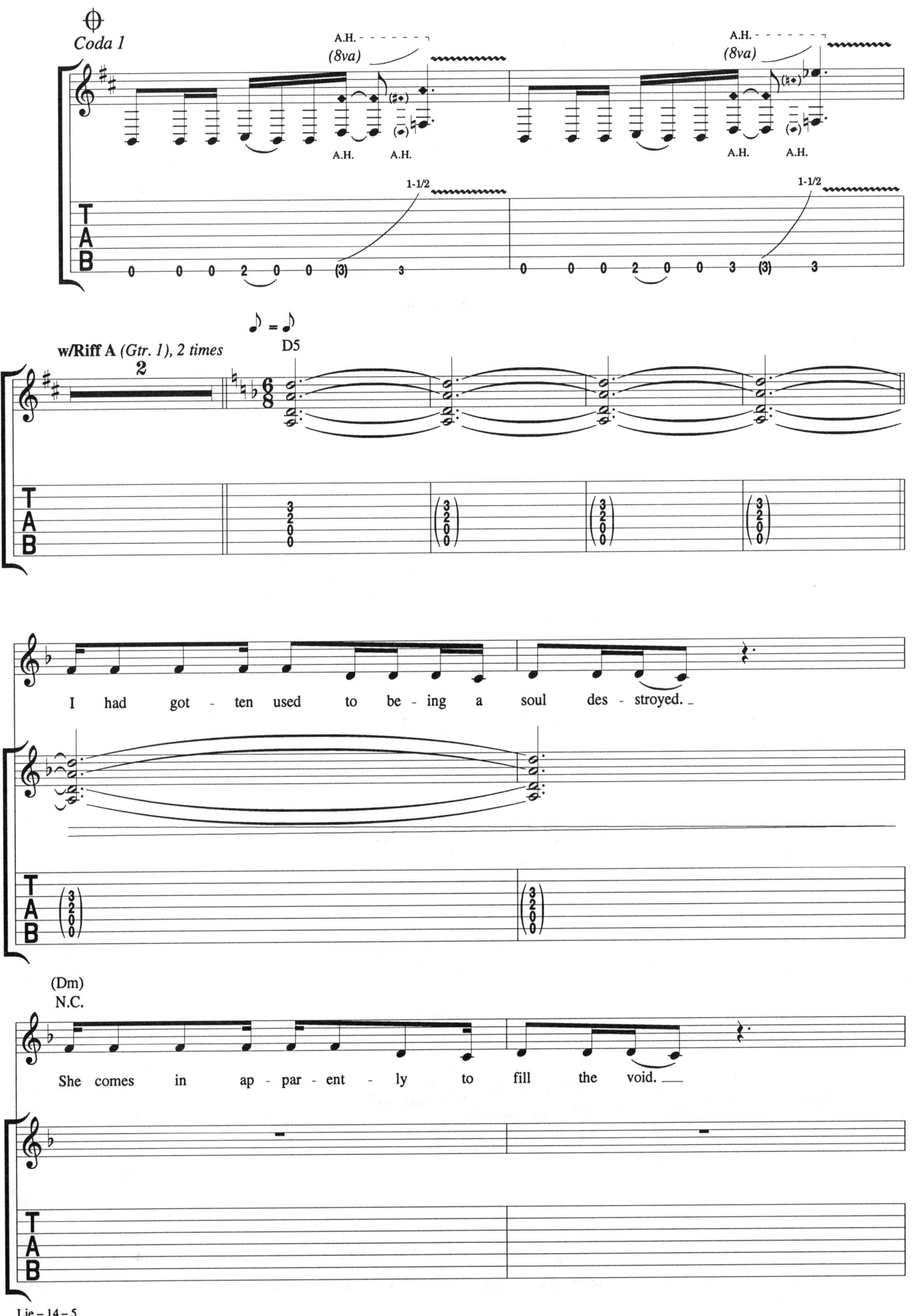

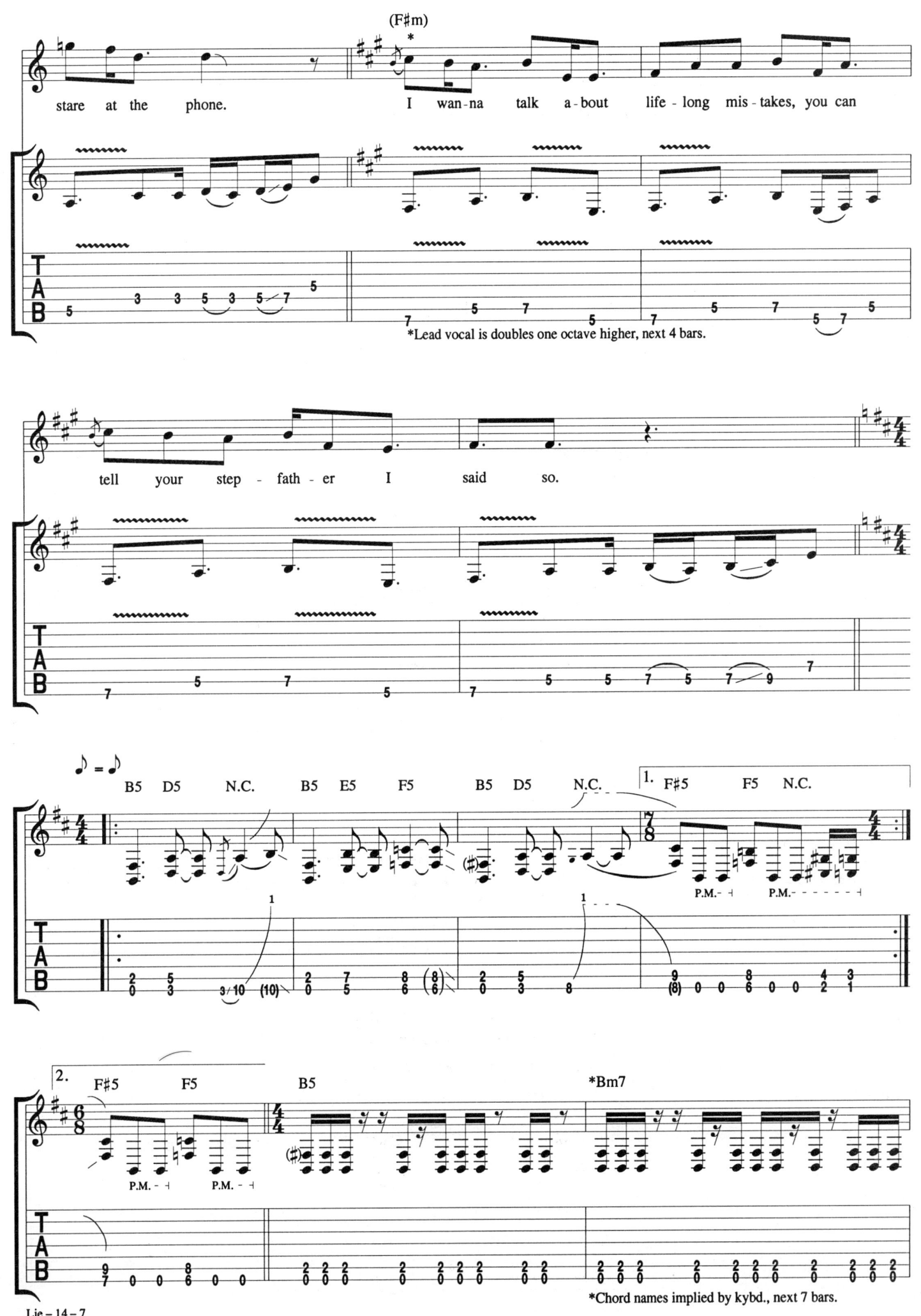

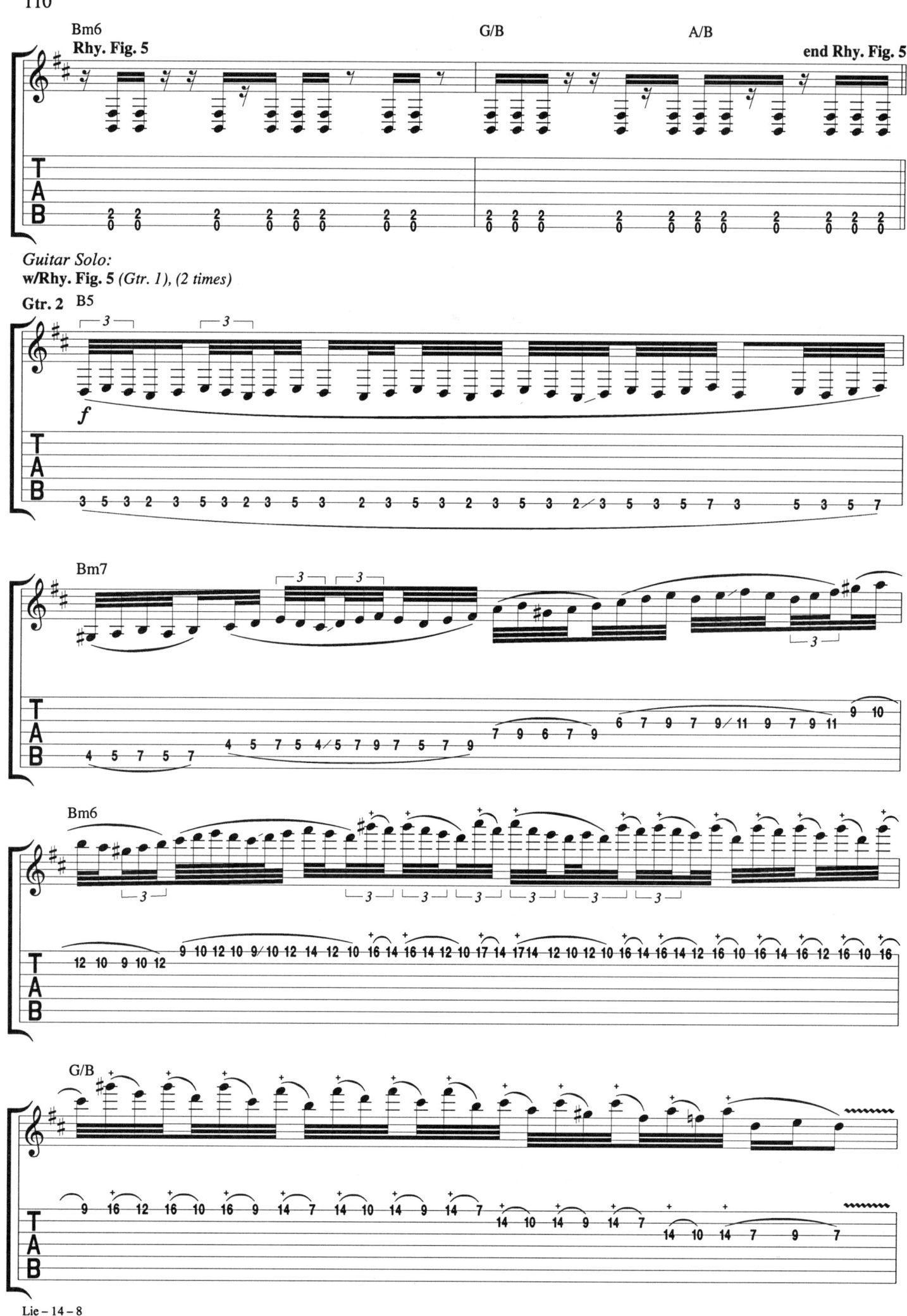

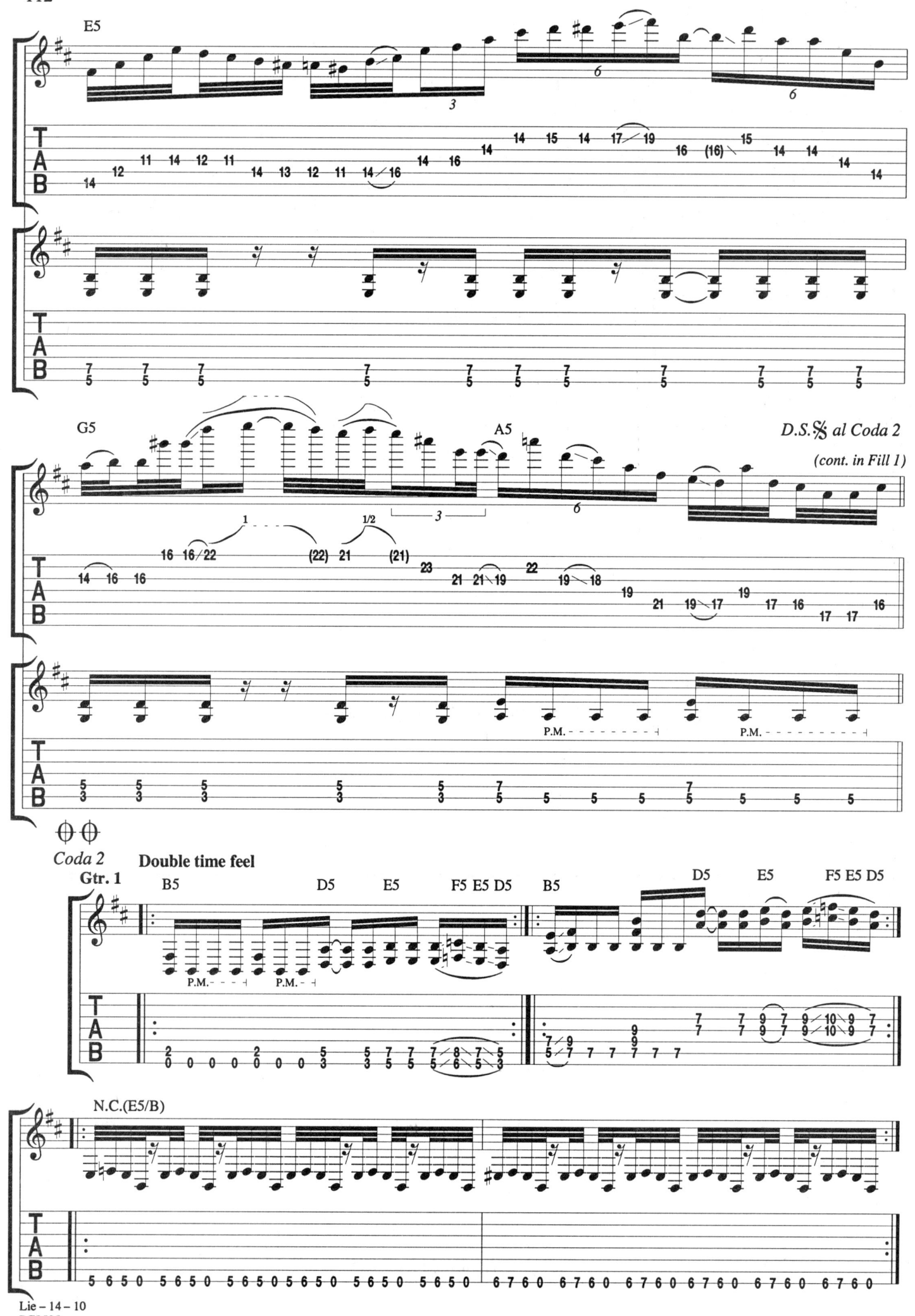

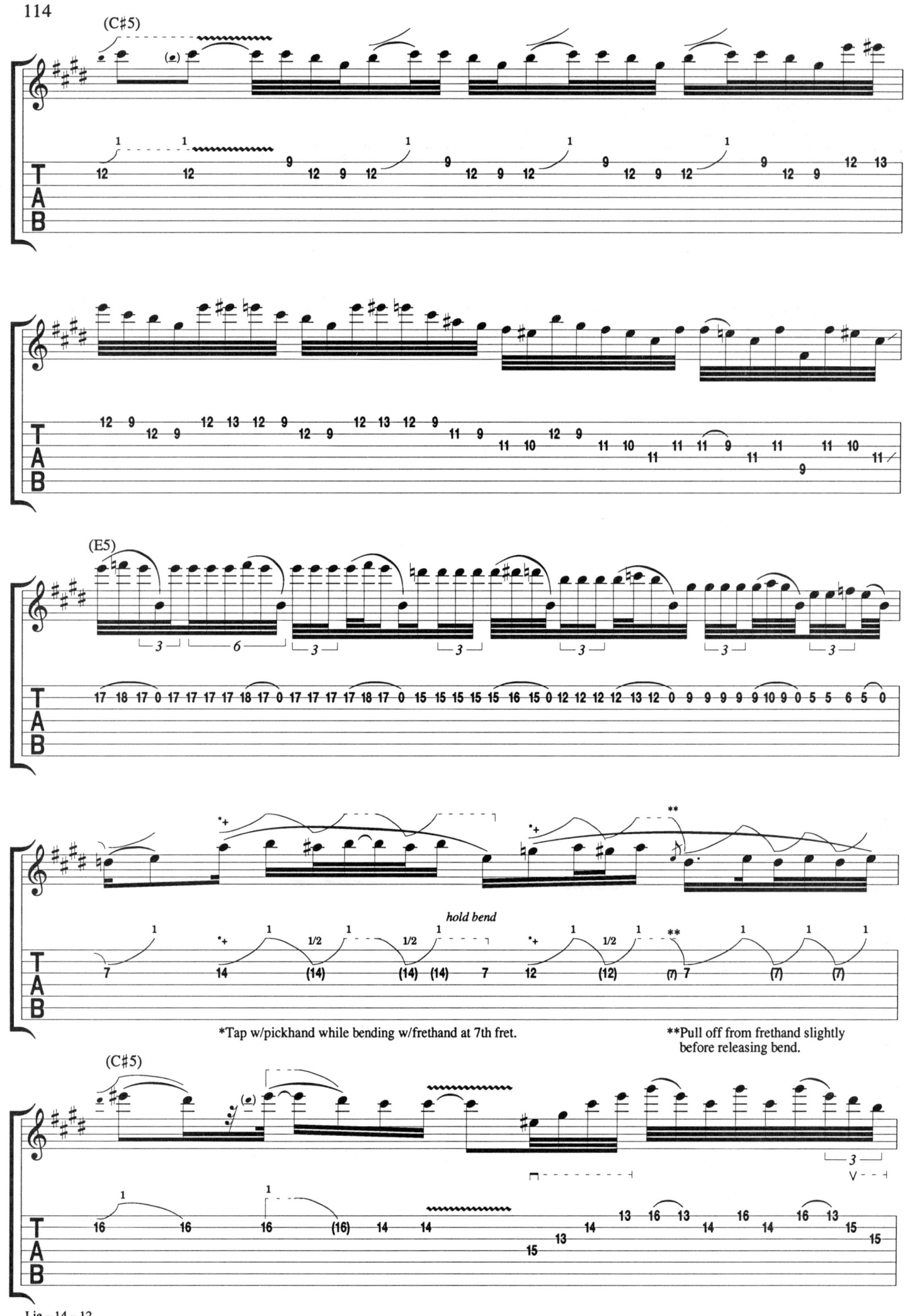

*Tap w/pickhand while bending w/frethand at 7th fret. 　　　　　　　**Pull off from frethand slightly before releasing bend.

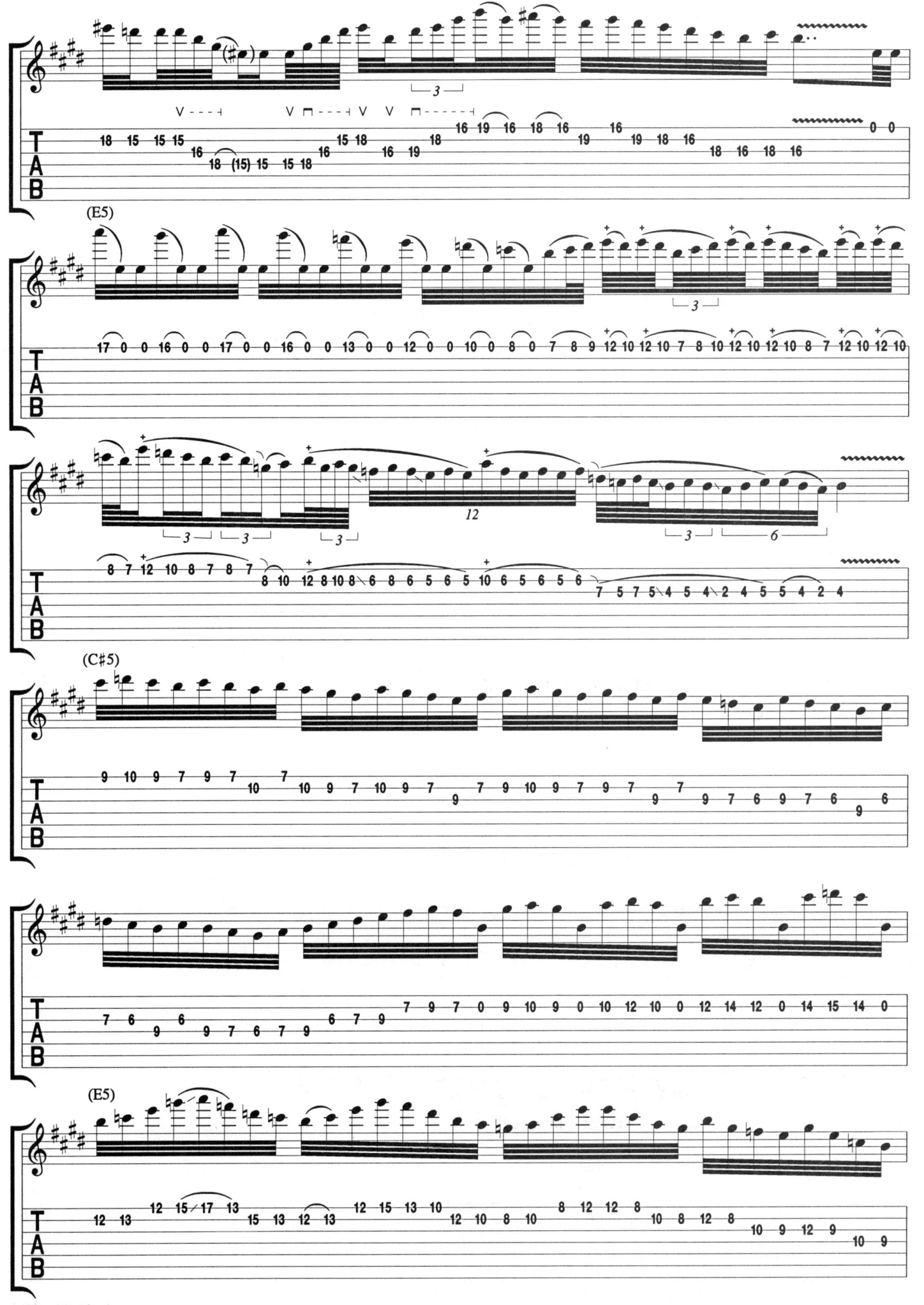

116

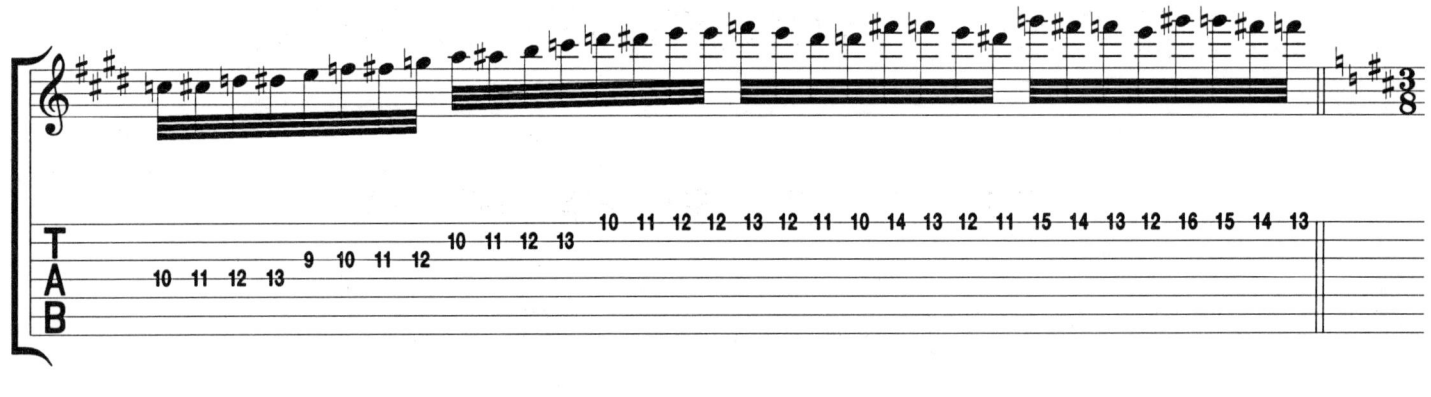

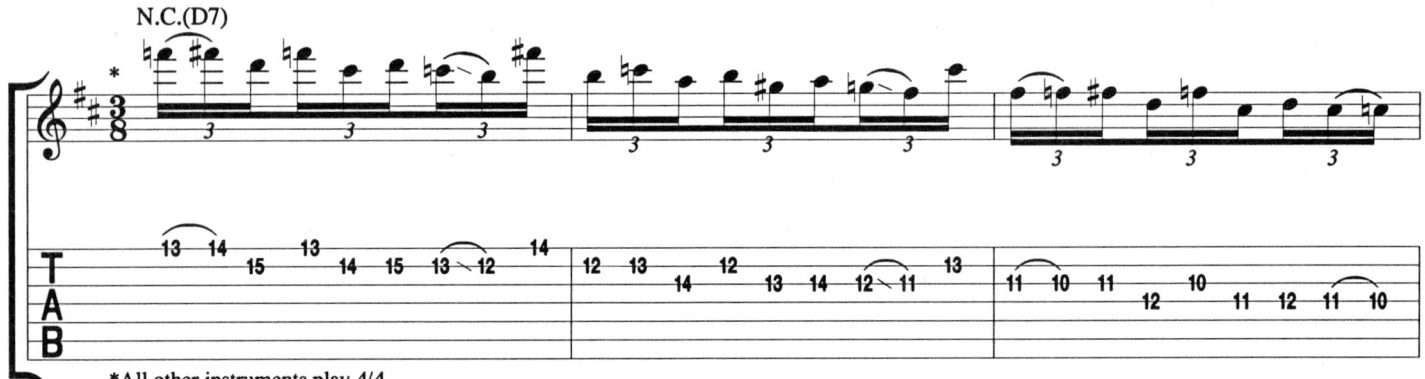

*All other instruments play 4/4.

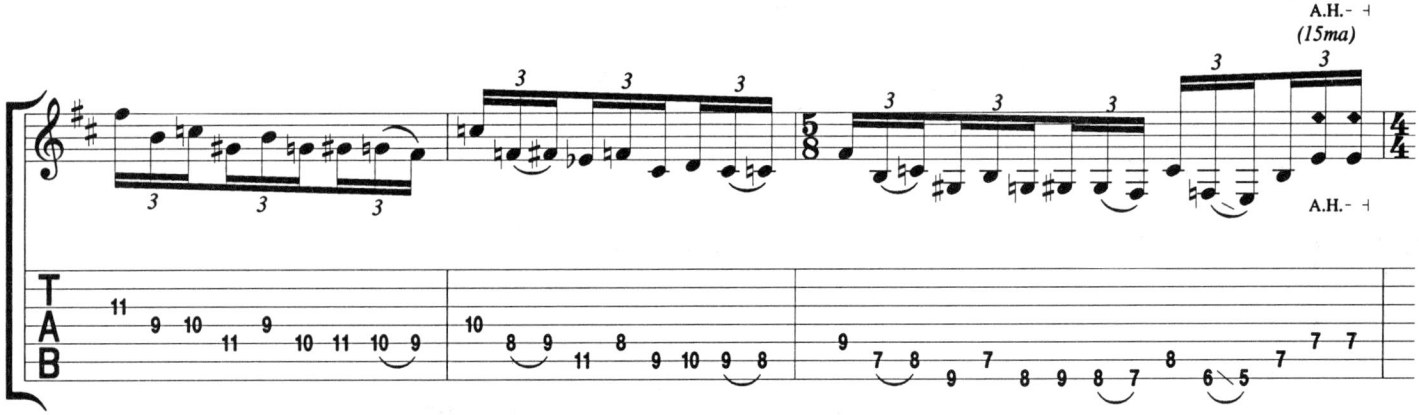

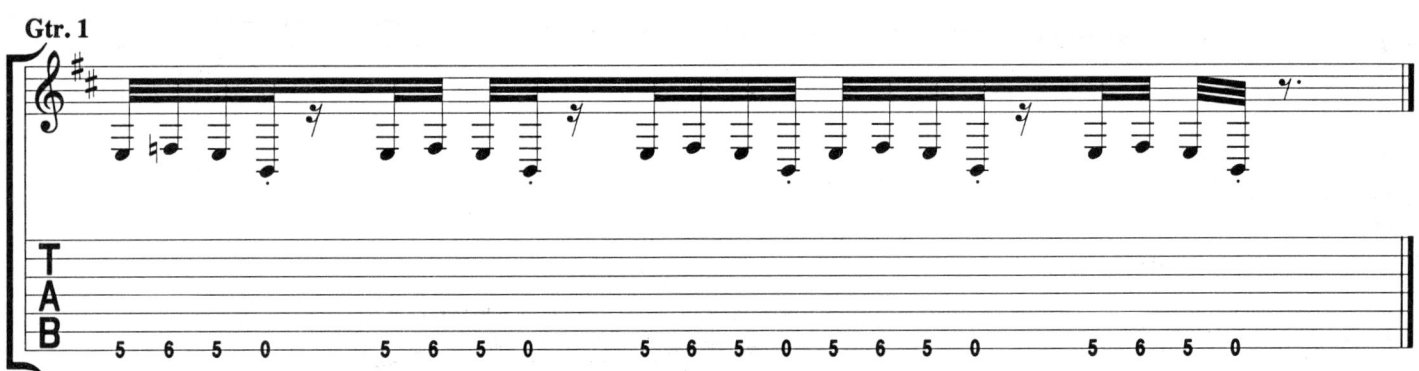

2. Doing fine, but don't waste my time.
   Tell me what it is you want to say.
   You sin, you win, just let me in.
   Hurry, I've been out in the rain all day.
   So you tell me, "Trust me," I can trust you
   As far as I can throw you.
   And I'm trying to get out of a shadow of doubt,
   'Cause I don't know if I know you.
   (To Chorus:)

LIFTING SHADOWS OFF A DREAM

Words and Music by JAMES LABRIE
KEVIN MOORE, JOHN MYUNG,
JOHN PETRUCCI and MICHAEL PORTNOY

*w/Digital delay set on single repeat at 416 milliseconds. Echoed notes are in parenthesis and occur three 16th notes after primary attack. Delay volume is slightly higher than guitar volume.
**Cue note sounds on repeats only.

*Cue note sounds at repetition of Riff A.

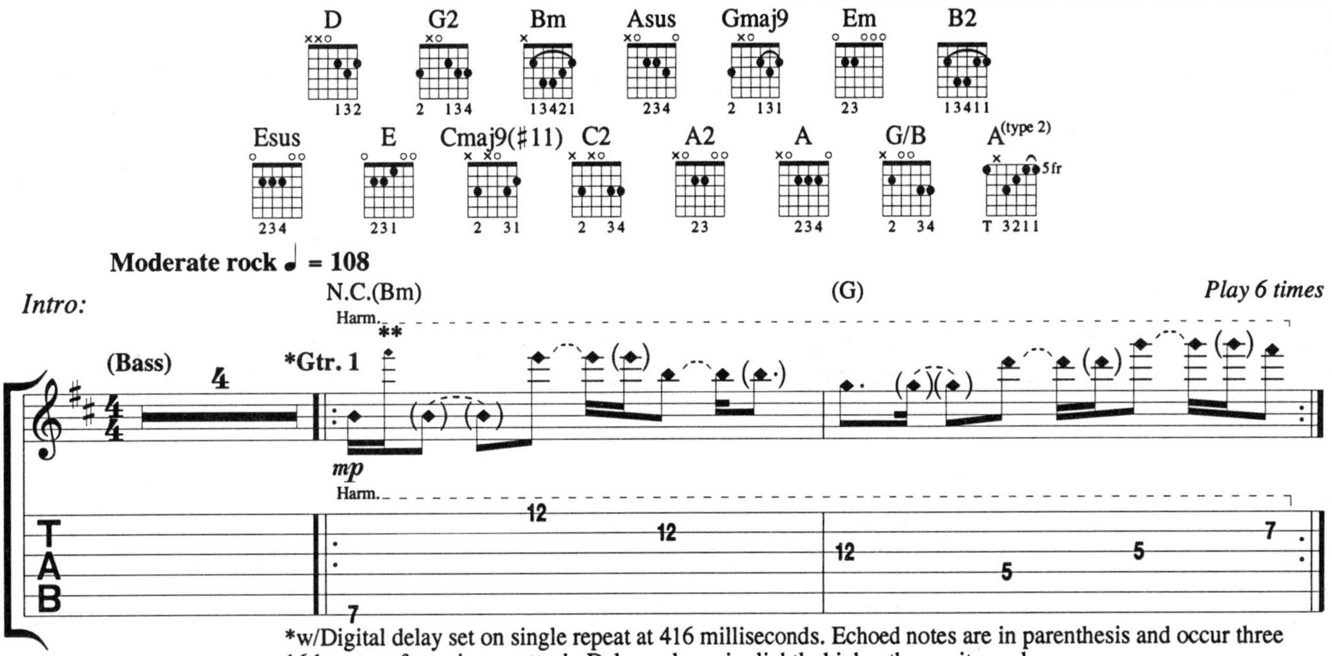

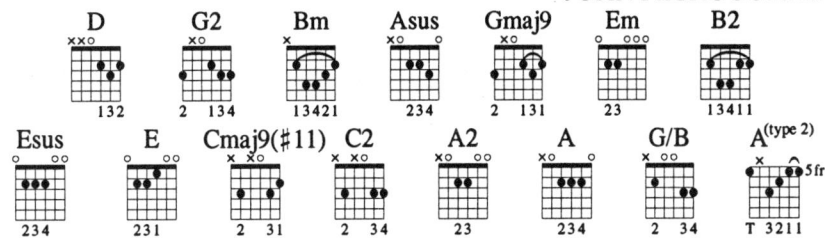

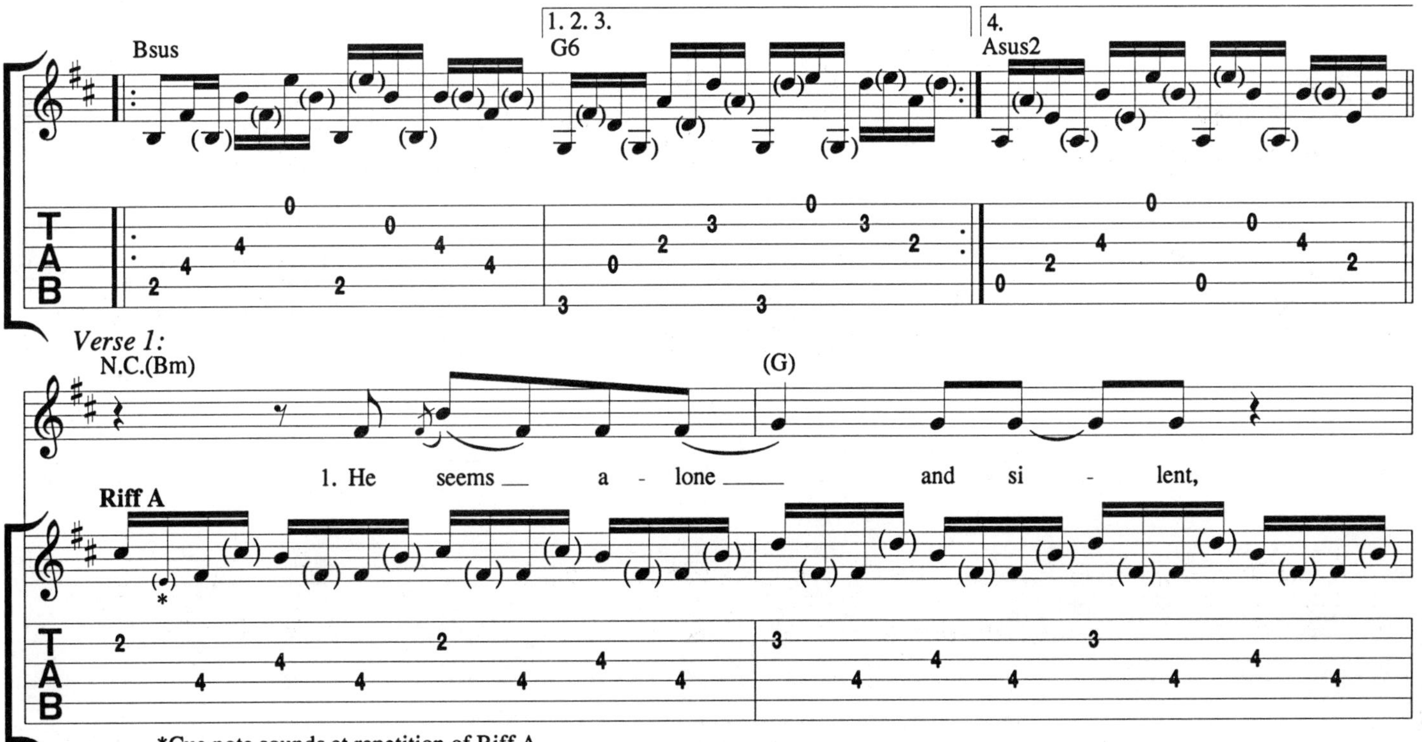

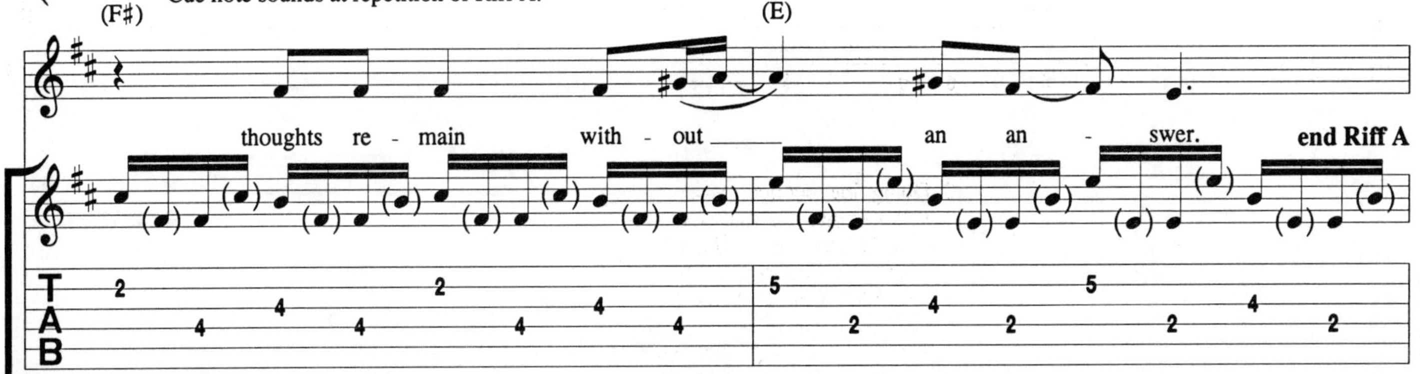

118

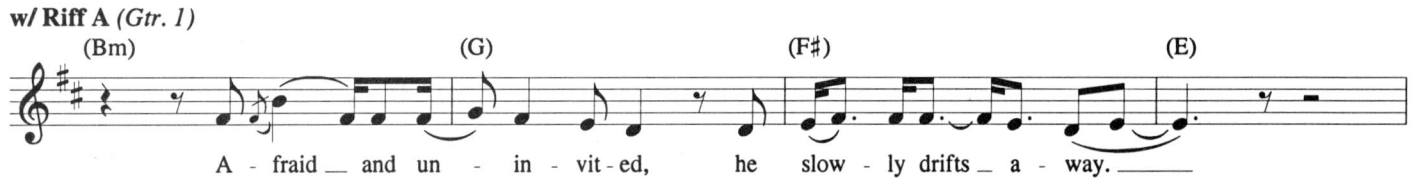

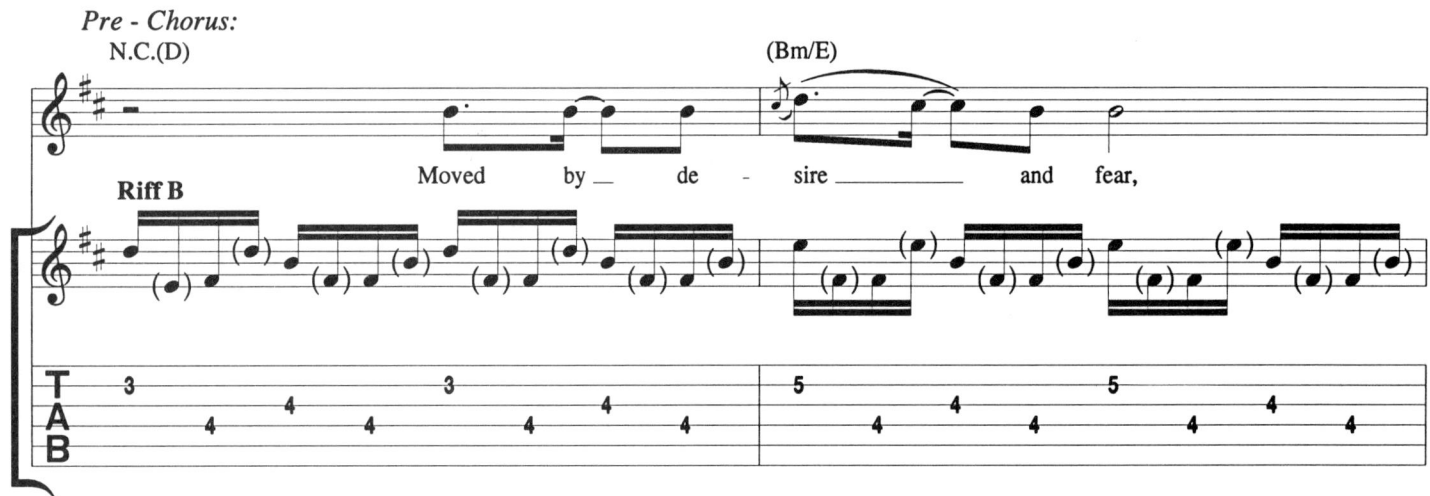

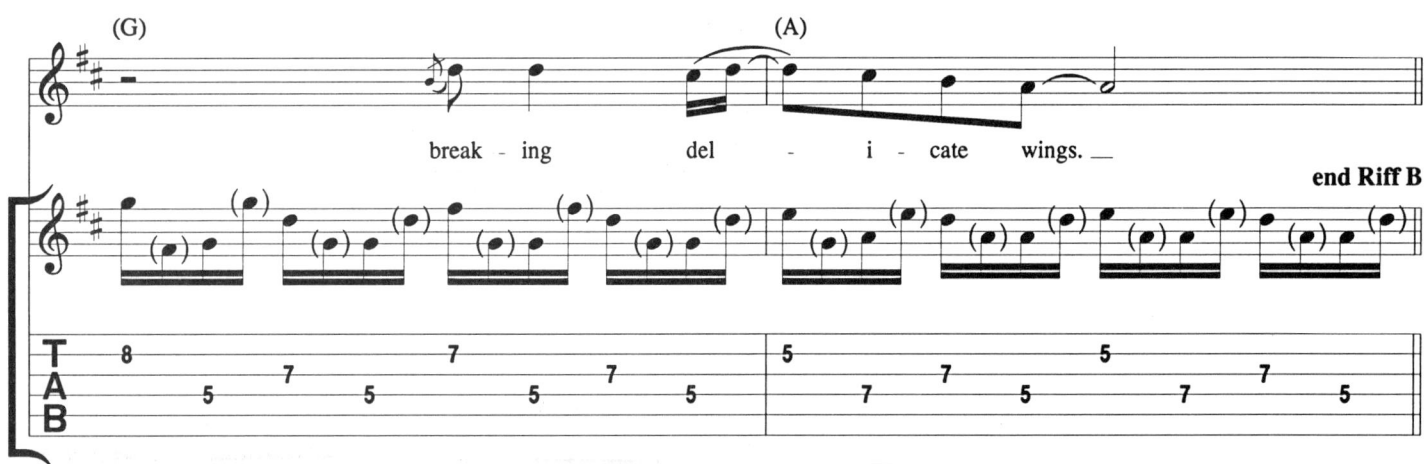

*Cue note sounds at repetitions of Riff C.

Lifting Shadows Off A Dream – 9 – 2

PG9505

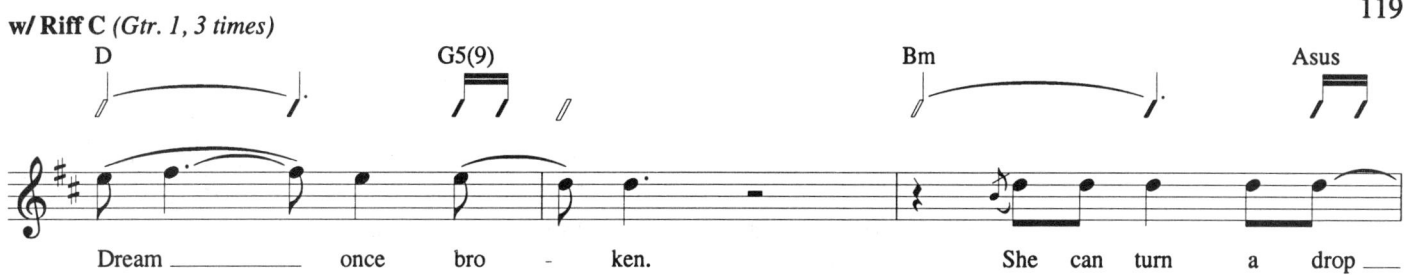

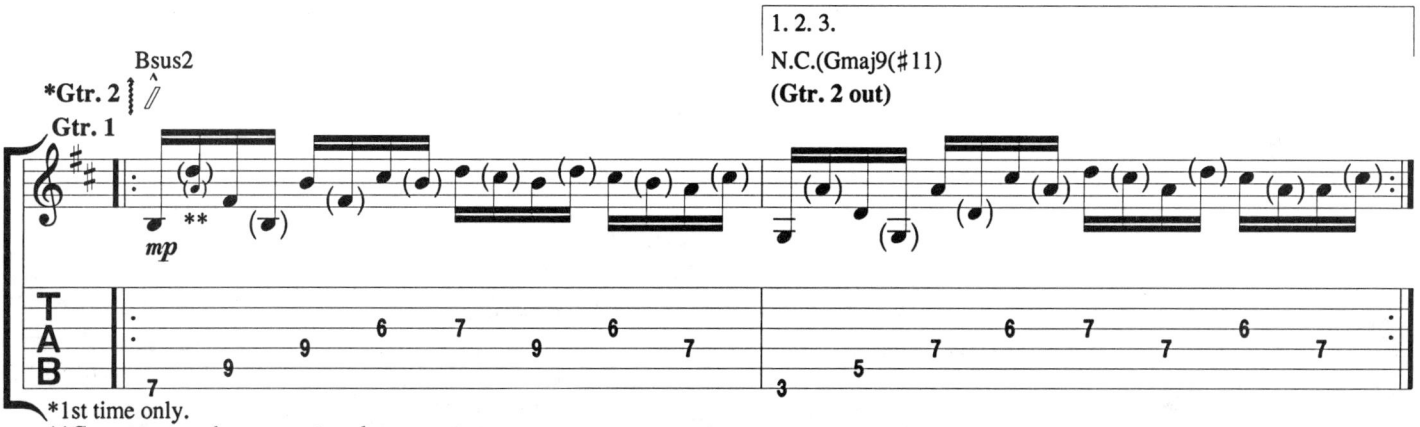
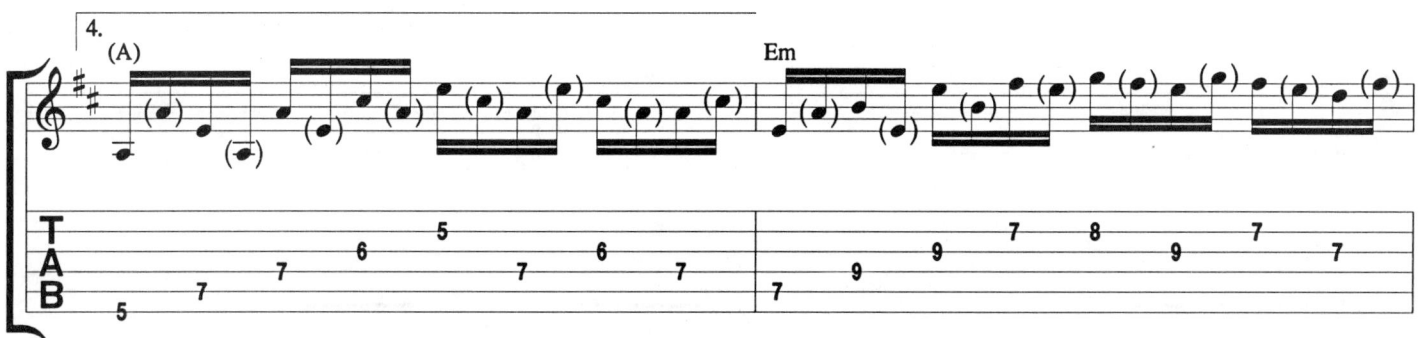
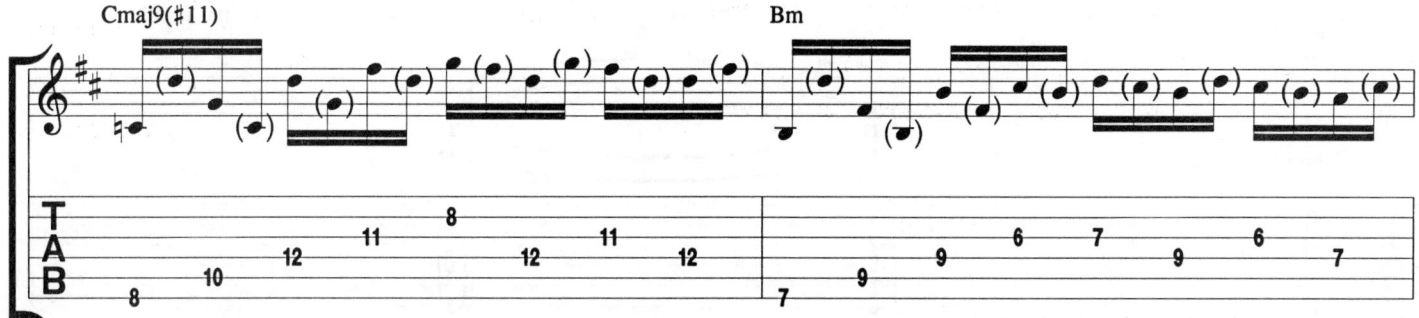

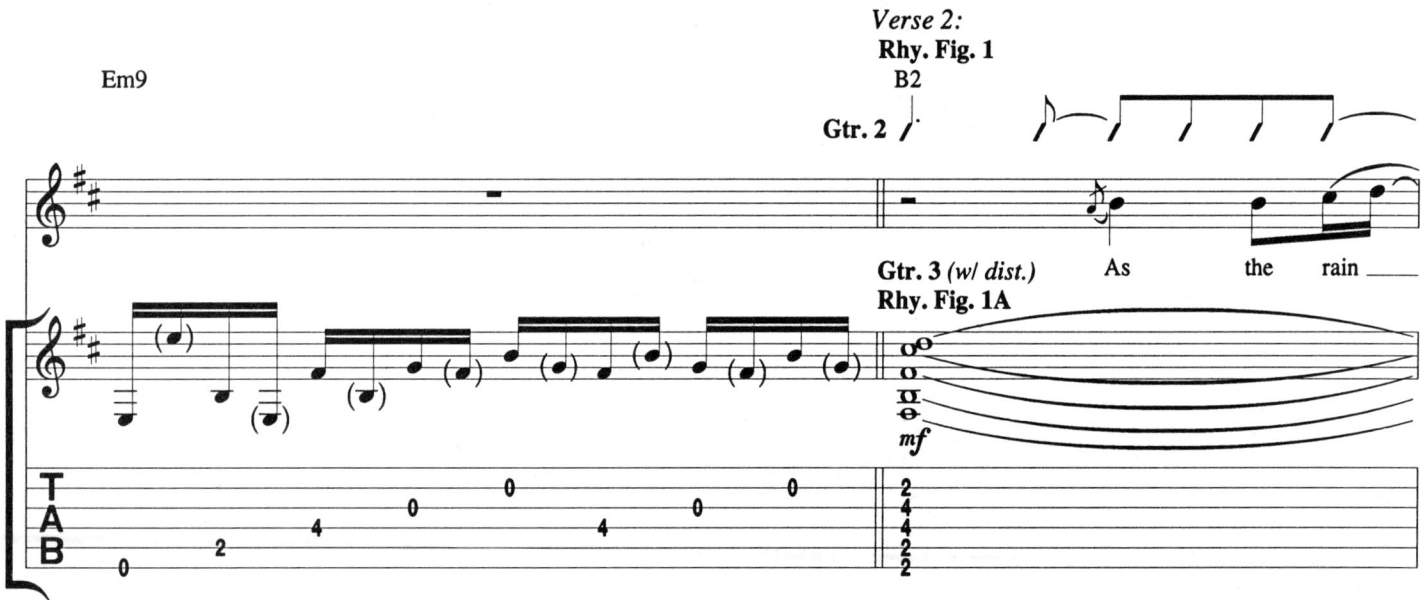
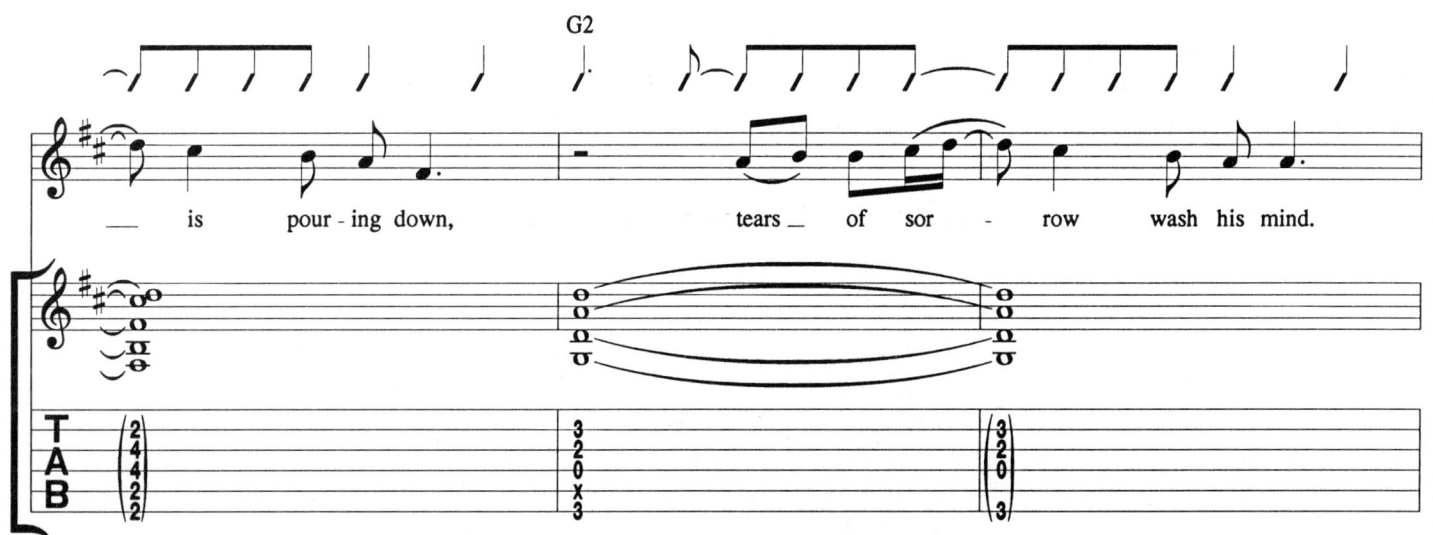

Lifting Shadows Off A Dream -9 -4
PG9505

SCARRED

By JAMES LABRIE, KEVIN MOORE,
JOHN MYUNG, JOHN PETRUCCI and MICHAEL PORTNOY

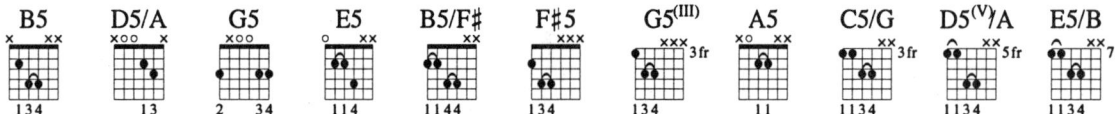

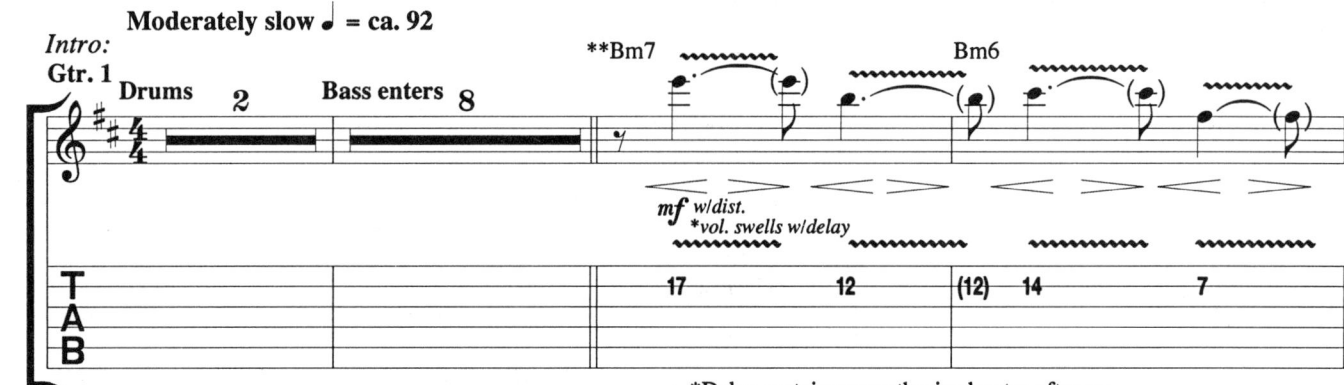

*Delay sustains parenthesized notes after >.
**Chords implied by bass.

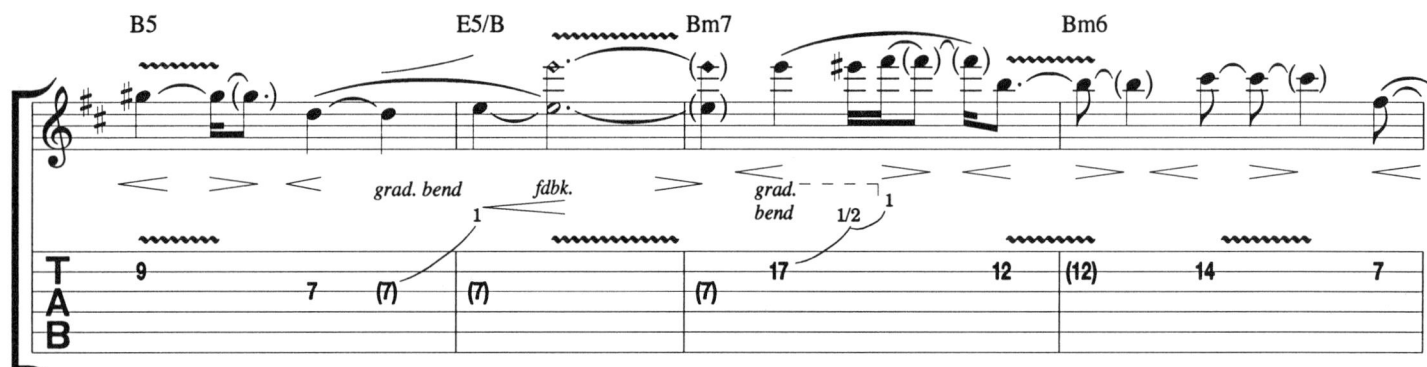

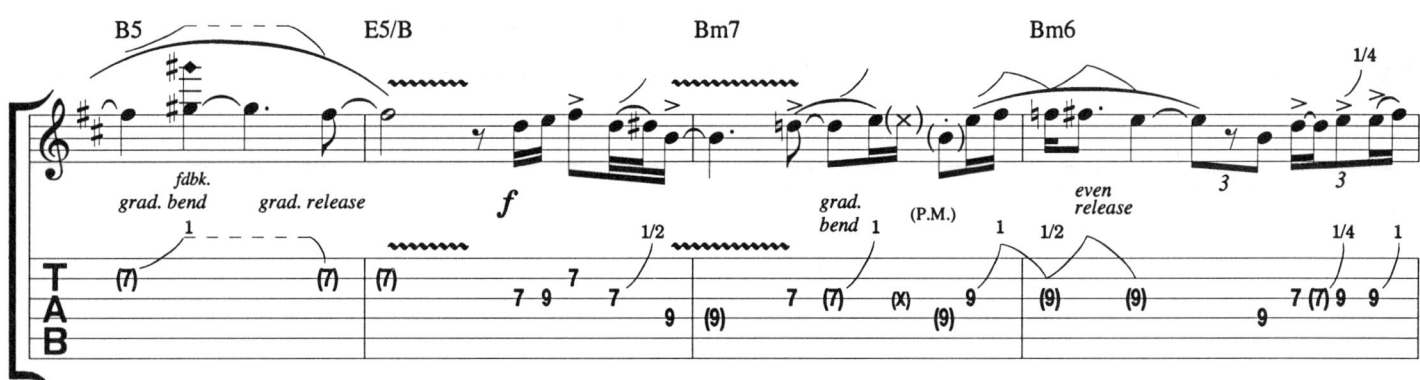

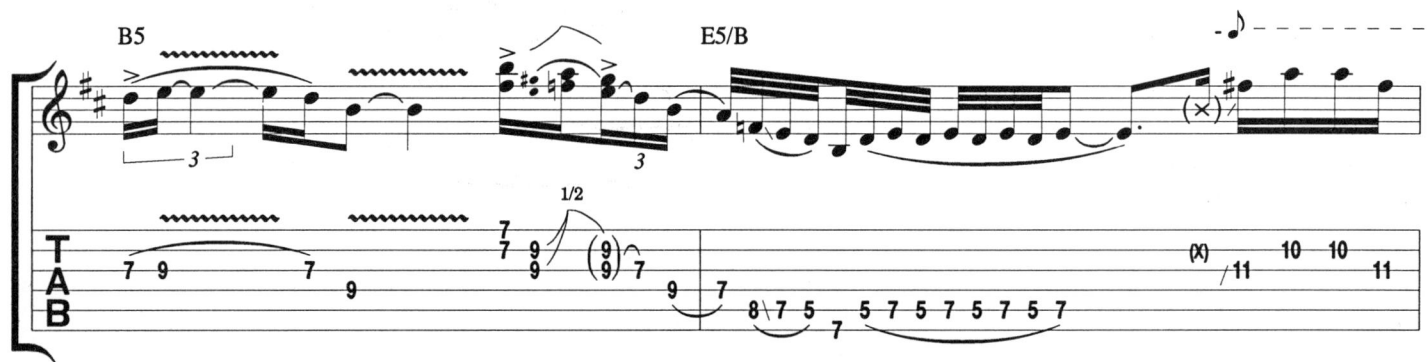

© 1994 OCTA MUSIC, INC. (ASCAP), YTSE JAMS, INC. (ASCAP)
All rights on behalf of OCTA MUSIC, INC. & YTSE JAMS, INC. administered by WB MUSIC CORP. (ASCAP)
All rights reserved

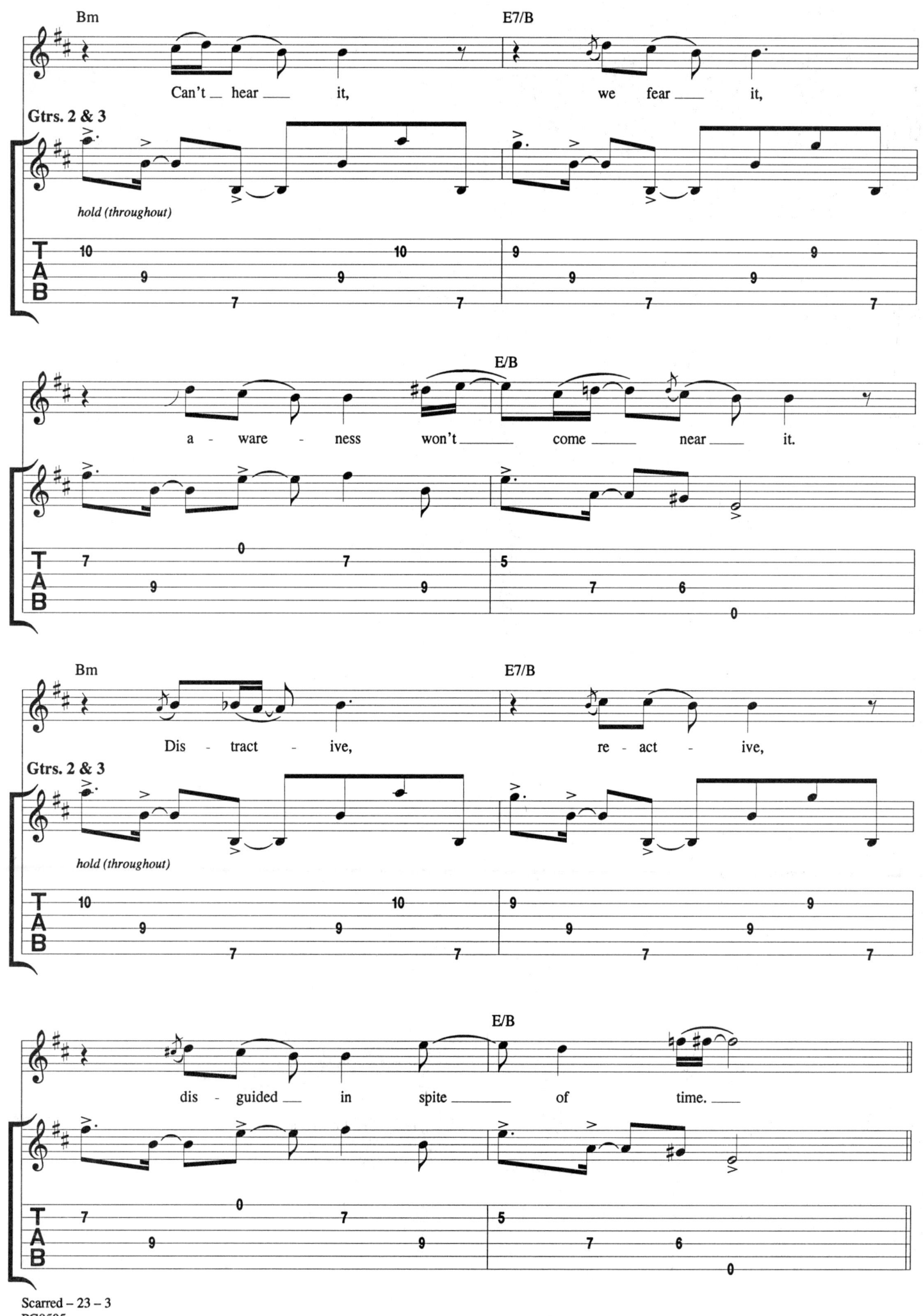

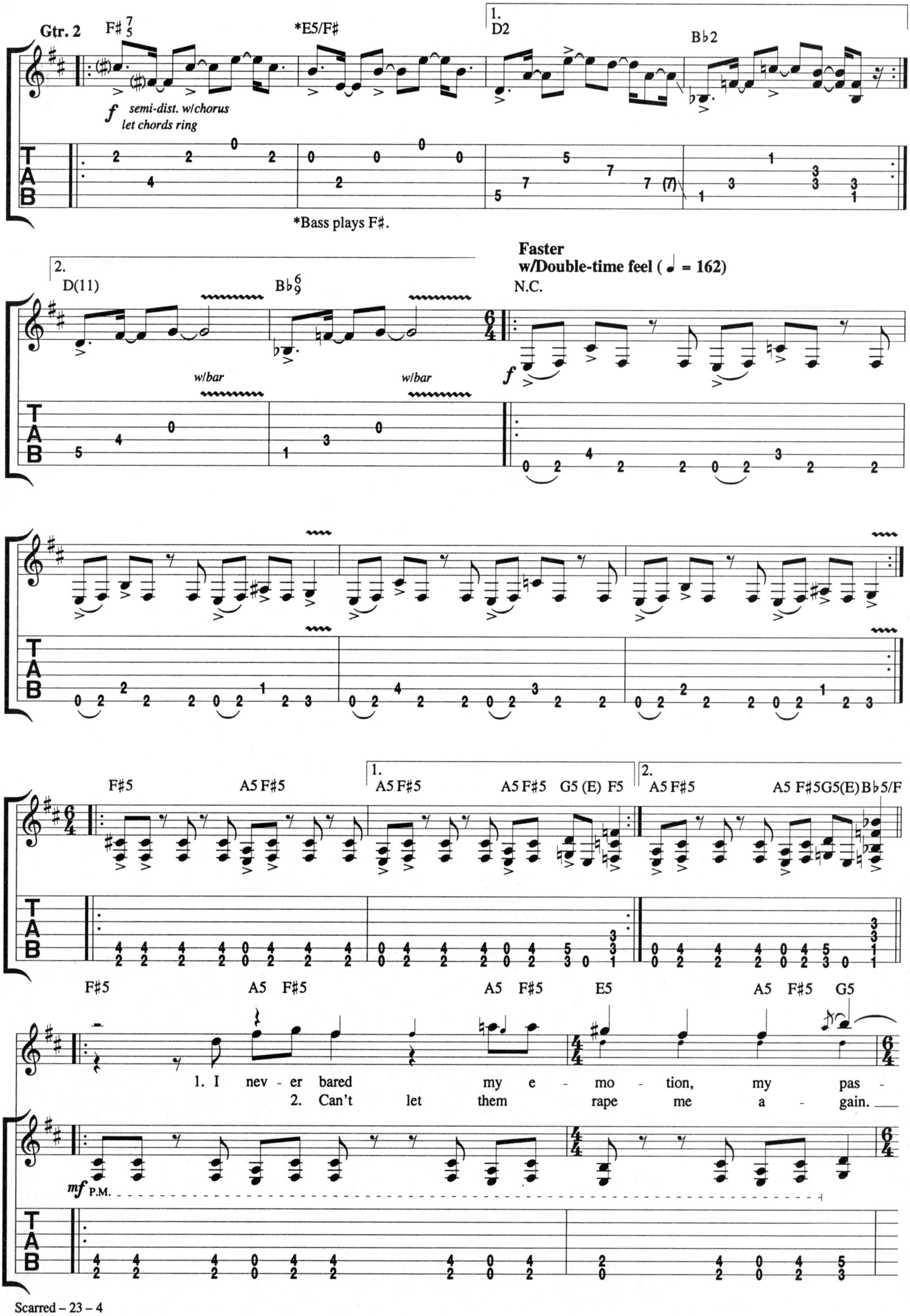
Gtr. 2
F♯ 7/5
*E5/F♯
1.
D2
B♭2
semi-dist. w/chorus
let chords ring
*Bass plays F♯.
2.
D(11)
B♭ 6/9
w/bar
Faster
w/Double-time feel (♩ = 162)
N.C.
F♯5
A5 F♯5
A5 F♯5
A5 F♯5 G5 (E) F5
A5 F♯5 G5(E) B♭5/F
E5
A5 F♯5 G5
1. I nev - er bared my e - mo - tion, my pas -
2. Can't let them rape me a - gain.
P.M.

F♯5 A5 F♯5 A5 F♯5 A5 F♯5 A5 F♯5 F5 D5/A F♯5 A5 F♯5 A5 F♯5
sion al - ways strong. I nev-er lost my de -
Your ven-om's not fam - i - ly here. Won't let them
mf P.M.
A5 F♯5 A5 F♯5 G5 F♯5 A5 F♯5 A5 F♯5 1. A5 F♯5 E5 F♯5 F5 D5/A
vo - tion but some - where fate went wrong.
fill me with fa - tal - is - tic rem - e - dies.
F♯5 A5 F♯5 A5 F♯5 A5 F♯5 G5 (E) F5
F♯5 A5 F♯5 A5 F♯5 A5 F♯5 G5 (E) B♭5/F
TAB

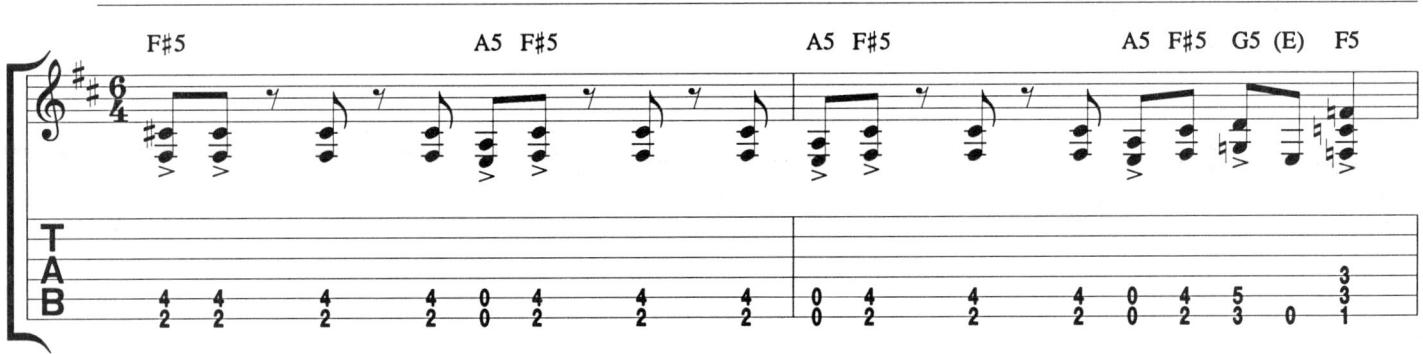

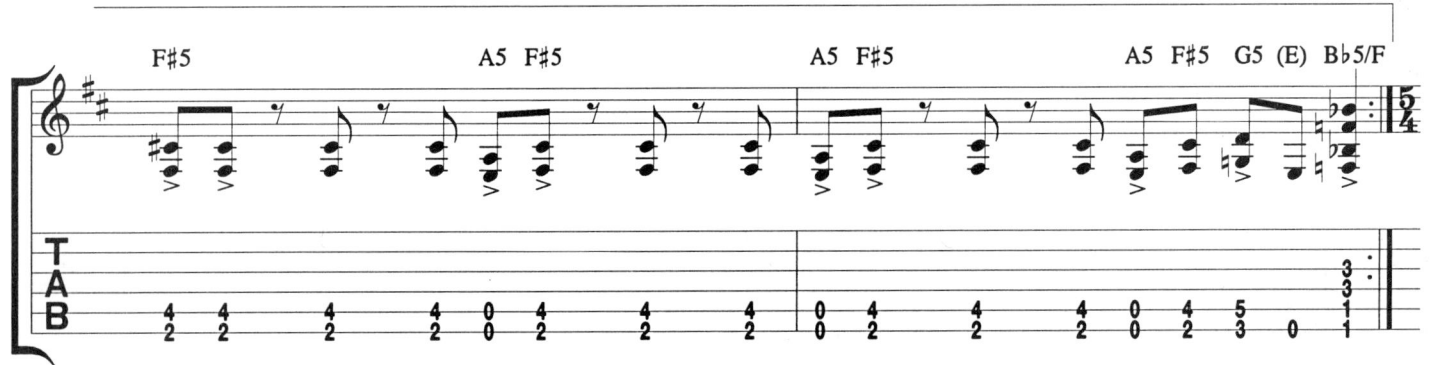

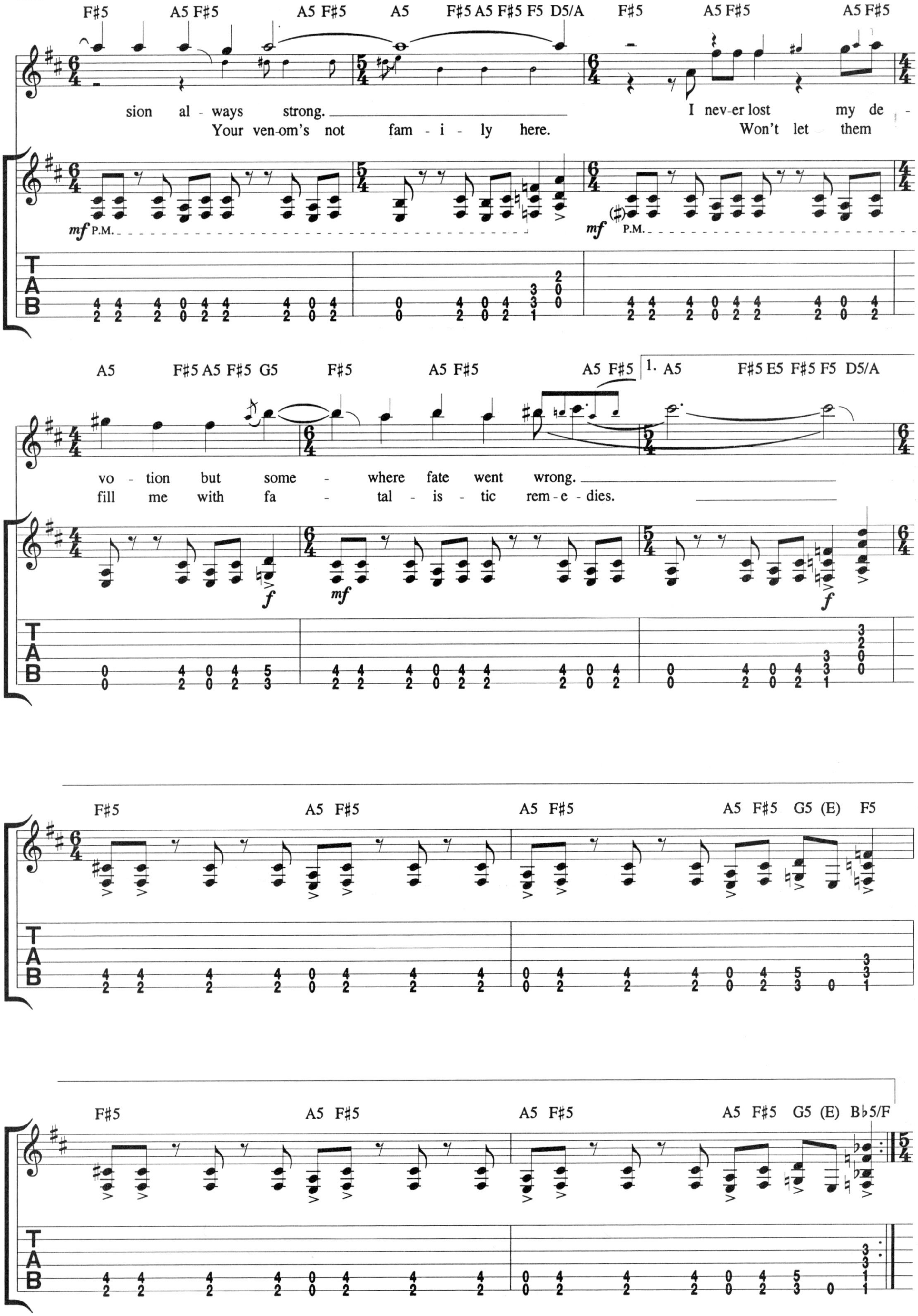

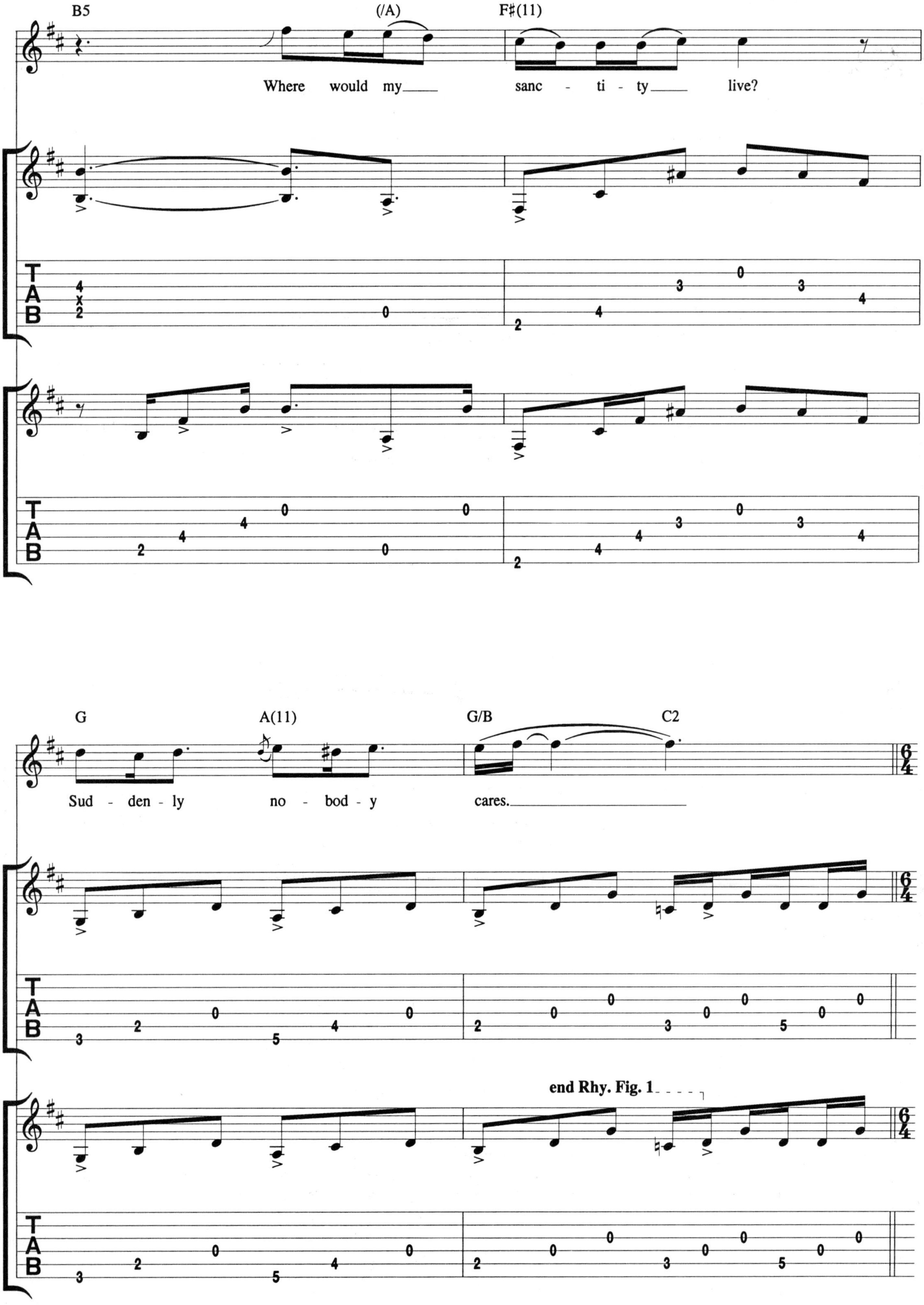
B5
(/A)
F♯(11)
Where would my sanc - ti - ty live?
G
A(11)
G/B
C2
Sud - den - ly no - bod - y cares.
end Rhy. Fig. 1

134

Scared – 23 – 9

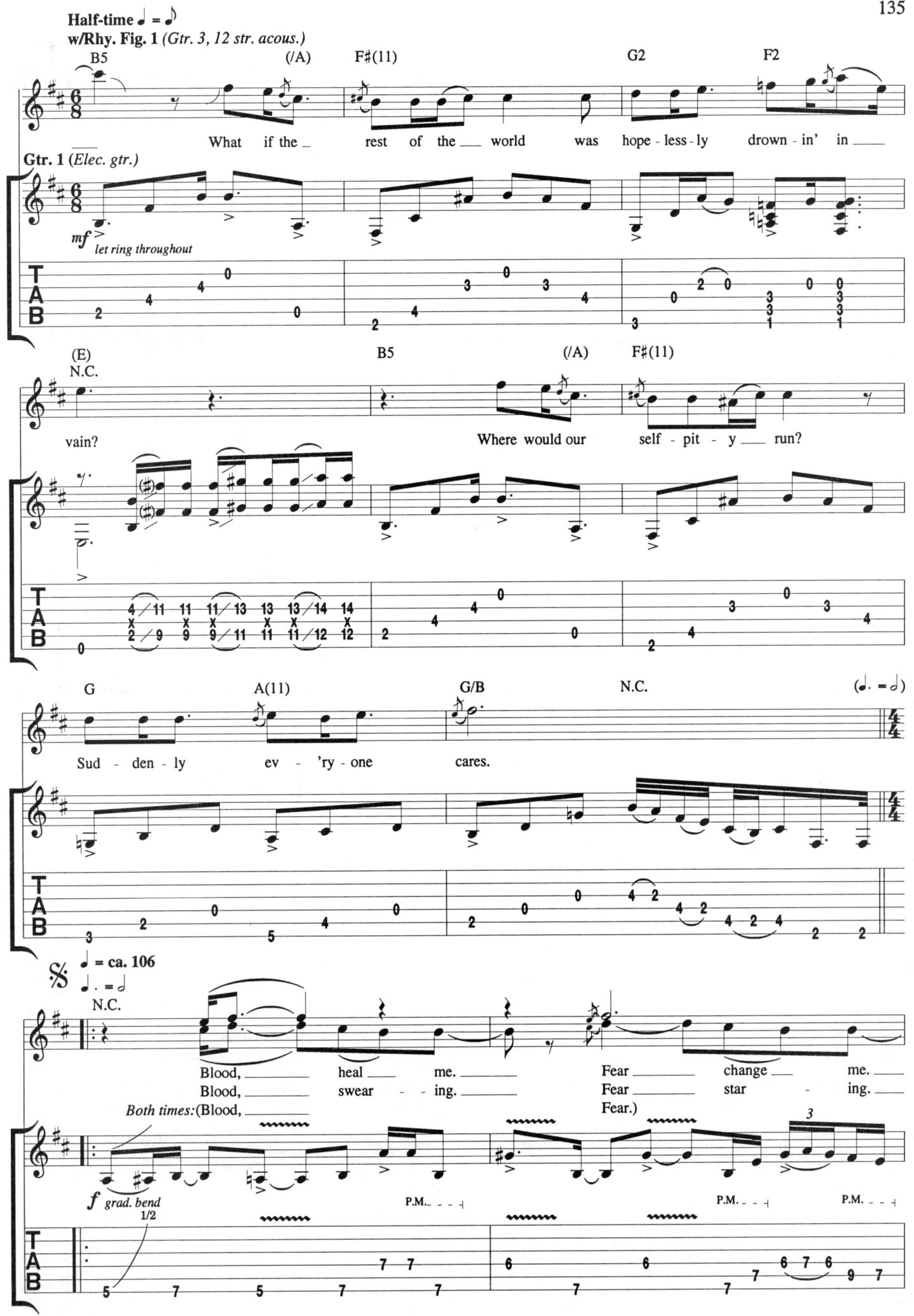

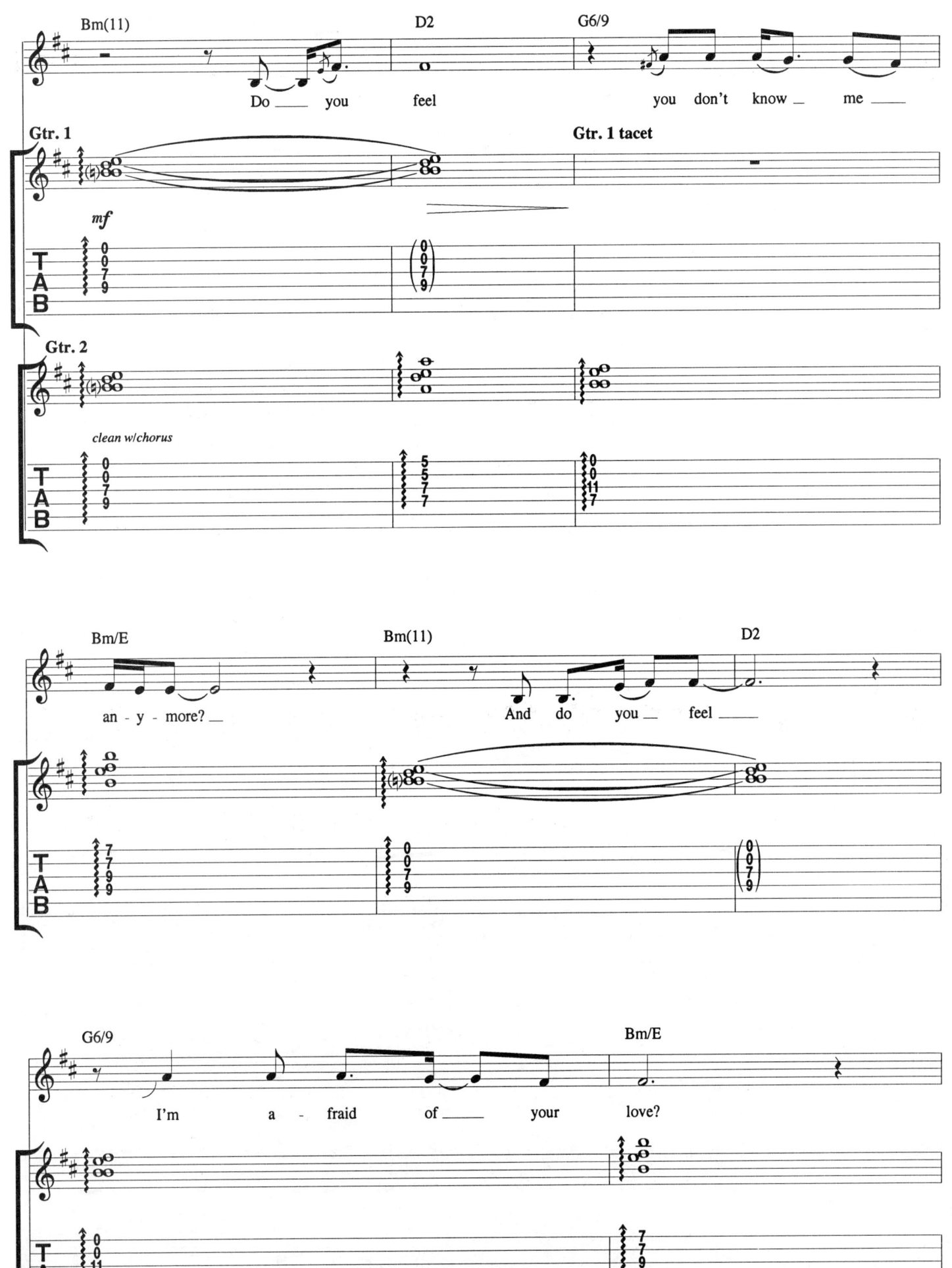

Coda 1
(♩ = ca. 104)
N.C.
mf
P.M.
Gtr. 1
Gtr. 2
f
Gtr. 3
f
(P.M.)

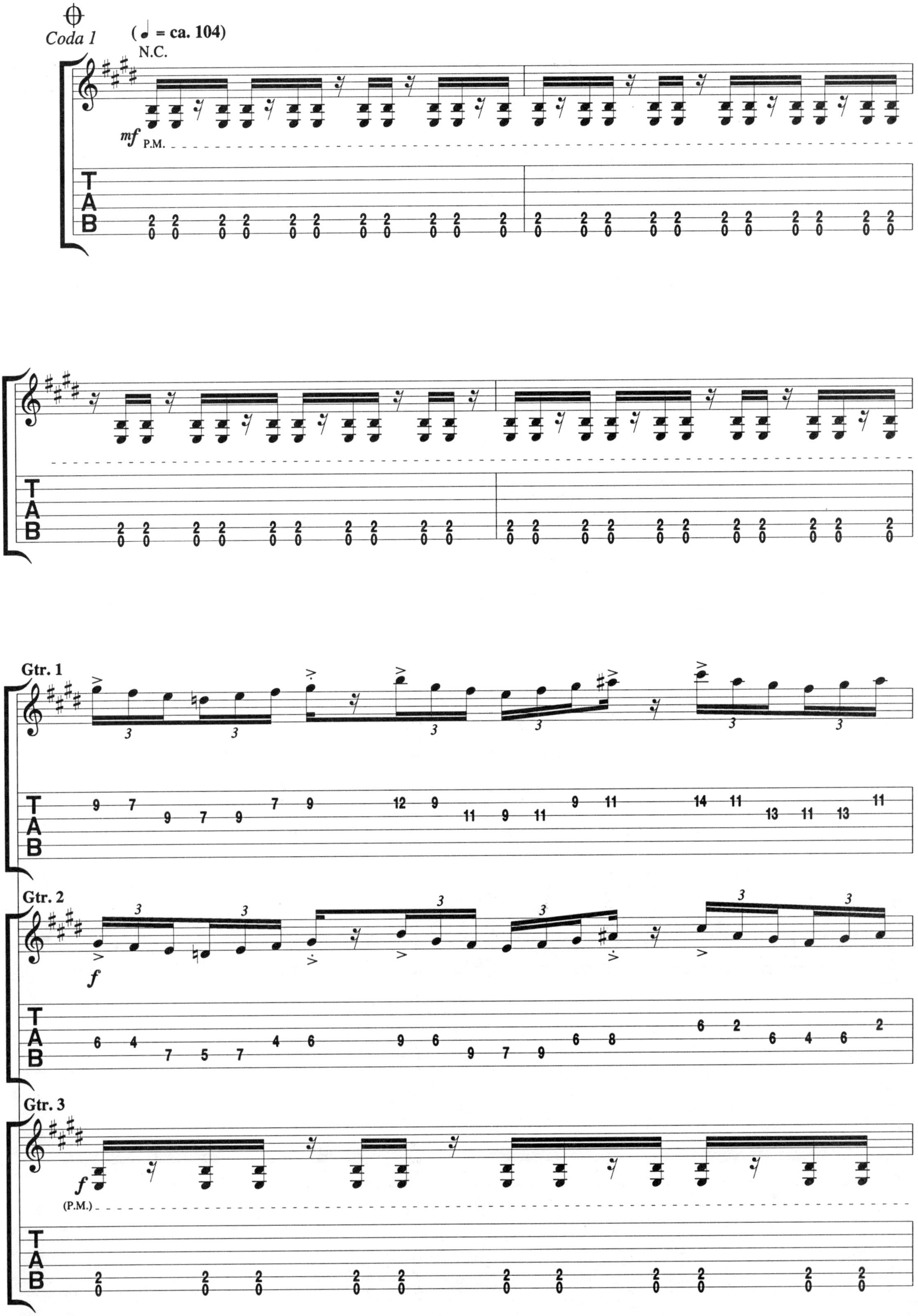

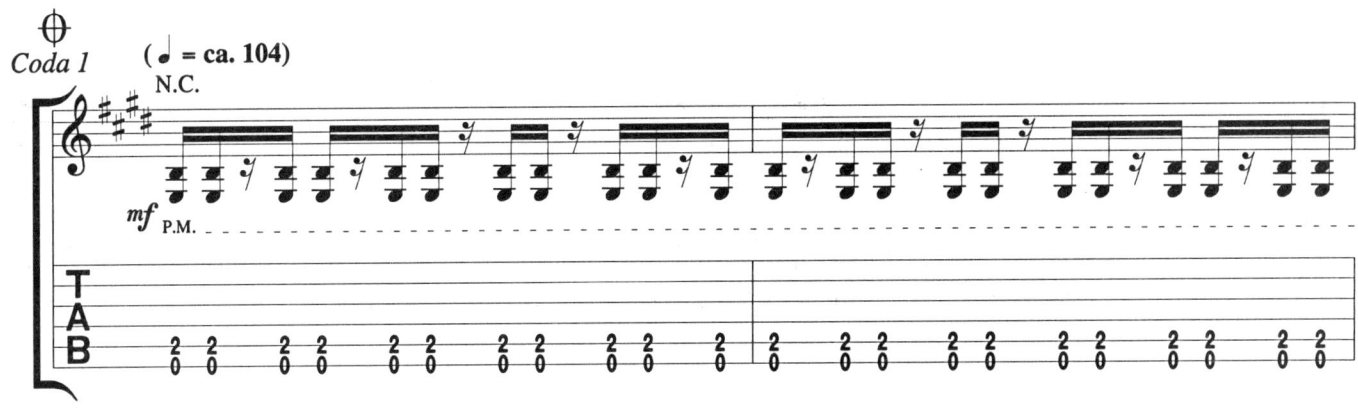

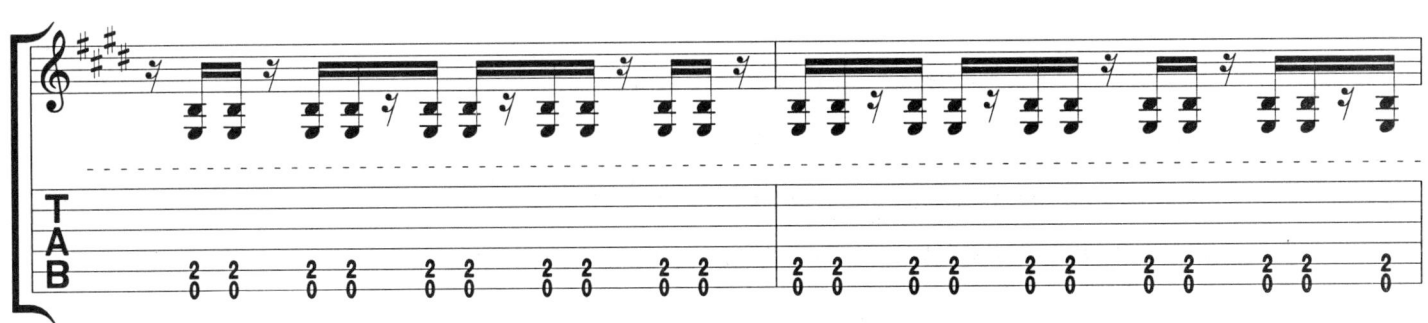

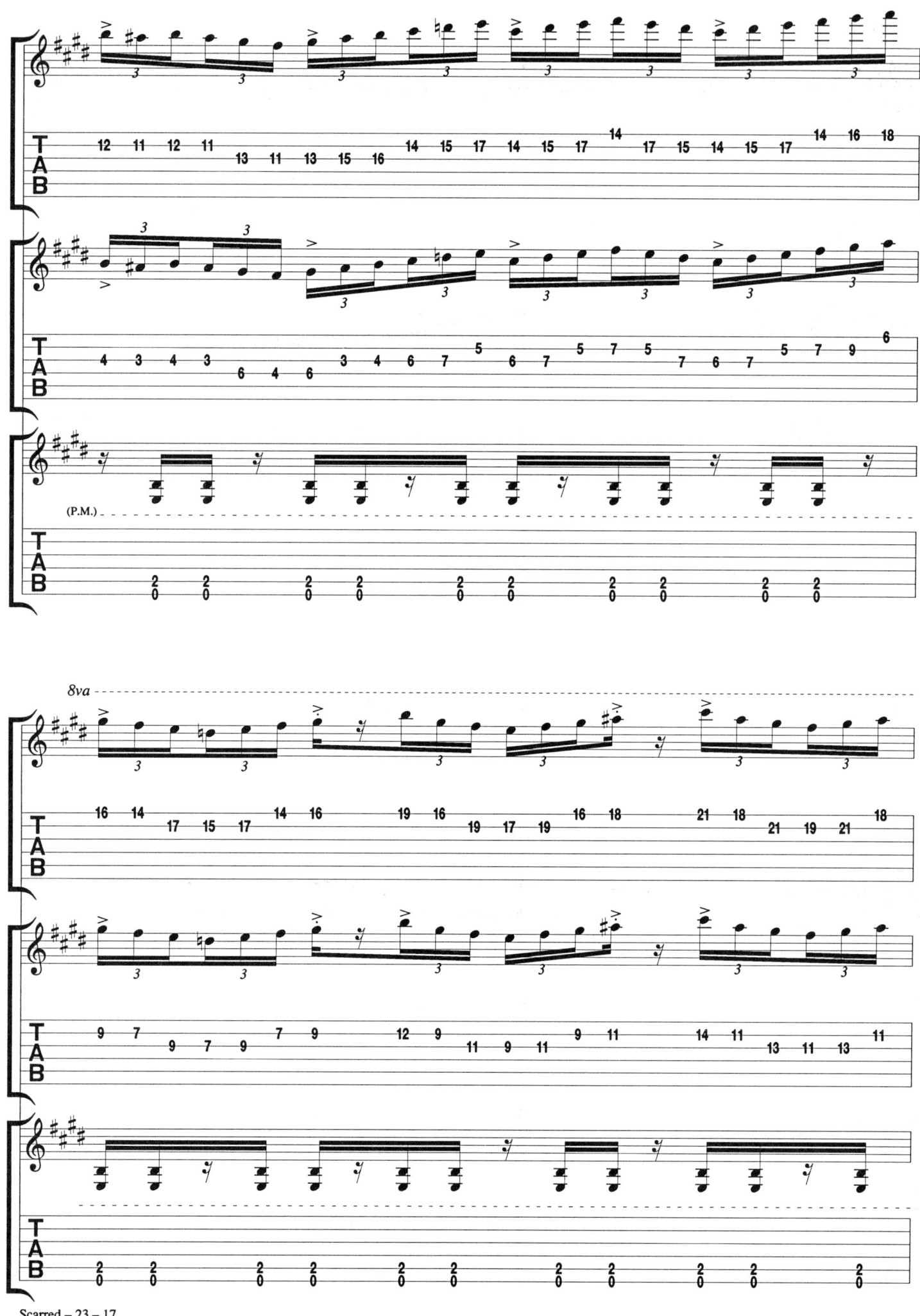

(8va)
(P.M.)
Gtr. 3 tacet
Gtr. 1
loco
Gtr. 2

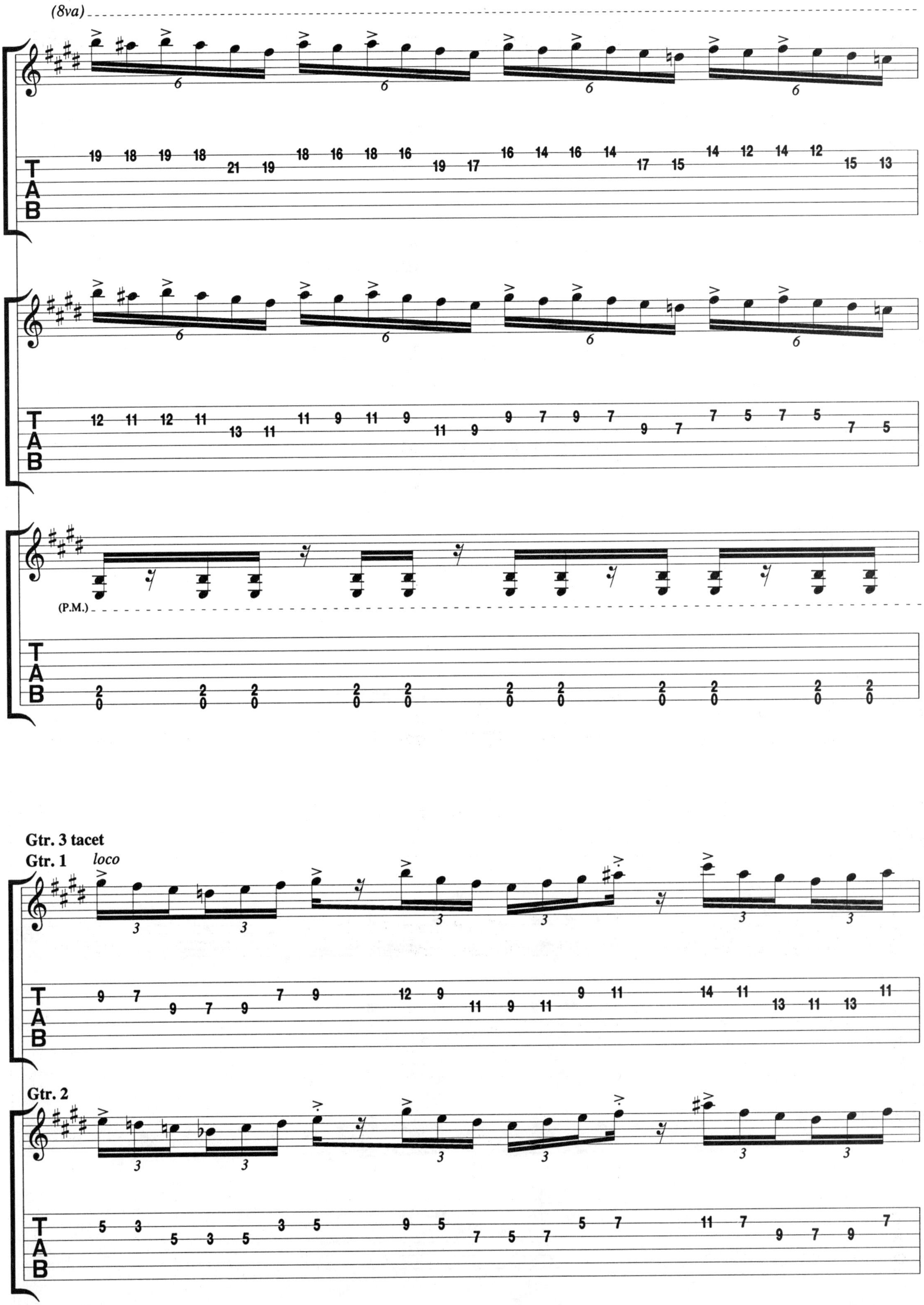

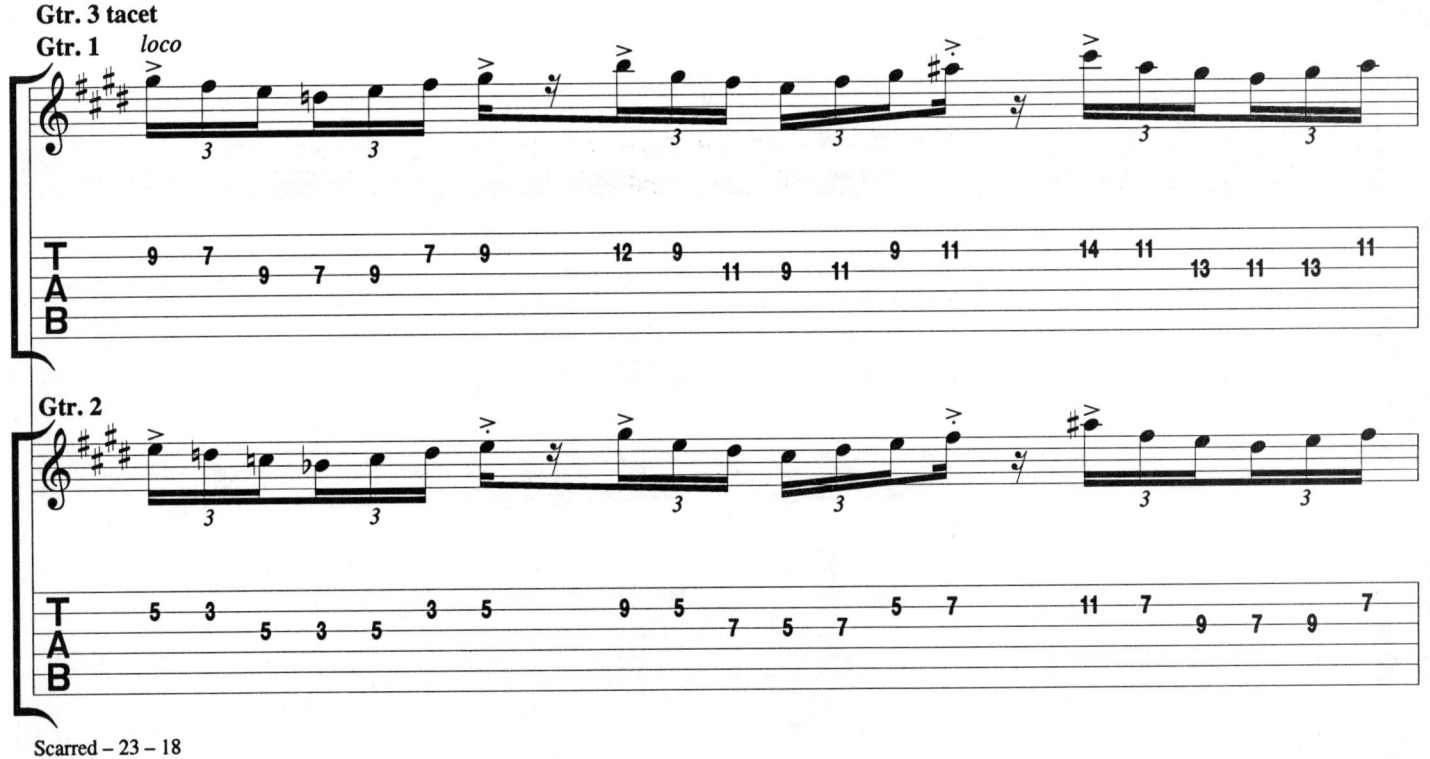

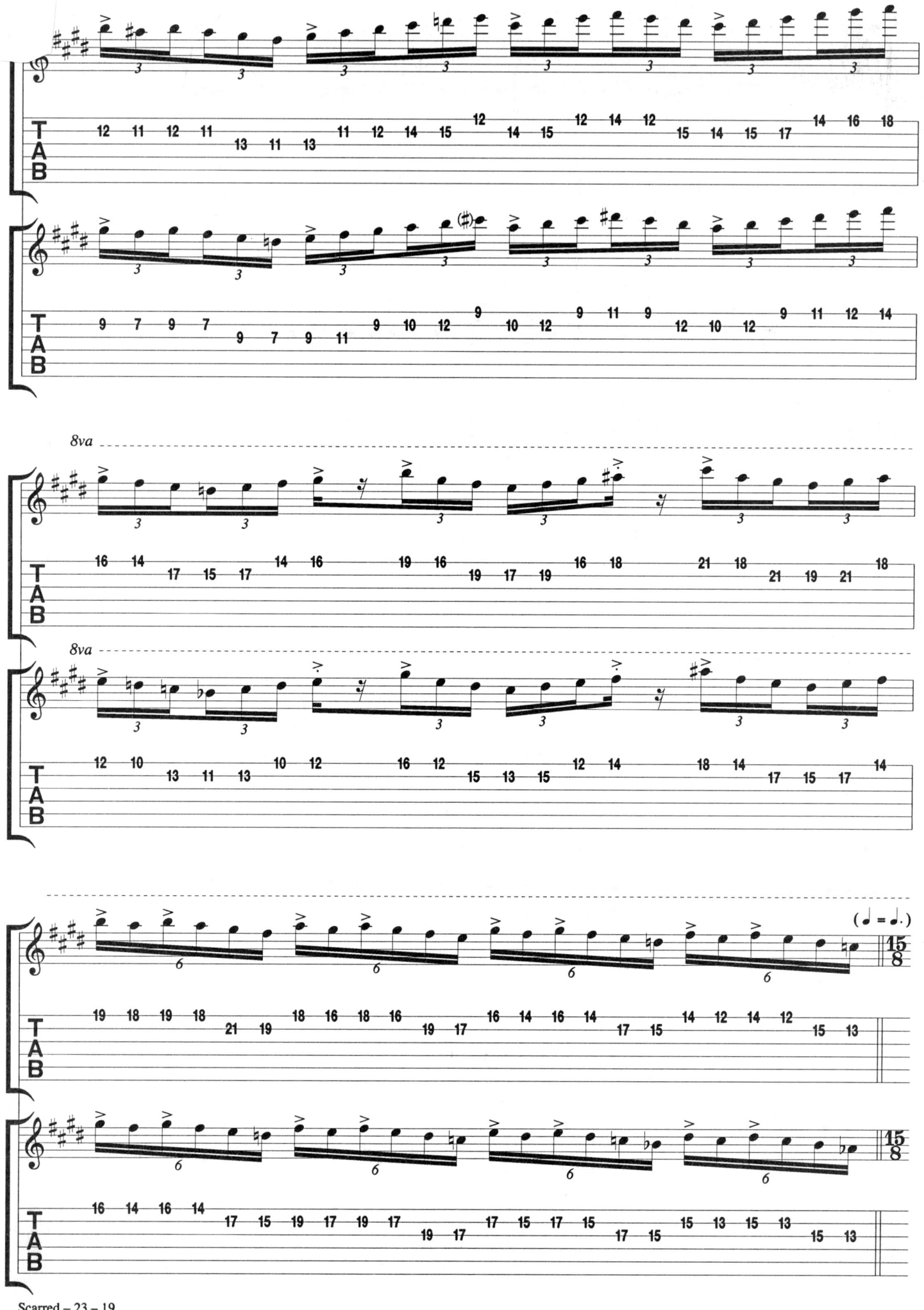

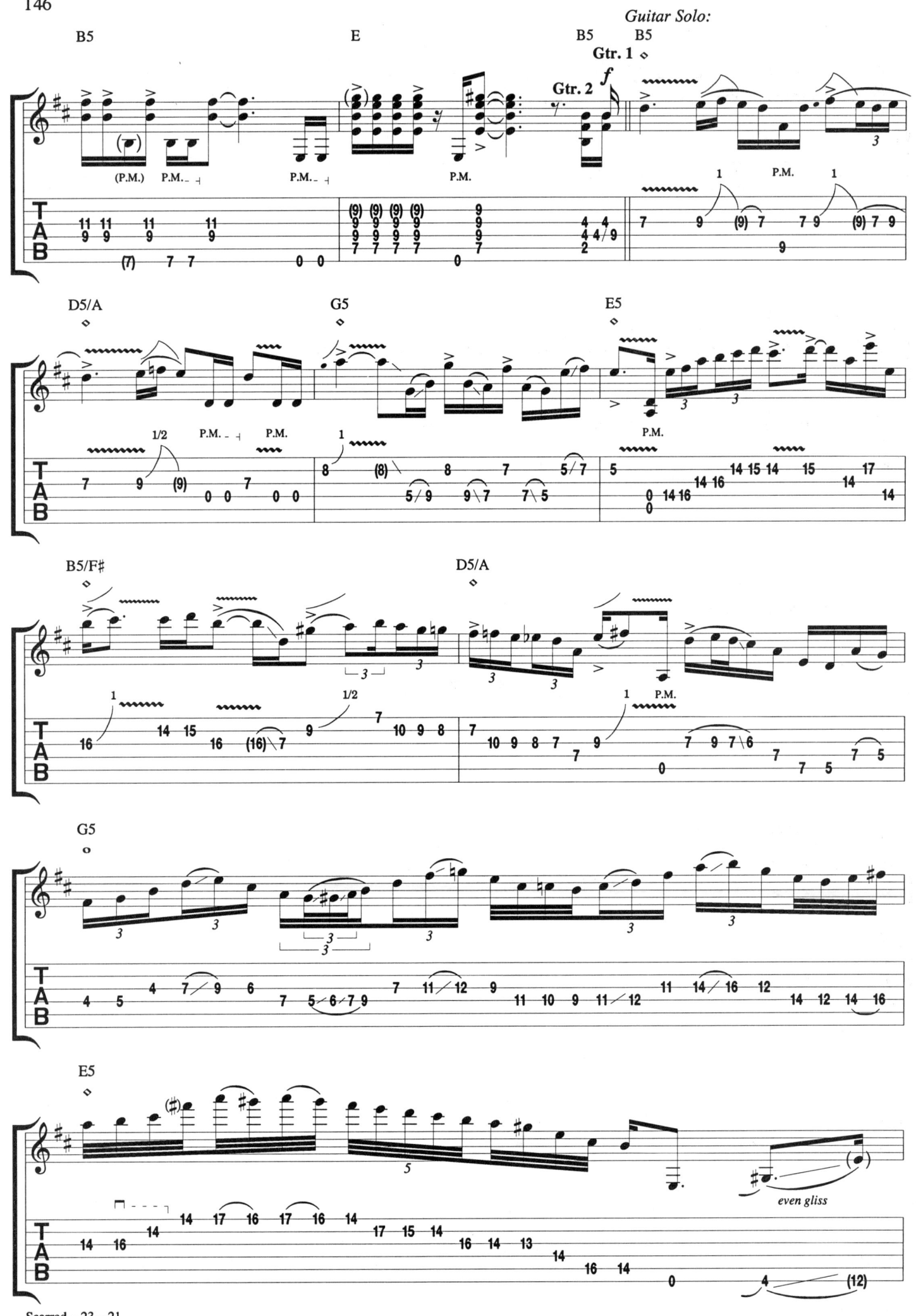

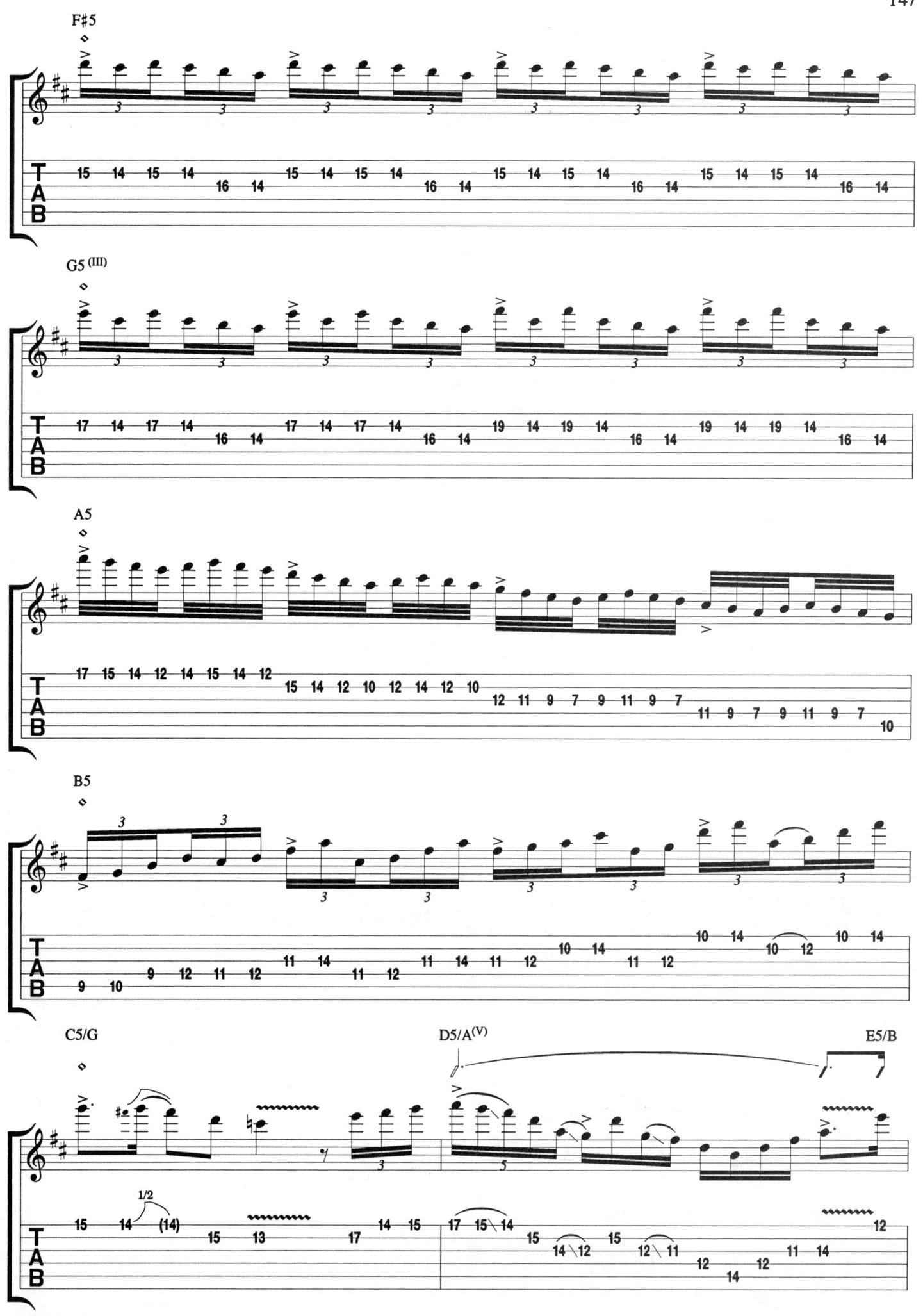

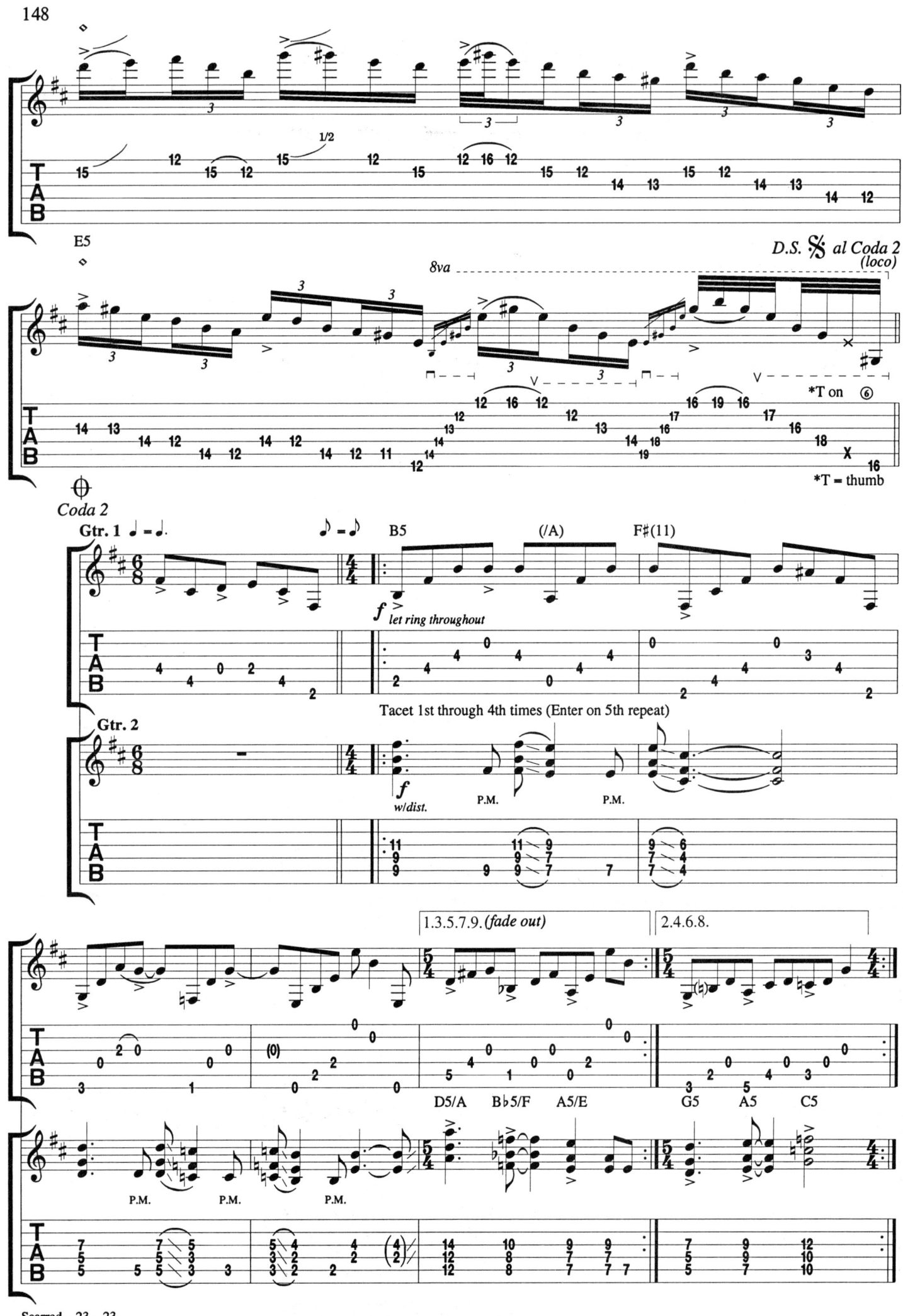

SPACE - DYE VEST

By KEVIN MOORE

149

*Piano arranged for fingerstyle guitar.

*Allow sympathetic D harmonic on ⑥ to ring in order to maintain same pitch of open ④ once B♭ is fretted.

* Harp harmonic.

© 1994 OCTA MUSIC, INC. (ASCAP), YTSE JAMS, INC. (ASCAP)
All Rights on Behalf of OCTA MUSIC, INC. & YTSE JAMS, INC.
Administered By WB MUSIC CORP. (ASCAP)
All Rights Reserved

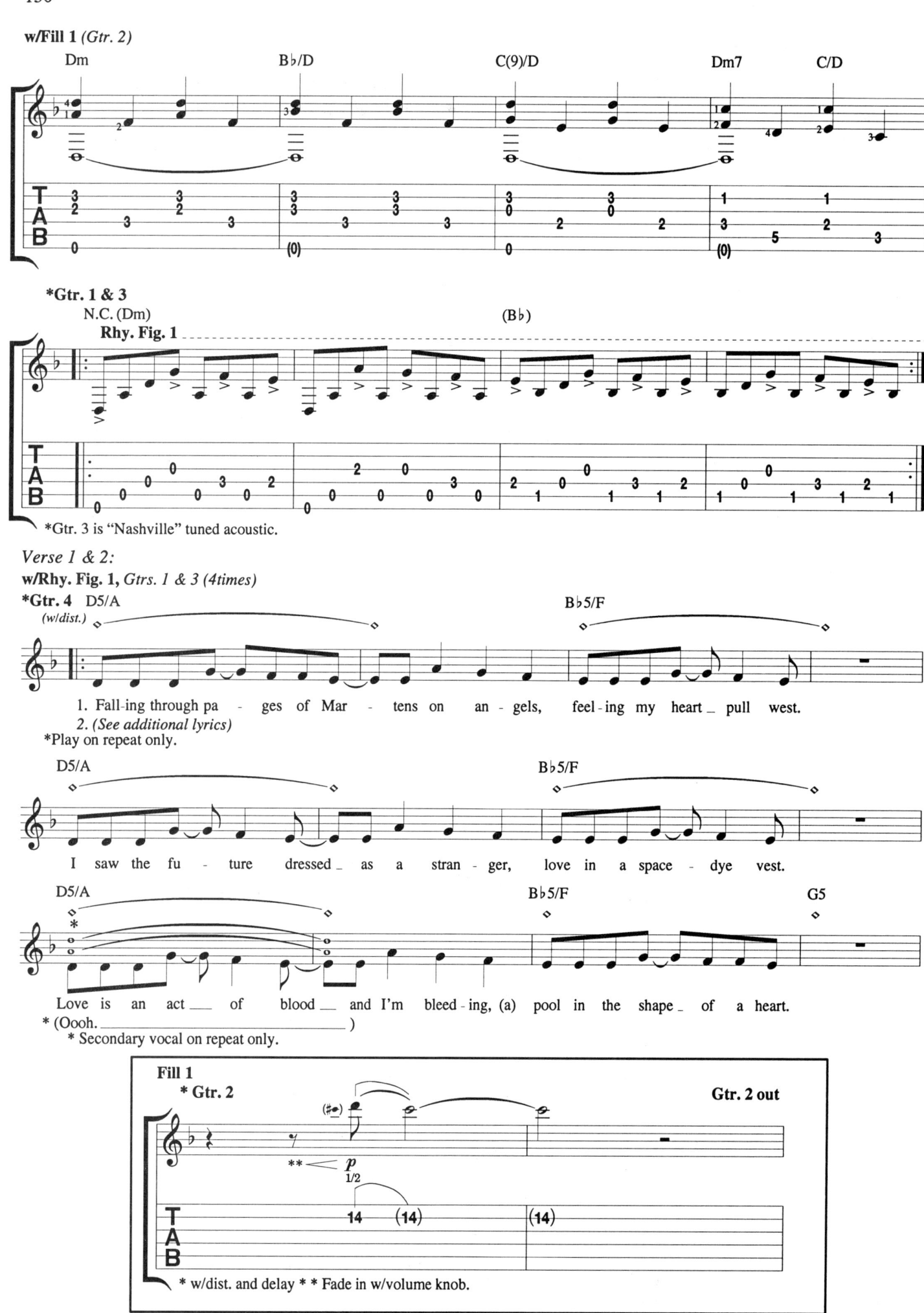

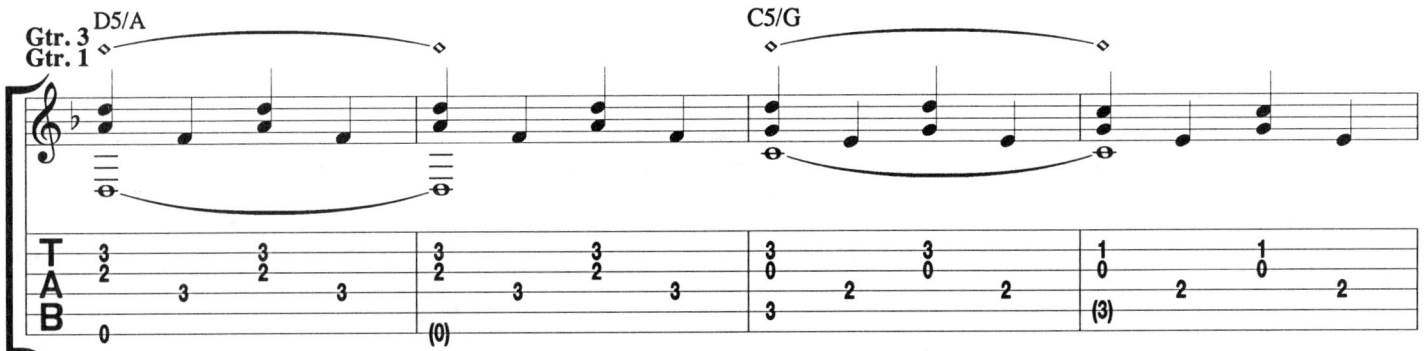

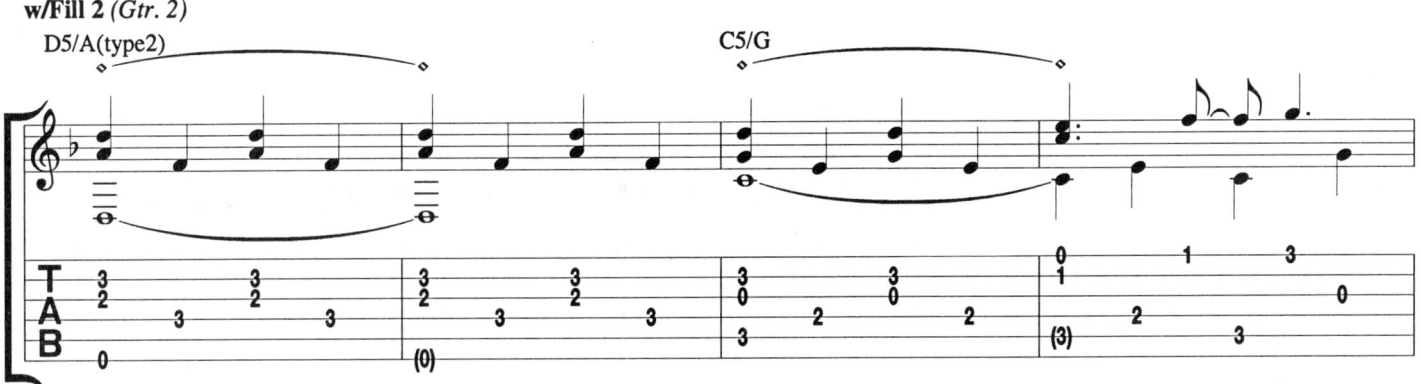

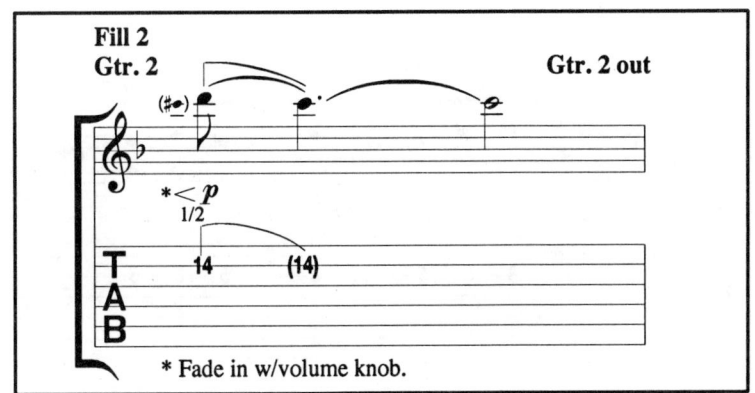

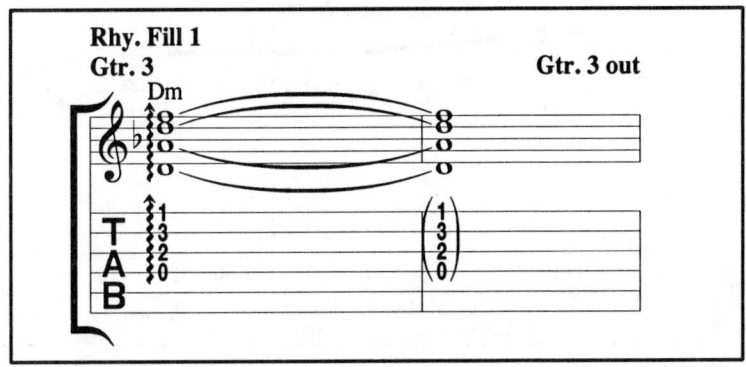

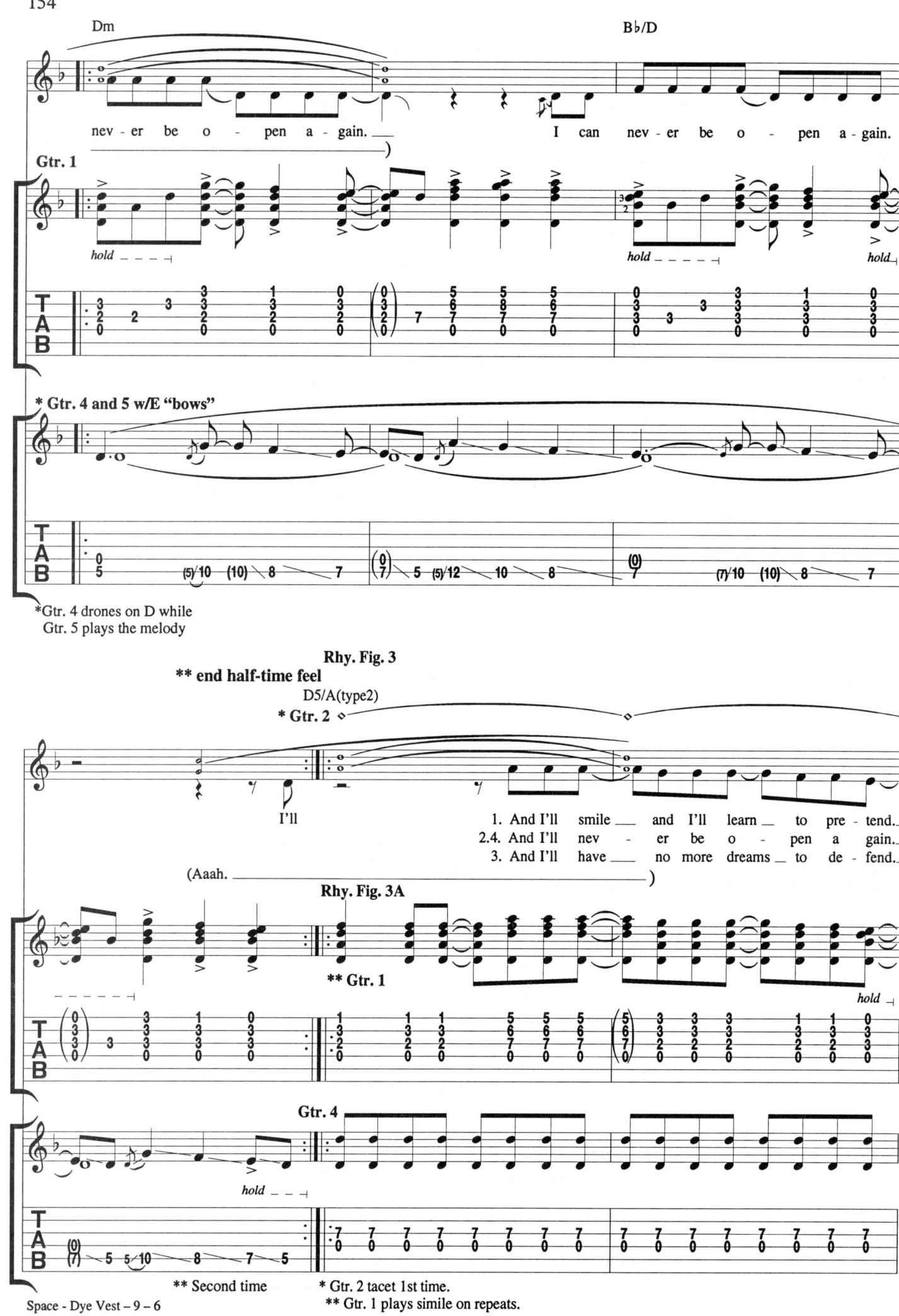

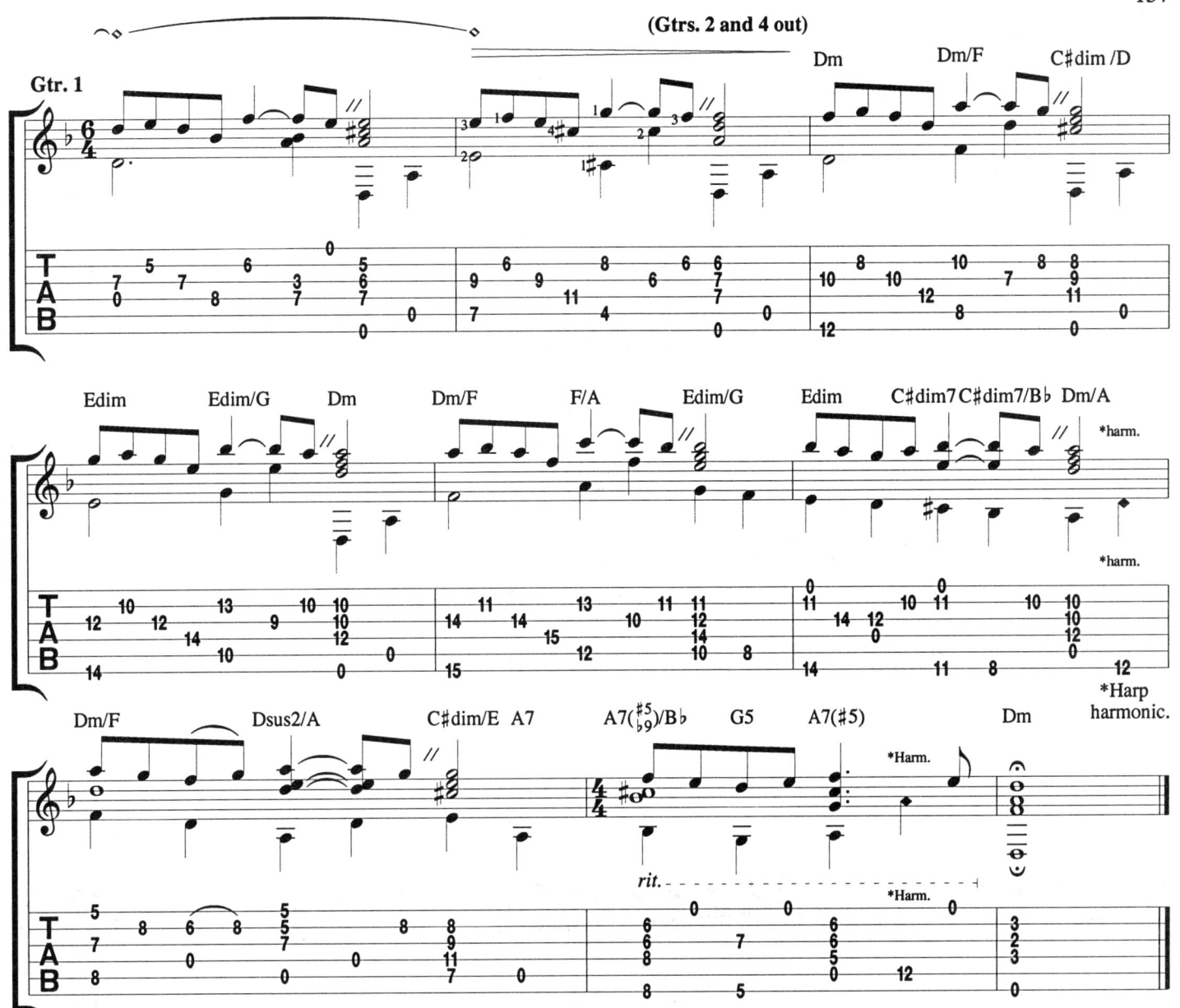

Verse 2:
Now that you're gone I'm trying to take it,
Learning to swallow the rage.
Found a new girl, I think we can make it,
As long as she stays on the page.
This is not how I want it to end.
And I'll never be open again.

Recitation 1:
But he's the sort who can't know anyone intimately, least of all a woman.
He doesn't know what a woman is.
He wants you for possession - something to look at like a painting or an ivory box.
Something to hold and to display.
He doesn't want you to be real - to think and to live.
He doesn't love you, but I love you.
I want you to have your own thoughts and ideas and feelings,
Even when I hold you in my arms.
It's our last chance.

Recitation 2:
I can be on my own, get a job, get my own place.
Go to the mall whenever I want.
No one to tell me I'm too young.
Some people, my advice before, about facing facts, about facing reality.
And this, without a doubt, is his biggest challenge ever.
He's going to have to face it.
He's going to have to try and get some help here.
I mean, no one can say they know how he feels.
So they say that in Houston or something.
They say, "Yes, it's 180 degrees, but it's a dry heat."
In Houston they say that?
Oh, maybe not. I'm all mixed up.
Dry until they hit the swimming pool.

GUITAR TAB GLOSSARY **

TABLATURE EXPLANATION

READING TABLATURE: Tablature illustrates the six strings of the guitar. Notes and chords are indicated by the placement of fret numbers on a given string(s).

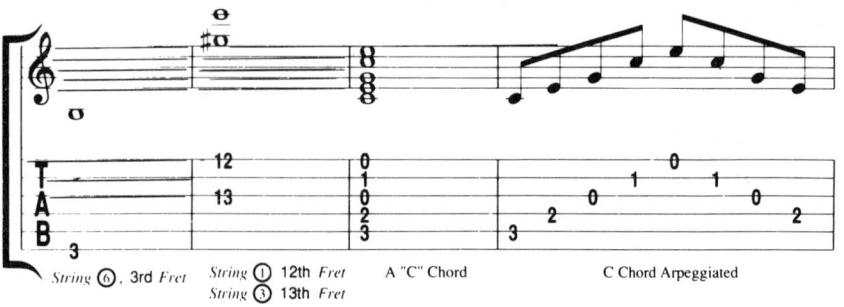

String ⑥, 3rd Fret   String ① 12th Fret   A "C" Chord   C Chord Arpeggiated
String ③ 13th Fret

BENDING NOTES

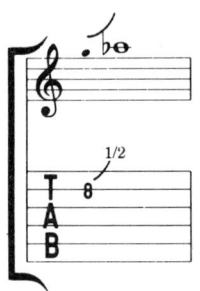

HALF STEP: Play the note and bend string one half step.*

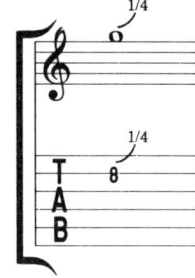

SLIGHT BEND (Microtone): Play the note and bend string slightly to the equivalent of half a fret.

BEND AND RELEASE: Play the note and gradually bend to the next pitch, then release to the original note. Only the first note is attacked.

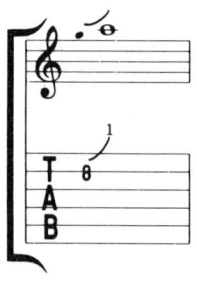

WHOLE STEP: Play the note and bend string one whole step.

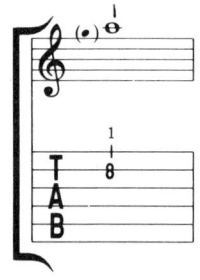

PREBEND (Ghost Bend): Bend to the specified note, before the string is picked.

BENDS INVOLVING MORE THAN ONE STRING: Play the note and bend string while playing an additional note (or notes) on another string(s). Upon release, relieve pressure from additional note(s), causing original note to sound alone.

WHOLE STEP AND A HALF: Play the note and bend string a whole step and a half.

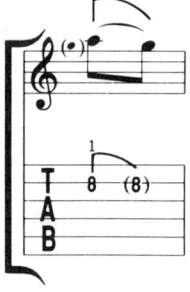

PREBEND AND RELEASE: Bend the string, play it, then release to the original note.

BENDS INVOLVING STATIONARY NOTES: Play notes and bend lower pitch, then hold until release begins (indicated at the point where line becomes solid).

UNISON BEND: Play both notes and immediately bend the lower note to the same pitch as the higher note.

TWO STEPS: Play the note and bend string two whole steps.

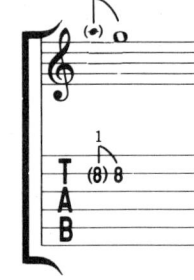

REVERSE BEND: Play the already-bent string, then immediately drop it down to the fretted note.

DOUBLE NOTE BEND: Play both notes and immediately bend both strings simultaneously.

*A half step is the smallest interval in Western music; it is equal to one fret. A whole step equals two frets.

© 1990 Beam Me Up Music
c/o CPP/Belwin, Inc. Miami, Florida 33014
International Copyright Secured   Made in U.S.A.   All Rights Reserved

**By Kenn Chipkin and Aaron Stang

RHYTHM SLASHES

STRUM INDICATIONS: Strum with indicated rhythm. The chord voicings are found on the first page of the transcription underneath the song title.

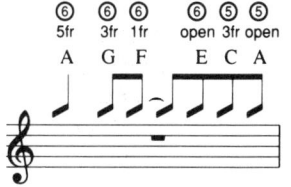

INDICATING SINGLE NOTES USING RHYTHM SLASHES: Very often single notes are incorporated into a rhythm part. The note name is indicated above the rhythm slash with a fret number and a string indication.

ARTICULATIONS

HAMMER ON: Play lower note, then "hammer on" to higher note with another finger. Only the first note is attacked.

LEFT HAND HAMMER: Hammer on the first note played on each string with the left hand.

PULL OFF: Play higher note, then "pull off" to lower note with another finger. Only the first note is attacked.

FRETBOARD TAPPING: "Tap" onto the note indicated by + with a finger of the pick hand, then pull off to the following note held by the fret hand.

TAP SLIDE: Same as fretboard tapping, but the tapped note is slid randomly up the fretboard, then pulled off to the following note.

BEND AND TAP TECHNIQUE: Play note and bend to specified interval. While holding bend, tap onto note indicated.

LEGATO SLIDE: Play note and slide to the following note. (Only first note is attacked).

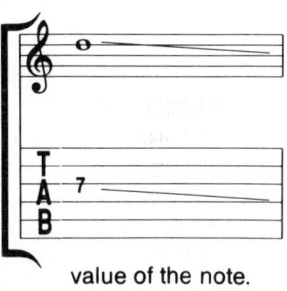

LONG GLISSANDO: Play note and slide in specified direction for the full value of the note.

SHORT GLISSANDO: Play note for its full value and slide in specified direction at the last possible moment.

PICK SLIDE: Slide the edge of the pick in specified direction across the length of the string(s).

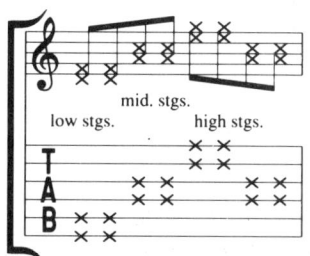

MUTED STRINGS: A percussive sound is made by laying the fret hand across all six strings while pick hand strikes specified area (low, mid, high strings).

PALM MUTE: The note or notes are muted by the palm of the pick hand by lightly touching the string(s) near the bridge.

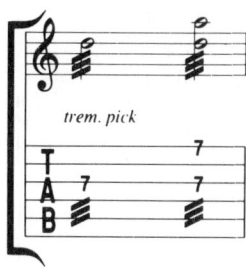

TREMOLO PICKING: The note or notes are picked as fast as possible.

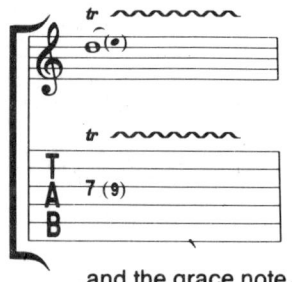
TRILL: Hammer on and pull off consecutively and as fast as possible between the original note and the grace note.

ACCENT: Notes or chords are to be played with added emphasis.

STACCATO (Detached Notes): Notes or chords are to be played roughly half their actual value and with separation.

DOWN STROKES AND UPSTROKES: Notes or chords are to be played with either a downstroke (⊓) or upstroke (v) of the pick.

VIBRATO: The pitch of a note is varied by a rapid shaking of the fret hand finger, wrist, and forearm.

HARMONICS

NATURAL HARMONIC: A finger of the fret hand lightly touches the note or notes indicated in the tab and is played by the pick hand.

ARTIFICIAL HARMONIC: The first tab number is fretted, then the pick hand produces the harmonic by using a finger to lightly touch the same string at the second tab number (in parenthesis) and is then picked by another finger.

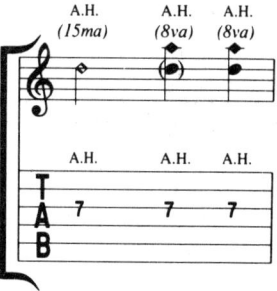
ARTIFICIAL "PINCH" HARMONIC: A note is fretted as indicated by the tab, then the pick hand produces the harmonic by squeezing the pick firmly while using the tip of the index finger in the pick attack. If parenthesis are found around the fretted note, it does not sound. No parenthesis means both the fretted note and A.H. are heard simultaneously.

TREMOLO BAR

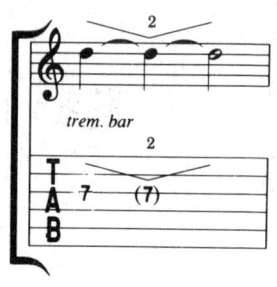
SPECIFIED INTERVAL: The pitch of a note or chord is lowered to a specified interval and then may or may not return to the original pitch. The activity of the tremolo bar is graphically represented by peaks and valleys.

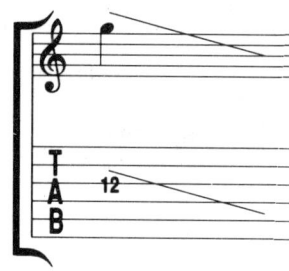
UN-SPECIFIED INTERVAL: The pitch of a note or a chord is lowered to an unspecified interval.